Napoleon's Hussars and Chasseurs

To Keith Rocco

Thank you for your friendship, encouragement and support of my research

Napoleon's Hussars and Chasseurs

Uniforms and Equipment of the Grande Armée, 1805–1815

Paul L. Dawson

Frontline Books

First published in Great Britain in 2023 and reprinted in 2025 by
Frontline Books
An imprint of Pen & Sword Books Limited
Yorkshire – Philadelphia

ISBN 978 1 39903 078 6

A CIP catalogue record for this book is available from the British Library

Typeset by Mac Style
Printed and bound in India by Replika Press Pvt. Ltd.

MIX
Paper | Supporting responsible forestry
FSC www.fsc.org FSC™ C016779

The Publisher's authorised representative in the EU for product safety is
Authorised Rep Compliance Ltd., Ground Floor, 71 Lower Baggot Street,
Dublin D02 P593, Ireland.
www.arccompliance.com

For a complete list of Pen & Sword titles please contact

PEN & SWORD BOOKS LIMITED
47 Church Street, Barnsley, South Yorkshire, S70 2AS, England
E-mail: enquiries@pen-and-sword.co.uk
Website: www.pen-and-sword.co.uk
or
PEN AND SWORD BOOKS
1950 Lawrence Rd, Havertown, PA 19083, USA
E-mail: uspen-and-sword@casematepublishers.com
Website: www.penandswordbooks.com

Contents

Acknowledgements

This book and its companion volumes marks the culmination of almost two decades of research, and a combined period of almost four months of daily study in the French Army Archives in Paris. In December 2004 I first walked through the gate house of Chateau de Vincennes as the clock above me chimed nine o'clock. I explained the nature of my visit, and was guided by an army officer through an arched doorway and up a flight of stairs in what was an 1830s barrack block. Waiting for me was the muster list of the 1e regiment of Grenadiers a Pied of the Imperial Guard. I was visiting the archives to find out as much as I could about Grenadier Simplet, whose uniform is on display in the Musée de l'Armée, and what source material existed to tell me about what the regiment wore: a whole new world of primary sources was opened up to me, most of which I had never seen referenced before. Thus began my love affair with wanting to find out exactly how Napoléon's men were dressed.

For the last 200 years, it has been assumed that army-level regulation has been the primary source for the appearance of the armed forces. However, this did not answer key questions of how the regulations were interpreted, how the regulation was changed and above all how each regiment introduced the regulation, a factor that far outweighed the dictates of the War Ministry or other official publication. To answer these questions, perhaps, 1,000 archive boxes needed to be consulted. Such an extensive degree of research was only possible through collaboration with a core team of friends who supported me in my endeavour.

I am indebted to Jean-Charles Lair, Sally Fairweather and Yves Martin for their most generous and gracious assistance with, and photographing of, archival material at the Archives Nationale and Service Historique de la Défense Armée de Terre, in Paris. Without their help, this book could not have been written. Yves is also to be thanked for his friendship, advice and most generous provision of illustrative material. My esteemed friend and research colleague Robert Cooper is to be thanked for his steadfast friendship and comments on my essay and critical comments on my thought processes in understanding the archive sources and supply issues for the army.

Jerome Croyet must be thanked for his permission to reproduce the photographs I have taken of the former Brunon collection. He is also to be thanked for provision of research notes.

Also, to be thanked is Bertrand Malvaux for permission to use images of items in his collection.

The long-suffering staff at Service Historique de la Défense Armée de Terre in Paris need to be thanked for answering questions and locating items of research that have made this book possible.

To Jose Luis Canibe I am eternally grateful. His digital art works have brought to life what the archive documents say in his wonderful graphics. Without these many hundreds of illustrations, the book would not be the 'ultimate reference book' that I hope it is for the light cavalry.

Paul L. Dawson, Paris, 5 December 2022

Introduction

The cavalry in the French Army comprised of three main types of formation: light cavalry used primarily for scouting and reconnaissance work, dragoons, and heavy cavalry, which provided the shock troops of the period on the battlefield. Each type of cavalry required horses specific to the function of the cavalry regiment. Light cavalry units, particularly the *hussars*, were also known to have an extremely bold and audacious reputation. To further enhance their mystique, the *hussars* were the most flamboyantly dressed cavalry units, and sported long hair and fearsome moustaches. The *chasseurs* thought themselves as being equal to the *hussars*; the *hussars* however thought otherwise. Frequent quarrels arose between the two on the most trifling pretext.

The light cavalry was primarily charged with providing accurate reconnaissance reports on the enemy as well as seizing key terrain. In addition, the light cavalry also screened the movement of the main body of the army, preventing the enemy from knowing Napoléon's true troop dispositions. All of these actions helped shape the battlefield. During battle, Napoléon's heavy cavalry was typically held in reserve to be committed at the critical place and time to deliver the decisive blow against the enemy. Often out of necessity, as at Essling and Waterloo, the light cavalry charged alongside the *cuirassiers* and *carabiniers*. Thus, the cavalry's commitment to the main battle tended to prove decisive. Following the main battle, light cavalry was used to pursue elements of the enemy's troops and complete the total destruction of the enemy's force, which was Napoléon's habitual objective. Therefore, with sufficient and well-trained cavalry, Napoléon's victories tended to be decisive, as in the Jena-Aüerstadt Campaign of 1806. The regiments could be subdivided into smaller-sized units for use as pickets and vedettes (mounted sentinels deployed forward of an outpost). Napoléon relied on his light cavalry to gain and maintain contact with the enemy, as well as to screen his movements. A successful cavalry screen would deny the enemy valuable information with regard to the location, size, and composition of Napoléon's forces. The light cavalry could also be employed as couriers and to secure the lines of communication of the French Army. One of the most significant contributions the light cavalry made to Napoléon's campaigns, after their reconnaissance and courier work, was in the role of pursuit. This could prove to be decisive in completing the destruction of the enemy force. For example, on 8 February 1814 a half squadron of 31e *Chasseur* captured 150 Austrian infantry near Massimbona. Another squadron captured 300 infantry between Marengo and Roverbella. Even the scouts of the regiment did something to be proud of, they captured an Austrian baggage column, which was moving into Villafranca with its escort.

The horses for the *chasseurs*, *hussars* and train horses were to come from the Ardennes, Cantal, Corrèze, Finistere, Morbihan, Nievre, Nord, Puy-de-Dôme, Pyrénées and Haute-Vienne for similar reasons. The age of the horse upon reception was determined by its breed type and the area of the army it was needed. All foreign-bred horses, and those from the Ardennes, Calvados, Dyle, l'Eure, Finistere, Manche, Meuse inferieure, Morbihan, Nievre, du Nord, Orne, Outre and Seine Inferieure, were to be aged 4 years. Those horses that came from the Cantal, Correze, Puy-de-Dôme, Pyrénées and Haute Vienne were to be at least 6 years old as they matured later than the horses from the areas noted previously. The horses were to stand 140cm (13.3hh) to 147cm (14.2hh) and cost 360 francs.[1] Another 150 francs was needed for the track. As well as his horse and saddle, a cavalry trooper needed his uniform, boots, equipment and arms.

As the state provided the uniform through stoppages in the men's pay, in consequence this and their equipment was tightly regulated and was issued on a controlled basis. Each item of clothing had a specified duration period. A *habit* had to last two years, a bearskin twenty years, a pair of *culottes* a matter of months. Every year a regiment would be inspected, and the condition of the clothing assessed. A return of all the clothing to be struck off/disposed of was made, and the appropriate number of new items ordered. Clothing and equipment needing repairs was also logged, as was how many items had been repaired since the last inspection. The soldier was responsible for the repair of their own clothing and any costs associated. Likewise, if they lost items, they had to purchase replacement items – in many ways a soldier ended up paying to be in the army when these deductions were taken into consideration. Every year half of the regiment's cloth work was replaced, so every twenty-four months a soldier received a new habit. It was very much make do and men by the time the cloth items of equipment were coming to the end of their service life. These inspection returns are a fantastic resource for outlining what a regiment actually wore rather than the theory based on the regulations. The two often did not agree in practice. Clothing and equipment was overseen by the regiment's clothing officer. His work was overseen by an inspector general. Items of clothing had a specific lifespan. Each time an item was inspected it was classed as either new, in need of repair, due to expire, or expired and in need of replacement. Upon joining the army, men were issued their first complete set of uniform (*1e Messe*), which came from stoppages in their pay. The masse *d'habillement*, literally clothing fund, set a yearly quota of money available to a colonel to pay for clothing renewals and repairs. In addition, the regimental Council of Administration drew its necessary funds to buy raw materials, equipment and headdress, as well as to pay the regimental workmen. It also covered sundry items such as the epaulettes of the adjutant-sous-officiers, lace for rank stripes, service chevrons, musicians and drummers lace, plumes and pompoms. The fund was to provide a soldier with his full issue of uniform and equipment. A solider, in addition to his basic issue, needed more than a single shirt, stock and pair of shoes. This was paid for with more stoppages from his pay being sent to the Linen and Shoe Fund. The fund was paid for at the rate of 12 centimes a day for sous-officiers (sergeant-major, sergeant, and fourrier: corporals are not considered non-commissioned or sous-officiers) and 7 centimes for other ranks.[2] The men were paid, in theory, weekly, according to rank and status. In all cases, the pay was subject to a number of deductions for communal funds (masses), which left very little actual pay. The purpose of the pay was actually not to give the soldier pocket money to spend on wine, women and gambling but so he could pay for fines, pay repair bills for his clothing and equipment, purchase soap and cleaning equipment and if needed buy new items of clothing. All repairs were carried out under the auspices of the *caporal-fourrier*. Minor repairs were to be carried out to clothing and equipment by the soldier, for more major repairs, the *caporal-fourrier* took the solider and his damaged items to the captain clothing officer, who authorised the regimental workmen to undertake the repair. If the repair was judged to be necessary through the negligence of the soldier, he had to pay for the work or a replacement item from his pay.[3]

We now turn our attention to what the men wore, both the idealised theoretical appearance from the dress regulations and reality.

Chapter 1

Chasseurs à Cheval

Since 1789, the number of light cavalry regiments in the French Army had more than doubled in number, with twenty-six regiments; light cavalry was of increasing importance in picket and patrol work as well as screening the army, leaving the heavy cavalry for the shock of the charge. The *chasseurs à cheval* cost less to clothe and equip and train. As the First Empire progressed, more regiments were raised, the 27e on 29 May 1808 from the Belgian Chevau-Legers d'Arenberg; the 28e in Tuscany in January 1808; the 29e, formed in late 1810 from the 3e Provisional regiment of Light Cavalry; the 30^{e} on 3 February 1811, but were in theory lancers, and finally the 31^{e}, formed on 7 September 1811 by amalgamating the 1^{e} and 2^{e} Provisional regiments of Light Cavalry.

A 'Provisional' title indicated that the battalion or regiment unit was consciously intended to be engaged in battle in that formation. This system was applied both for infantry and cavalry. During the 1806 campaign, eleven provisional regiments of cavalry were formed by adding a fifth squadron to each cavalry regiment. These men were to be equipped and trained at their *dépôts* in France, and then dispatched as provisional squadrons to Magdeburg, Cassel or Potsdam, with their horses coming from France. During the march to the forward *dépôt*, the men were to undergo on-the-job training. During the new year Napoléon busied himself with the remounting of his cavalry. By 25 February 1807, the remount *dépôt* at Cassel had processed 10,977 horses and held some 866 more. The remount *dépôt* at Potsdam needed 6,962 horses to mount dismounted men. Furthermore, between 1 December 1806 and 25 February 1807 Potsdam had sent 3,500 to 3,800 horses to each army corps and had mounted 7,000 men.[4] At the start of March 1807, Napoléon ordered Marshall Kellerman to form four provisional regiments of cavalry from the men at *dépôts* in France who were equipped, mounted and trained and had arrived at Potsdam. Each regiment was to have five companies. In each regiment the first company were to be *hussars*, the second *chasseurs à cheval*, the third and fourth companies dragoons and finally a fifth company to be either *carabiniers* or *cuirassiers*. Each company was to have 120 men, the regiment 600 men.[5] Things changed in 1807 when provisional regiments of each arm were created. The 1e provisional *chasseurs* mustered 600 men from the 1e, 2e, 5e, 7e and 11e regiments. The second provisional regiment again of 600 men was formed from detachments of the 12e, 13e, 16e, 20e and 21e regiments. In addition, *régiments de marche* were formed. These were general administrative groupings for moving troops from rear areas to field armies and are titled *marche* companies, squadrons, battalions etc. When reaching the designated corps or similar formation, these units were usually broken down or distributed among the existing units (usually part of their parent regiment). For example, at Perpignan in 1808 a *marche* squadron of *chasseurs à cheval* formed from men held in the dépôts of the 3e, 14e and 24e *chasseurs à cheval* regiments, which totalled some 200 horses.[6]

With the abdication of Napoléon in 1814, the Royal Ordinance of 12 May 1814 disbanded the Imperial Army.[7] All three arms were culled. Only the senior regiments of cavalry and infantry were to be taken into the new Royal Army. The cavalry was reduced from 110 regiments to 56. The 16e through to 31e *Chasseurs à Cheval*, and the 7e to 14e *Hussar* regiments were disbanded.[8] The 7e survived the cull and became the *Hussard du Orléans*. During the Hundred Days a hastily raised 16e *Chasseurs* was created. These regiments were disbanded with the decree of 25 September 1815.

In terms of dress, from 1801 onwards the *chasseurs* had been allowed to wear light cavalry style *dolmans*, but not the *pelisses* or sabretaches of the *hussars*. In undress they wore a single-breasted *surtout* (jacket with long tails). The building block for the uniform of the *chasseur* regiments during the course of the First Empire came with the decree of 22 February 1802:

> The Consuls of the Republic, on the report of the Minister of War; the state council heard,
> Stop:
>
> Art. I. The mass of clothing of the troops will remain fixed, for the year X, at the rate which was determined by the law of the 28 Fructidor year VII.
>
> It will be paid in full for each body by the decree of Vendémiaire, year X.
>
> The accounts and the administration of this mass will remain fixed as they were by the decree of 9 Thermidor year VIII.
>
> II. The effects of clothing and equipment to be distributed in year X, on the funds of the mass of clothing, are those named below, and they will not be renewed until the periods hereafter determined.
>
> XIV. *Chasseurs à Cheval.*

objects.	duration.
Dolman:	4 years.
Broadcloth *veste*:	4.
Culottes hongroise:	2.
Surtout:	2.
Manteau:	8.
Schakos:	4.
Stable trousers:	1.
Sabre belt:	6.

Boots: 2.	
Giberne and belt:	20.
Carbine belt:	20.
Porte-manteau:	8.
Saddle, breastplate, crupper, girth surcingle, stirrups and irons, bridle, head collar:	20.
Wool saddle blanket:	8.
Schabraque:	8.

Non-commissioned officers (sergeant, *fourriers* and sergeant majors), corporals and *chasseurs* will provide, at their expense, the repair of their boots.

Each non-commissioned officer and soldier will receive, each year, a *veste* made from the old clothing.

The provisions of Articles IV, V, VI, VIII, IX and X are common to the *chasseurs*, viz:

IV. Non-commissioned officers and soldiers will be required to provide *bonnets de police* at their expense.

VI. The clothes and jackets that will be replaced in year X, will belong to the regiment; the best will be kept for the clothing of the new soldiers, for the guard – house, the prison and the discipline room.

VII. Non-commissioned officers and soldiers will be allowed to provide white linen breeches for the summer, while complying with the provisions of the instruction which will be written and addressed to each regiment by the Minister of War.

VIII. The administrative council will take steps to procure for each ordinary or barrack room, a number of canvas smocks for the men to wear on fatigues.[9]

From this basic building block, colonels were free to pick and choose what their regiment wore. Nothing official had been written down about the dress of trumpeters.

Dolmans, Habits or Surtouts?

The *dolman* was a costly and flamboyant garment, and in order to reduce the cost of clothing the cavalry, in October 1804 the War Ministry ordered that they were to be taken out of service and replaced with a *surtout* that was to have short tails. It seems this sombre garment was the cause of much complaint by regimental colonels and the decree of 6 July 1806 stated that the *chasseurs à cheval* were to do away with the *surtout*, which were henceforth replaced by the *habit-surtout* i.e., a short-tailed *habit* with rounded-headed, point-ended *revers*, and at the same time the infantry *schakos* was to be adopted.[10] Under both the *habit* and *surtout* a white broadcloth *veste* (sleeveless waistcoat with V notch to centre front) or *gilet* (flat-bottomed, sleeveless waistcoat) lined in serge was worn. The front was closed by ten small uniform buttons. Under the terms of the decree, all the existing *surtout* were to be re-made as *gilet d'ecuries* (stable coats) by the simple act of cropping off the tails. The official tariff for the *habit-surtout* for the years 1806 to 1812 was as follows:[11]

Item	Cloth	1806, 1807, 1808, 1809, 1810	1811, 1812
Habit	Green broadcloth	1m 68[cm]	1m 56
	Facing cloth	0m 10	0m 15
	Facing colour serge	3m 26	2m 12
	Linen for lining	0m 80	1m 10
	Small Buttons	22	6
	Large Buttons	6	16
Veste	White broadcloth	1m 9	1m 9
	White serge	1m 56	
	Linen for lining	0m 29	1m 30
	Buttons	12	12
Gilet d'ecuries	Green broadcloth	Made from old *surtouts*	1m 10
	Facing cloth		0m 6
	Linen		1m 34
	White serge		
	Small buttons		24
Culottes hongroise	Green broadcloth	0m 89	1m 10
	Linen	0m 40	0m 40
	Lace	3m 57	4m

The changeover to the new regulation would have taken time to complete. It is very unlikely that any new clothing was made in 1806 and issued before the 1806–07 campaign began and made its way to the squadrons on active service. Inspected on 1 June 1807 we find:[12]

3^e^ *Chasseurs*: 606 *habits* and *vestes* in service
7^e^ *Chasseurs*: 610 *habits* and *gilets* in service
11^e^ *Chasseurs*: 749 *gilet d'ecurie*s were worn as service dress
13^e^ *Chasseurs*: 598 *habits* and 562 *gilets* in service
19e *Chasseurs*: 609 surtouts and *gilets* in service
20e *Chasseurs*: 589 *surtouts* and *gilets* in service
22e *Chasseurs*: 508 *surtout*s and 510 *gilets* in service

The lack of further archive sources inhibits any further discussion on this, but is likely that *dépôt* squadrons had new-issue clothing and the war squadrons only received new issue once back in France at the end of 1807, and assuming they had had time to re-equip before heading to fight in Spain. At the end of 1807 we find that:

1e *Chasseurs*: 455 *surtouts* and 741 *gilets* in service[13]
2^e *Chasseurs*: 720 *habits* and 854 *vestes* in service[14]
3^e *Chasseurs*: 907 *habits* and *vestes* in service[15]
4^e *Chasseurs*: 580 *surtouts* and 810 *gilets* in service[16]
6^e *Chasseurs*: 803 *surtouts* and 802 *gilets* in service[17]
9^e *Chasseurs*: 582 *habits* and 657 *vestes* in service[18]
12^e *Chasseurs*: 1020 *surtouts* in service[19]
16^e *Chasseurs*: 1103 *surtouts* in service[20]

Clearly *habits* and *surtouts* were used side by side. Therefore, it would take time to harmonise the *chasseurs* into a single, uniform, order of dress. For example, the 16e was given a shake-down inspection on 25 January 1808. The inspecting general authorised the regiment to adopt *habits* in lieu of *surtouts*, and agreed 808 be purchased, phased in over the next two years.[21]

In January 1810, the light cavalry were officially authorised to adopt *pantalons à cheval*: these were overalls made from tricot, opening at the side seam with bone buttons with the inner leg and the bottom of the leg reinforced with leather. These had been used unofficially since 1802: the 22e *Chasseurs* had these in 1807 recorded as *pantalons d'ecurie en drap*, which neatly describes their appearance.[22] More changes followed. In March 1811, the War Ministry decreed that *habits a revers* were to be discontinued, and all regiments were to have the *kinski*, i.e., the short-tail *surtout*, which is what many regiments were already wearing. With the savings made on the cheaper *kinski* compared to the *habit*, the 'spare money' was authorised to be used to pay for *gilet d'ecuries* to be made from new material.[23]

As before, changeover will have taken time: all garments had a regulated lifespan, so a brand-new *habit a revers* issued 1 October 1810 would not be scheduled to be replaced until October 1812. The regiments must have presented a very mixed and far from uniform look as they marched to Russia. A complete route and branch reform of the dress of the French Army was begun in 1811, headed by General Bourcier, with Major Bardin as secretary. The resulting regulation issued 15 February 1812 carried Bardin's name. Under the terms of the Bardin regulation, the stable trousers – *pantalons d'ecurie* – were to be suppressed and the money allocated to make them used to produce *pantalons à cheval.* In their place, simple *pantalons de route* – linen canvas overalls – were to be adopted.[24]

Bardin

Under the terms of the 1812 regulations, the *chasseurs* adopted the *habit-veste.* Details about the dress of the *chasseurs à cheval* can be found in Part 3, Section 4 of the regulations, which was heavily amended in April 1813. We reproduce the regulation as it is written down in 2022:

Art 1 Clothing

1395. The clothing of the *sous-officiers and chasseurs* will ~~comprise wi~~ll [three lines redacted text rendering it totally illegible] be of the general dispositions viz. No. 298.

1396. The *habit-veste* will be in Imperial Green broadcloth and will conform ~~of the model issued to the light infantry viz. No. 648~~ to the general model viz. No..4, however the sleeves will be slightly wider [sentence redacted] and the cuffs will be in the form affected for the light troops as shown in engraving No. 1648 and will be garnished with four large buttons and twenty small.

1397. The pockets will not be figured on the outside edges and instead a patch will be placed in the pleats placed below the small of the back, and the top of the patch will be cut into three points garnished with piping; the pocket will be lined. The pocket will descend the length of the retroussis; they will be 200mm long from the top edge of the highest point. The patch will be 20mm wide, piping included. The escutcheon will be 40mm and will be placed on the button small of the back. There will be placed a second button 100mm lower than the first, measured from the centre of this button See the engraved design No. 1397. The ~~retroussis~~ [rest illegible]

1398. The *gilet* is to be cut from white broadcloth ~~it will have no sleeves, and will have a collar with no hooks and eyes and be 25mm tall.~~ It will conform to general model No. 301.-

1399. The *gilet d'ecurie* will be made from green tricot and will conform to the general model Viz. No. 304.

1400. The *culottes hongroise* will be made from green broadcloth and the same cut as those of the *hussars*, with the exception of the braid which will extend to the waistband.

1401. The *caleçon* will conform to the general model of the infantry Viz. No. 21.

1402. The *pantalons à cheval* will be in green tricot and conform to the general model Viz. No. 308.

1403. The stable trousers will conform to general model No. 311

1404. The sleeved cloak will be in green broadcloth and conform to the model No. 320.

Art 2. Headdress

1405. The headdress of the *sous-officiers* and *chasseurs* will comprise a *schako* and a *bonnet de police*. The Elite companies will wear *schakos* the same as the grenadiers of the infantry Viz. No. 37.

1406. The *schakos* will be the same as that of the infantry Viz. No. 32; the plate ~~will be of the form in the engraved drawings as will be the~~ and chinscales which will be in the colour of the uniform buttons.

1407. The *bonnets de police* will be in broadcloth the same colour as the body of the habit and will conform to the model. Viz. No. 45.

Art 3. Distinctive Markings

1407. The distinctive marks of the *sous-officiers* ~~and those of the corporals~~ will be in silver ~~as detailed as for the *hussars*~~ and as detailed in general dispositions Viz. No. 355 and 337. The corporals will wear the same stripes as the light infantry, placed the same. The distinctions of the veterinarians and farriers will conform to No. 328 and 340.

1408. The trumpeters of the *Chasseurs à Cheval* will conform in all points to general dispositions No~~. 338 and 399~~ 341. Their *habits* will be the same as description No. 83, except that the form will be that of light troops.

Art 4. Weapons and Equipment

1409. The armament of the corporals and *chasseurs* will comprise a sabre a ~~pair of~~ pistols and a *mousqueton* with bayonet. The sergeants, *fourriers*, trumpeters and farriers are armed the same except they don't have the *mousqueton*.

1410. The equipment comprises a *giberne*, a *porte-giberne*, a *banderolle-porte-mousqueton*, a sabre belt, a sabre knot a pair of boots with spurs and a porte manteau.

1411. The *giberne* is exactly the same as that for the ~~*hussars*~~ light artillery, Viz. No. 1234 and 1244.

1412. The *porte-giberne* will conform ~~to that of the *hussars* Viz. No. 1302~~ to No.1245.

1413. The *banderolle-porte-mousqueton* will conform to general dispositions No. 365. [6 lines of text redacted]

1414. The waistbelt for the sabre is the same as for the light artillery, Viz. No. 1250 to 1257.

1415. The sabre knot is the same as the general model Viz. No. ~~350~~ 353.

1416. The boots and spurs are of the general model Viz. No. 1372.

1417. The *porte manteau* is made from Imperial Green broadcloth and to conform to the general model Viz. No. 350.

Art 5. Petit Equipment, Linen and Footwear

1418. The petit equipment will comprise ~~a musette, a pair of black gaiters, three shirts, two stocks, three rabats, two handkerchiefs, [illegible] and will conform to the general dispositions, Viz. No. 370~~ the general dispositions No. 372.

Art 6. Harness

1419. The harness for the horses of the *chasseurs* will be strictly the same as for the light artillery, Viz No. 1262 to 1300 except that it will also include the porte canon as described in dispositions No. 1381.[25]

The Bardin-regulation *schako* was also introduced on 17 September 1812. It was 240mm in diameter and 190mm tall. Those of grenadiers and *carabiniers* were 200mm tall and 250mm in diameter. New *schako* plate designs were introduced to replace the diamond plate of 1810. For elite companies, the colpack was removed from use, and they wore grenadier *schakos*, as used by the infantry, or at least in theory. The *schako* differed from the standard design as it sported a scarlet wool lace top band 40mm wide with a pair of 20mm-wide V chevrons, to be 10mm wide at the bottom measured inside the lace, and 90mm at the top. A second V chevron was placed 10mm outside the inner V chevron. It was also taller than the standard *schako*, being 20cm tall and 25cm in diameter. On the back of the *schako*, where a copper buckle was fitted to hide the join in the leather bottom band on a standard model, rather than a buckle a small copper grenade was substituted. The regulations also don't give any dimensions of this. An *aigrette* 18cm tall and made from dyed horse hair bound to a wire core was authorised for use for the by the elite company in lieu of the feather plume. Scarlet fringed epaulettes were authorised to be used and any other design of shoulder decoration removed from use – at least in theory.[26]

Officers

Bardin decreed the following for officers' dress:

Section 7: Clothing and Headdress of the Officers

1419. The clothing of the officers of the *chasseurs* will be made as described in the general dispositions No. 427 to 438. The *frac*, ~~redingote~~ and manteau are green.

1420. The headdress will comprise a *schako*, a *chapeau* for undress and a *bonnet de police*: these will conform to the general dispositions No. 439 to 448. The lace on the *schako* will be in silver.

1421. The distinctive marks of the officers will conform to the general dispositions No. 450; the epaulettes sword knot, sabre knot will be in silvered thread and conform to details No. 451 to 452.

1422. The foot wear of the officers will conform to the general dispositions No. 458.

1423. The officers will be armed according to the general dispositions No. 459. The sabre is the same as those used by the light artillery No. 1306.

1424. The equipment of the officers is described in the general dispositions No. 465 to 469. The *porte manteau* is in green broadcloth laced in silver. The waistbelt is as follows.

1425. The sword belt is made from green Moroccan leather, lined on the interior with yellow leather. It is the same as for the officers of light artillery, except the lacing is in silver, the fittings carry the head of the lion and silvered and will conform to engraved designed No. 1425. On campaign officers may use a sword belt of the same design but made from varnished black leather.

1426 … the *schabraque* are made from green broadcloth laced in silver and is the same form as used by the officers of light artillery see No. 1321.[27]

Officers did not have sheepskin *schabraques*, and interestingly the officers were not authorised to carry a *giberne*. They were allowed to wear in undress a narrow white buff leather waistbelt to carry an épée, which was adorned with a silver sabre knot.

Bardin Mark 2. The 1813 Collation

Bardin regulation was ordered into production on 17 September 1812, to be in place by 3 February 1813. For the *chasseurs à cheval*, immediate changes were to the elite company, which were to have '*schako et aigrettes de grenadier*' and no epaulettes. Trumpeters likewise were ordered into Imperial Livery, so too the *hussars*, who also had the grenadier model *schako* and *aigrette* for the elite company. The 'light cavalry' was authorised gaiters made from linen and oil cloth covers for headdress. Despite being designed, nothing was said to authorise the production of 'Bardin' pattern leather work.[28] A document of 14 October 1812 advised the Emperor that old-pattern clothing would be allocated to regiments in Spain, and old-pattern clothing held in *dépôt* in Germany would also head to Spain if the logistics could be organised.[29]

Again, as a cost-cutting and common sense approach to the situation, regiments were ordered to use up all existing stocks of clothing and equipment before embarking on the production of new apparel.[30] Having to rebuild the army from scratch almost, it was quickly discovered that France simply did not have sufficient resources to reclothe and equip the mounted arm. A report, dated 18 February 1813, by the commander of the 12e Military District based at La Rochelle illustrates the chaotic situation that regimental *dépôt* workshops found themselves in, and is no doubt representative of regimental *dépôt* throughout the Empire at this time:

> 5e Chasseurs: The workshop comprises 25 labourers. The tailors aren't able to make any items as they have no cloth or other materials. This is because H.E. has only allowed sufficient funds for the regiment to buy materials, which are due to arrive by 10 March, to dress 150 men. In total the regiment needs to clothe and equip 325 men. It is important that H.E. gives the orders to issue the funds so the regiment can cloth and equip these 325 men.
>
> 10^e^ Chasseurs: 22 labourers actively employed in production of clothing, equipment and saddles.
>
> 13^e^ Chasseurs: The materials needed for the uniforms for the 1812 conscripts arrived on January 28th. The regimental labourers are now actively making uniforms.

> 22e Chasseurs: There are 50 complete uniforms in stores and the regimental tailor and labourers are working on making another 163. Furthermore, the regimental saddler is busy making the equipment authorised by H.E. and have passed contracts to have 163 sets of harness and saddles produced for the sum of 61,203 francs. However, I regret to say, the regiment has only received 14,000 francs from H.E.
>
> 27e Chasseurs: The regimental tailor is busy making 188 uniforms for the conscripts. The regiment has taken measures to acquire enough tack for 188 horses.
>
> 31e Chasseurs: The regimental saddler and labourers are actively working on making the 307 sets of harness and saddles required. It is uncertain if they'll be ready for 1 March as H.E. ordered.
>
> 1e Hussars: The master-tailor will soon be inactive if H.E. doesn't send the necessary materials to make pantalons etc ... The master-saddler is making 163 saddles; however, the regiment has not been able to make the 165 sets of harness required due to lack of materials.
>
> 2e Hussars: The regimental labourers are actively making uniforms, equipment and tack.
>
> 3e Hussars: Since the start of the month, the regimental tailor reports that his workshop has made 45 pelisses, 87 dolmans, 106 stable jackets, 229 pairs of trousers and 65 complete harnesses. The regiment is finding it difficult to recruit labourers.
>
> 9e (bis) Hussars: The regimental workshop has 24 labourers. The master tailor reports that the uniforms for 50 conscripts of the Class of 1813 have been completed. The master saddler and labourers are working on making 50 sets of equipment. The master-saddler has committed himself to make 156 complete schabraques by 1 March and by the 15th, it is hoped that they'll have another 198.[31]

Despite these obstacles, the Emperor was able to field a rejuvenated mounted arm at the battles of Lützen and Bautzen.

On 10 April 1813, the Bardin decree of February 1812 was comprehensively rewritten. All trumpeters – except the *hussars* – now wore the same pattern *habit* as the line infantry: away went the *revers* with laced edging used by the dragoons, lancers and *chasseurs*. More changes occurred two months later or thereabouts. On 22 June 1813, Count de Cessac wrote to the commissary inspectors, sub-inspectors and regimental colonels:

> 1. The light infantry regiments, *chasseurs à cheval*, *hussars*, artillery train battalions, engineer and equipment train, irregular troops, veteran battalions, coast-guards and national guards that, as a result of my decision, are to buy leather accoutrements made from black cowhide in lieu of buff leather;

2. Line infantry regiments, *carabiniers*, *cuirassiers*, dragoons, *chevau-légers*, foot and horse artillery are exempted from the above decision and will continue to use buff leather.[32]

In theory, the light cavalry and troops of the train adopted blackened cow hide leather work. The last major change to the dress of the *chasseurs* came on 25 January 1814. Due to an acute shortage of green broadcloth, the War Ministry allowed that *manteaux-capote* were to be made from chestnut brown, white, *blanc picque de bleu* and *brun-beige* broadcloth and tricot.[33]

Bardin Mark 3. The 1814 Collation

By the end of spring 1814, after three campaigns, the army was exhausted. Bardin regulation had evolved, many aspects not being implemented due to lack of time and lack of funds. Bardin was not in universal use, nor was every change fully implemented by the time the Emperor rode away from Fontainebleau. The War Ministry *Circulaire* of 22 April 1814 stated that the decree of 19 January and 7 February 1812 for the dress of the army was to be enforced. Any clothing not made to these regulations was to be removed from use. The War Ministry as part of the 'rebranding' exercise made the following amendments to the Bardin regulations, the fifth such major change:

> On the retroussis of the habits the crowned N will be removed and replaced by a fleur des leys, 70mm tall (2 pouces ½ or thereabouts) and of proportionate width.
>
> The crowned N will be removed from the *schako* plates
>
> The crowned N will be removed from the *gibernes*
>
> The crowned N will be removed from sabretaches
>
> The crowned N will be removed from the buttons of the gendarme
>
> The drummers, trumpeters and musicians will abandon the colour green and will use bleu de Roi in its place for habits and will use the Livery of the Royal Household.
>
> All other aspects will be in strict conformity to the two decrees.[34]

At the same time, a second circular from the War Ministry ordered that all the codicils that made up the Bardin collation of orders generated from January 1812 through to June 1813 were to be deleted:[35]

1. Black leather work was to be replaced
2. *Pokalems* were undress headgear
3. All *gilets* were to be made from broadcloth
4. Elite companies had scarlet epaulettes, *aigrettes* and grenadier *schakos*. Colpacks were abolished
5. All pre-Bardin clothing to be taken out of service

In essence, all non-standard clothing and equipment was to be replaced. This was the first time that the War Ministry had the chance to impose onto the armed forces the Bardin regulation, and vast sums of money were allocated to the task of remaking the Imperial Army in the Royalist mould.

Bardin Mark 4. The 1815 Collation

On 8 February 1815, the War Ministry issued a new dress regulation to dress the army in the new Royalist manner. The regulations were framed on the Bardin regulation of 1812. It was the first time that the army had chance to be totally re-equipped with new-pattern clothing and equipment. One notably innovation was the fact the War Ministry ordered the light cavalry to abandon *culottes hongroise* and *pantalons à cheval* in favour of overalls worn over the boots, the same as used by the heavy cavalry, made from *gris-beige* broadcloth.[36]

A huge reclothing programme began in spring 1815, but any chance of rolling out the new regulation came to a juddering halt with Napoléon's return. At the start of the Hundred Days, yet another collation of dress regulations appeared. According to the decree of 28 March 1815, the two decrees of 19 January and 7 February 1812 were to be reinstated: drummers and trumpeters were to wear green with Imperial Livery, the Royal Cypher and *fleur-de-lys* were abolished in favour of the crowned 'N'.[37]

How far these changes were implemented can only be judged by looking at their implementation at regimental level. What follows is a discussion of the uniform of every regiment of cavalry and ancillary troops where archive paperwork can found.

Chapter 2

Chasseurs à Cheval – Regulations in Practice

Despite whatever the War Ministry may have said about dress regulations, how these were implanted at regimental level was another matter. In order to assess how regulations were actually enacted upon we now look at the regiments of *chasseurs* to assess theory and practice of the implementation of the various uniform decrees across the period. Throughout the course of the Empire a total of thirty-two *chasseur* regiments existed, the last numbered being raised in 1814.

1e *Chasseurs à Cheval*

Formed in 1651, it became a dragoon regiment in 1776, and from 17 March 1788 the *Regiment du Chasseurs d'Alsace*. The 1e *Chasseurs* from 1791, the regiment was inspected at Verdun on 25 May 1803:[38]

Item	In Good Repair	In Need of Repair	To be Written Off	Total	Total made since 28 January 1802	To be Replaced
Habits	Nil					
Dolmans	594	22		616	616	
Pelisses	Nil					
Surtouts	113			113	114	
Manteaux	174	191	120	485	130	
Gilets in broadcloth	539	77		616	299	
Gilet d'ecuries	372	120	174	666	372	
Culottes hongroise	174		360	534	174	
Stable trousers	628			628	694	
Chapeaux	Nil					
Schakos	59	350	239	638	59	
Bonnets de police	350		248	598	350	

The *dolman* we suppose was used for parade dress, and the *surtout* for everyday use but clearly not every man had *surtouts*, perhaps reserved for sous-officiers only? Rather than a *capote*, the cavalry used a *manteau* (large cloak made from green broadcloth). At first this was a cape with a standing collar, introduced in 1791. By 1801 the garment had developed a short shoulder cape. The front of the cape was closed by a row of six hooks and eyes. The lining of the shoulder cape, the front opening at the body, and the

pl. 40
Troupes Françaises
150
Chasseurs à cheval
1er Régiment

Chasfeur à Cheval du 1er Regiment.

Chasseurs à cheval 1812. 1er Rég.

Pl. 40
Troupes Françaises
Chasseurs à cheval
1. Régiment

back vent were lined in the facing colour of the regiment. When folded and placed on the cantle of the saddle it was hidden under the *schabraque*.

Cloth and other materials in the *dépôt* comprised:[39]

Item	In *Dépôt* 1802	Purchased since 1802	Total	Amount Used	Remaining in *Dépôt*
Green broadcloth	720m 59	1,033m 13	1,753m 72	1,365m 15	388m 57
White broadcloth		130m 28	130m 28	130m 28	
Scarlet broadcloth	9m 3	70m 23	79m 26	79m 26	
Treillis	The regiment has none				
Green tricot	693m 84	1,349m 92	2,043m 76	2,043m 76	
Scarlet tricot	The regiment has none				
White serge	845m 45	448m 63	1,294m 8	1,294m 8	
Linen	2,708m 14	2,540m 78	5,438m 92	5,248m 92	
Large buttons	304 doz	315 doz	649 doz	649 doz	
Small buttons	1795 doz	1,199 doz	2,995 doz	2,995 doz	
Bone buttons for stable trousers	The regiment has none				

The cloth list does not provide us with any surprises. The tricot was used to make *porte-manteaux* and *culottes hongroise*. No *treillis* or bone buttons existed to make new pairs of stable trousers. Furthermore, the *dépôt* held 234 old habits and had produced 616 new items, like wise 244 old *gilets* existed and 299 had been made new and issued. The inspecting general authorised the production of 193 new *dolmans*, 86 *manteaux* and 386 new *surtouts*, as well as 1,493 *gilets*, 772 pairs of *culottes hongroise* and stable trousers. Armament wise, the regiment had 597 carbines but not a single *banderole-porte-carabine* to carry them, 607 pistols and 637 sabres. No man had their regulation issue of linen *caleçon* (underwear).

Opposite: Four contemporary images depict the evolution of the uniforms of the regiment's centre companies.

Firstly, Martinet shows a trooper of the 1[e] *Chasseurs* as they appeared from 1803 to late spring 1805. The regiment was ordered to remove the *dolman* from service on 2 October 1804. The only men to wear *dolmans* by this date were the trumpeters: presumably these were scarlet-faced green.

In our second image is an eyewitness coloured sketch of a trooper by Zimmermann executed in 1808. Zimmermann shows us the detail of the long-tailed *habit*, which has uniquely white metal fish scale epaulettes. Of interest is that the trooper still wears the old-fashioned *queue*, and, despite not being elite company, wears a moustache.

Thirdly, an eyewitness painting of the 1[e] *Chasseurs* as they appeared before and during the Russian campaign. Our artist is Charles Jean Bregeot, born 1 October 1782, who was conscripted into the 16[e] *Chasseurs* in 1800, was promoted to sergeant major on 6 April 1809 and lieutenant on 3 July 1812. Captured during the Russian campaign, he languished in prison until he returned to France in spring 1815 and took no part in the Hundred Days' campaign. His artwork seems to be very reliable, as it can be cross referenced with the 1[e] *Chasseurs*' paper archive. Lastly, we have an image by Martinet published in 1814, showing the regiment as it appeared shortly before the First Restoration. (*Collection KM*)

Reconstruction of centre company trumpeters from a note by General Vanson housed in the *Musée de l'Armée*. On the left the trumpeter is wearing campaign dress, Vanson notes in 1805: the habit is in reversed colours and he wears the campaign legwear. Presumably in full dress, the trumpeters wore *culottes hongroise*. In the centre we see a trumpeter as they appeared from 1812 onwards, Vanson notes. Commandant Boucquoy – based on Vanson – also presents the same uniform but with an uncovered *schako*. Lastly, we present a reconstruction of a centre company trumpeter from the regiment's paper archive of 1813–14.

Inspected again on 2 October 1804, the regiment was reviewed at Gand. Clothing then in use as was follows:[40]

Item	In Good Repair	In Need of Repair	To be Written Off	Total	Total Made Since 25 May 1803	To be Replaced
Habits	The regiment has none					
Dolmans	35		548	583	35	
Pelisses						
Surtouts	614			614	614	
Manteaux	184		285	469	15	
Gilets in broadcloth	400	7	134	541	400	
Gilet d'ecuries	324		566	890	324	
Culottes hongroise	614		54	668	614	
Stable trousers			565	565	565	
Bearskins	84	16		100	36	
Schakos	258		392	650	258	
Bonnets de police	245		528	773	245	

By 1804 the *dolman* was clearly no longer in use bar 35 examples in good condition – were these for trumpeters and sous-officiers we wonder? – as 548 examples were to be written off. Clearly the regiment was not dressed in *surtouts*. Cloth and other materials in the *dépôt* comprised:[41]

Reconstruction of elite and centre company troopers based on the regiment's paper archive. On the left we see an elite company trooper wearing the 1808 issue *habit* that replaced the *surtout*, and he also wears the colpack. In the centre, we see the elite company as they appeared in 1813–14. The archive presents the use of plumes and *schako* cords, Martinet tells us the plume was black. Lastly, we see a centre company trooper from 1808 to 1814. At the end of the Empire a mix of Bardin and pre-Bardin *habits* were in service.

Item	In *Dépôt* 1803	Purchased since 1803	Total	Amount Used	Remaining in *Dépôt*
Green broadcloth	388m 57	2,635m 60	3,024m 17	2,213m 90	810m27
White broadcloth		425m 80	425m 80	384m 30	41m 50
Scarlet broadcloth		128m 54	128m 54	128m 54	
Treillis	The regiment has none				
White serge		1,971m 88	1,971m 88	1,770m 48	201m 40
Scarlet serge		586m 80	586m 80		586m 80
White tricot	The regiment has none				
Linen		3,992m 77	3,992m 77	3,992m 77	
Large buttons		1,600 ½ doz	1,600 ½ doz	1,299 doz	301 ½ doz
Small buttons		2,191 doz	2,191 doz	1,248 doz	9,432 doz
Bone buttons for stable trousers	The regiment has none				

The *dépôt* held 35 new *dolmans*, 54 new pairs of *culottes hongroise* and 50 pairs of stable trousers. Furthermore, 74 *surtouts* were in the *dépôt* awaiting repairs and 136 pairs of stable trousers were held waiting to be issued. The inspecting general authorised the production of 90 new *manteaux*, 404 *surtouts*, 202 *gilets*, 404 *gilet d'ecuries*, 808 pairs of *culottes hongroise* and stable trousers, 16 colpacks and 177 *schakos*. We also note that the regiment required 736 *banderole-porte-mousquetons*, of which only 37 were authorised for production along with 134 waistbelts, 37 *gibernes* with belts, 90 *manteaux*, 404 pairs of boots and 404 sword knots. The regiment possessed some 613 carbines, and yet had no shoulder belts to carry them and only 37 were to be made. Presumably these were for the elite company alone. A further 87 carbines were supplied from the Arsenal at Maubeuge. The regiment also had 586 pistols and 614 sabres for 720 men, so clearly over 100 men, presumably those in the *dépôt*, had no weapons at all. The regiment was also recorded as having 14 *enfant de troupe* as cadet trumpeters.

Some ten months later the regiment was inspected 22 July 1805:[42]

Item	In Good Repair	In Need of Repair	To be Written Off	Total	Total Made Since 2 October 1804	To be Replaced
Habits						
Dolmans		35		35		
Pelisses						
Surtouts	572		74	646		
Manteaux	53	55	140	237	52	
Gilets in broadcloth	493	100		590	180	
Gilet d'ecuries	290	324		614	192	
Culottes hongroise	607			607	607	
Stable trousers			136	136		
Bearskins	83	17		100		
Schakos	350	100	158	608	350	
Bonnets de police	46		185	301	46	

Cloth and other materials in the *dépôt* comprised:[43]

Item	In *Dépôt* 1804	Purchased since 1804	Total	Amount Used	Remaining in *Dépôt*
Green broadcloth	310m 27	1,449m 7	2,259m 34	1,354m 92	905m 29
White broadcloth	41m 50	161m 38	202m 82	202m 38	
Scarlet broadcloth		34m 61	34m 61		34m 61
Treillis	The regiment has none				
Green tricot		357m 30	357m 30	357m 30	
Scarlet tricot	586m 80	482m 48	1,069m 28		1,069m 28
White tricot	201m 40	989m 92	1,190m 72	1,067m 36	189m 36
Linen		2,019m 61	2,019m 61	2,019m 61	
Large buttons	301 ½ doz		301 ½ doz	301 ½ doz	
Small buttons	940 doz		940 doz	450 doz	484 doz
Bone buttons for stable trousers	The regiment has none				

The stocks of cloth again does not contain any surprises for us. Following the inspection 90 *manteaux*, 202 *surtouts*, 202 *gilets*, 404 *gilet d'ecuries* and 808 pairs of both *culottes hongroise* and stable trousers were authorised for production, as were 177 *schakos* and 17 bearskins. We assume the bearskins to be colpacks rather than a grenadier-style bearskin. The armament of the regiment does contain some surprised, as the regiment possessed 617 pistols, 688 cavalry carbines, 569 bayonets and 766 sabres, yet not a single *banderole-porte-carabine* existed to carry the carbine.

The regiment was inspected by General of Brigade LeBrun at Gand on 11 December 1807:[44]

Item	In Good Repair	In Need of Repair	To be Written Off	Total	Total Made Since 22 July 1805	To be Replaced
Surtouts	338	117		455	637	
Manteaux	383	300		633	640	
Gilets in broadcloth	330	411		741	629	
Gilet d'ecuries	471	227		698	1,029	
Culottes hongroise	144	136		280	938	
Stable trousers		300		300		
Colpacks			100	100		
Schakos	391	497		888	508	
Bonnets de police	255	58		313	765	

From the report, we see that insufficient pairs of *culottes hongroise* or stable trousers existed for each man to have a pair of each; it was a case of one or the other rather than both, which must have given the regiment a very varied look on parade. Unlike 1805, however, the regiment now had 591 *banderole-porte-carabine* in good condition. Forty had been so badly damaged in the recent campaign that they were to be written off, making a total of 631 examples, of which 430 had been made since 1805. The *dépôt* held 117 *surtouts* needing to be repaired, along with 300 *manteaux*, 319 *gilets* also needing repairs, and one new *surtout* and 154 new *gilet d'ecuries* yet to be issued. Cloth and other materials in the *dépôt* comprised:[45]

Item	In *Dépôt* 1805	Purchased since 1805	Total	Amount Used	Remaining in *Dépôt*
Green broadcloth	905m 23	5,386m 87	6,292m 10	6,025m 88	266m 72
White broadcloth		742m 82	724m 82	684m 61	40m 21
Scarlet broadcloth	34m 61	207m 19	241m 20	203m 20	38m 60
Treillis	The regiment has none				
White serge	123m 36	288m 8	3005m 44	3,004m 66	0m 78
Scarlet serge	1,069m 28	1,734m 57	2,803m 85	2,663m 42	140m 43
White tricot	The regiment has none				
Green tricot		834m 45	834m 45	753m 86	100m 59
Linen		4,952m 68	4,952m 68	4,873m 19	79m 49
Large buttons		1,877 doz	1,877 doz	1,409 doz	468 doz
Small buttons	434 ½ doz	1,669 doz	2,103 doz	1,791 doz	312 doz
Bone buttons for stable trousers	The regiment has none				

The inspecting general authorised the production of 124 new colpacks, 294 new *manteaux*, 474 *surtouts*, 188 *gilets*, 231 *gilet d'ecuries*, 649 pairs of *culottes hongroise* and stable trousers, 616 *bonnets de police*, 318 sabre belts, 240 *gibernes* and belt, 277 *banderole-porte-carabine*, 141 *porte-manteaux* and 523 pairs of boots. In terms of armament the regiment had 562 pistols, 944 carbines, 865 bayonets and 847 sabres. Since 1805, 322 pistols, 207 carbines, 207 bayonets and 215 sabres had been lost in action, but yet only 89 men had been killed in battle. Clearly a lot of equipment had simply been lost during the rigours of the campaign.

The regiment escaped the horrors of Spain, but instead suffered in Russia. It was re-formed in 1813 from conscripts, and the seven officers and fifty-seven men remaining at *dépôt*. Of these men, eight were to be sent to the infantry.[46] The re-formed regiment was clothed in the Bardin regulation.[47] We know very little about the dress of the regiment until it was disbanded in 1814 to form the *Chasseurs du Roi*:[48]

Item	In Service, but Due to Expire in the Next Year	In Need of Repair	To be Replaced in the Next Year	To be Replaced	Items Short
Habits	58	33	31	20	34
Gilets blanc	58	1	22	44	51
Gilet d'ecuries	58	18	16	40	44
Culottes hongroise	30	19	19	30	69
Stable trousers	41	6	47	26	56
Caleçon	43	2	67	25	39
Bonnets de police	71	6	24	26	49
Schako	103	7	29	22	15
Pantalons à cheval	46	23	43	29	35

Equipment passed to the new *Chasseurs du Roi* was as follows:[49]

Item	In Service, but Due to Expire in the Next Year	In Need of Repair	To be Replaced in the Next Year	To be Replaced	Items Short
Manteaux	84	18	12	29	33
Pair of boots	51	27	37	26	35
Pairs of gloves	64		22		90
Plumes	Nil				
Aiguilettes	Nil				
Waistbelts	87	23		23	43
Gibernes	101	28		11	36
Porte-gibernes	101	28		11	36

Item	In Service, but Due to Expire in the Next Year	In Need of Repair	To be Replaced in the Next Year	To be Replaced	Items Short
Porte-mousquetons	84	22		15	55
Sword knots	92	7		22	55
Fusils	66	9		43	
Sabres	87	13		21	
Pistols	55	11		27	

The inspector noted that the regiment accounts between 31 September 1812 and 9 March 1814 were incomplete and badly kept and that the regiment's colonel and Council of Administration were 'highly negligent' in their management. The *dépôt* of the regiment contained the following materials:[50]

0m 39 white broadcloth
40m 65 scarlet broadcloth
4m 75 green broadcloth
31m 58 scarlet serge
2m 84 white tricot
393m 57 linen
9m 78 trumpeters' lace
598m 80 linen lace
204m 41 flat wool lace
70m 55 *treillis*

In the regimental *dépôt* was a considerable amount of brand-new clothing ready to be issued: 3 trumpeters' *habits* – which were ordered to be burned and therefore adorned with Imperial Livery – 112 *habits a la chasseur*, 142 white *gilets* 25 pairs of *culottes hongroise*, and a solitary *gilet d'ecuries*, 148 pairs of stable trousers, 70 pairs of *caleçon*, 196 *bonnets de police*, 124 *schakos*, 66 *pantalons à cheval*, 135 *capotes*, 16 *schako* covers and 22 pompoms among other items.

In need of repair were 16 *habits a la chasseur*, with the same number of *culottes hongroise*, *pantalons à cheval*, *giberne* and belt, and to be written off were 31 *chasseur habits*, 60 *gilets*, 18 pairs of *culottes hongroise*, 6 *gilet d'ecuries* and 23 *porte-manteaux*. Other items in *dépôt* included 196 shirts, 14 black stocks, 29 white stocks, 60 pairs of wool stockings, 35 pairs of shoes, 44 *sacs a distribution*, 81 handkerchiefs, 10 spring clamps, 154 boxes of grease, 59 *habit* brushes, 36 *epinglettes*, 102 musket worms and 24 canteens among other items of grooming kit for the stables. The canteens are listed as wicker-covered bottles. Plumes are listed but none were in *dépôt*, so we suppose the regiment had these, counted with the *schakos* for elite company and trumpeters.[51] The '*habits a la chasseur*' are without a shadow of a doubt the short-tailed cutaway *habit a revers* used since 1806.

2e *Chasseurs à Cheval*

Formed in 1673 as a dragoon regiment, it was re-formed in 1788 as the *Regiment de Chasseurs de Évêchés*, becoming the 2e *Chasseurs* in 1791. Inspected on 28 July 1805, the regiment had the following clothing in use:[52]

Item	In Good Repair	In Need of Repair	To be written off	Total	Total made since 27 September 1803	Comment
Habits						
Dolmans						
Pelisses						
Surtouts	81	300	280	542	61	
Manteaux	200	58	61	317		
Gilets in broadcloth	79	210	216	505	79	
Gilet d'ecuries	444	85		529	244	
Culottes hongroise	193	52	250	499	198	
Stable trousers	311	143	86	541	118	
Colpacks	80			80	5	
Schakos	315	130	13	458	104	
Bonnets de police	453	22	66	541	53	

Most of the clothing was in tatters, and not every man had the regulation item of uniform. Despite this the elite company had colpacks made from bear pelt, according to the inspecting officer. To make good the clothing, 404 *surtouts* and *gilet d'ecuries*, 202 *vestes*, and 90 *manteaux* were authorised for production along with 808 pairs each of *culottes hongroise* and stable trousers, 17 new '*bonnets d'oursin*', 177 schakos and

We have reconstructed our elite company trooper of the 2e *Chasseurs* from the regiment's archive and also eyewitness observations. Our second image is a drawing by the artist Zimmerman, who shows the *surtout* and colpack, as well as the sabretache, at some time in 1808. Our third image by Berka adds more details to the rear of the uniform, and the appearance of the sabretache.

808 *bonnets de police*. The *dépôt* held 287m 83 of green broadcloth, 131m 32 of white broadcloth, 50m 2 of scarlet broadcloth as well as 61 new *surtouts*, 79 *vestes*, 244 *gilet d'ecuries*, 198 pairs of *culottes hongroise*, 118 pairs of stable trousers, 5 colpacks, 104 *schakos* and 50 *bonnets de police*.[53] By 24 September 1805, 560 new *surtouts* had arrived in the *dépôt* along with 6 *manteaux*, 347 *vestes*, 300 *gilet d'ecuries*, 51 pairs of *culottes hongroise*, 543 pairs of stable trousers – rather more than the authorised 118 pairs! – 11 colpacks, 75 *schakos* and 387 *bonnets de police*.[54]

Inspected on 23 November 1807, the regiment had the following clothing:[55]

Item	In Good Repair	In Need of Repair	To be written off	Total	Total made since 24 September 1805
Habits	714	6		720	571
Dolmans					
Pelisses					
Surtouts					
Manteaux	792	2		794	507
Gilets in white broadcloth	850	4		854	584
Gilet d'ecuries	1,012	11	11	1,034	1,034
Culottes hongroise	996	27	7	1,030	1,030
Stable trousers	985	20	16	1,021	1,021
Bearskins					
Schakos	991			991	829
Bonnets de police	1,000			1,000	873

Reconstruction of a trooper of the 2ᵉ *Chasseurs* based on the regiment's archive papers. At the time of the 1808 inspection, the regiment was wearing 720 *habits*, which had replaced *surtouts* issued in 1804. The old cutaway habits were still being worn in summer 1814, as we show here.

Reconstruction of a trumpeters uniform of the 2e *Chasseurs* said to be worn in 1818–14 based on notes by Rousselot housed in the library of the *Musée de l'Armée*. Secondly, a trumpeter as they appeared in 1814 to 1815 when ordered to adopt Royalist Livery, and lastly as they appeared in the Hundred Days.

Given that in 1805 no *habits* existed at all, and none were authorised for production, in the case of the 2e *Chasseurs*, judging by period iconography, *habit* must equal *surtout*. The *dépôt* held virtually no stocks of clothing, merely 8 pairs of *culottes hongroise* needing repairs, 1 waistbelt, 34 *giberne* and 10 *porte-gibernes*. Cloth held comprised 26m 80 of scarlet broadcloth, 174m 80 of white serge and 1,000m 70 scarlet serge.[56]

The regiment was decimated in the 1812 campaign. Reviewed on 27 April 1812, the *dépôt* held 7 officers, 4 master workmen and 137 other ranks. The regiment's major reported that the master workmen were busy making replacement clothing for the year 1812 and that the first shipment had been sent to the war squadrons.[57] We wonder if it ever arrived? Inspected on 27 July 1814, the regiment's clothing was in moderately good condition. Every man had his regulation uniform, even if it needed total replacement or repairs:[58]

Item	In Good Repair	In Need of Repair	Need Replacing in 1 Year	To be Replaced	Items Needed
Habits-vestes	71	36	43		
Gilet	173	18	29		
Veste d'ecurie	60	62	38		
Culottes hongroise	207	53			
Caleçon	52	98			
Pantalons à cheval	50	47	33		
Pantalon d'ecurie	38	16	106		
Manteaux	91	32	7		
Porte-manteaux	190	34	16		
Bonnets de police	172	64	34		
Schakos	125	37	8		
Pompom	Nil				

The men under arms had 502 shirts, and 140 black silk stocks – not a single pair of socks were in use. The men wore their boots over bare feet! Some 131 pairs of boots were in condition, 38 pairs needed repairs and 11 pairs were fit only for the rubbish tip. Remarkably some 230 *gibernes* were in use and not a single *giberne* belt! Likewise, not a single pair of gloves were in use or braces: we assume the belts for the *gibernes* were counted with the *gibernes* or were they hung off improvised belts made from string and other materials? The regiment was armed with 160 *mousquetons* in good condition and 14 needing repairs, 211 sabres in good condition, and 22 needing repairs and had 171 pistols. Materials in *dépôt* were very limited indeed, just 500m of lace for *culottes hongroise* and 90 dozen bone buttons! The inspector demanded funds so the regiment could be reclothed. The regiment was ordered 'to change its old *habits* to those currently worn in the line': we assume it was wearing the old cutaway *habits*.[59] Indeed, the inspector noted that the regiment had not adopted the uniform regulations as decreed on 19 January or 7 February 1812, nor had enacted the modifications of 23 April 1814 concerning the colour of trumpeter's *habits*.[60] Presumably the trumpeters wore Imperial Livery, but we cannot prove it, other than we know the trumpeters had not yet been reclothed in blue.

Disbanded in Strasbourg on 19 October 1815, the *dépôt* held 56 new *habits* and 1 needing repairs, 32 new *gilets*, 27 new *gilet d'ecuries* and 71 needing repairs, 57 *bonnets de police*, 42 new *manteaux* and 107 needing repairs, 92 *porte-manteaux in* good condition and 141 needing repairs, 32 pairs of *culottes hongroise* needing repairs, 32 new *schakos* and 15 needing repairs.[61]

A second report dated 25 November 1815 lists 1,430m 88 of green broadcloth, 135m of white broadcloth, 51m 97 of scarlet broadcloth, 74m 14 of green tricot, 160m 92 of *treillis*, 2m 70 of linen, 7m 80 of lace for sous-officiers, 89m 90 of worsted white lace and 977m 30 of lace for trumpeters – lace tended to come in rolls of around 560m, therefore we are clearly seeing two types of lace, no doubt Imperial and Royalist Livery under the same heading. Alas, we cannot tell the ratio of the lace types, but it is probably that both Royalist and Imperial Livery garments existed. Clothing comprised 4 *habits-vestes*, 35 *schakos*, 15 *manteaux*, 17 *porte-manteaux*, 109 *gibernes*, 71 *porte-gibernes*, 63 waistbelts. We also note that stores held 15 shirts, 45 pairs of wrist gloves, and 76 further pairs of stable trousers.[62] Not a single *aigrette*, *schako* or pair of epaulettes existed for the elite company. Clearly, the regiment only adopted Bardin in summer 1814 into spring 1815.

3e *Chasseurs à Cheval*

Formed in 1675 as a dragoon regiment, it became the *Chasseurs de Flandre* in 1788 and thence the 3e *Chasseurs* in 1791. The regiment had served in the 1798 Invasion of Ireland. General Charles Randon de Pully gave the 3e *Chasseurs à Cheval* a shake-down inspection on 21 October 1804.[63]

Officers of the 3e *Chasseurs* somtime in the period 1808–13. Reviewed in May 1811, General Nansouty tells us that the elite company were wearing *dolmans* and *colpcks*. Given that no more *dolmans* were to be made after 21 October 1804, the regiment's colonel clearly chose to ignore the utterances of the War Ministry and dressed his regiment how he wanted. Sabretache were never regulation, but were clearly used, so too *Pelisse*. In the background we see a trumpeter in a *bleu de ciel dolman*, red legwear and a red *schako*.

Item	In Good Repair	In Need of Repair	To be written off	Total	Total made since 24 May 1802	Comment
Habits						
Dolmans	454			454	28	
Pelisses						
Surtouts	487			487	579	
Manteaux	351		47	398	2	
Gilets in broadcloth	487			487	581	
Gilet d'ecuries	360		54	414	278	
Culottes hongroise	473		5	478	473	
Stable trousers	482		5	487	617	
Chapeaux						
Schakos	4,567			467	76	
Bonnets de police	450			450	196	

Judging by the numbers issued, the *dolman* we suppose was used for parade dress, and the *surtout* for everyday use, as per the regulation. Supporting this argument is the fact that just 25 *dolmans* were made between 1802 and 1804 compared to 570 *surtouts*. We note that at the close of the inspection, General Pully ordered that no more *dolmans* were to be made, and authorised the production of 404 new *surtouts*, 202 white broadcloth *gilets*, 404 *gilet d'ecuries* and 808 pairs each of *culottes hongroise* and stable trousers.

Cloth and other materials in the *dépôt* comprised:[64]

Item	In *Dépôt* 1802	Purchased since 1802	Total	Amount Used	Remaining in *Dépôt*
Green broadcloth	1,219m 76	1,868m 24	3,088m	1,954m 47	1,133m 53
White broadcloth	639m 59	229m 67	923m 66	651m 60	271m 76
Scarlet broadcloth	50m 44	32m 81	83m 25	69m 19	14m 6
Treillis	93m 55	960m	1,053m 55	1,053m 55	
Green tricot	1,249m 52		1,249m 52	1,249m 52	
Scarlet *tricot*	13m 6		13m 6	13m 6	
White serge	1,503m 69	816m 34	2,326m 2	1,609m 27	710m 75
Linen	998m 30	1,558m	2,556m 34	1,995m 27	561m 3
Large buttons		204 doz	204 doz	196 doz	8 doz
Small buttons	188 doz	3,366 doz	3,554 doz	1,816 doz	1,738 doz
Bone buttons for stable trousers	39 doz	2,576 doz	2,615 doz	2,615 doz	

The scarlet tricot is very much a curious addition to the list of cloth. Tricot was used to make *porte-manteaux* and *culottes hongroise*, therefore it seems the scarlet tricot was destined for trumpeters' *porte-manteaux* and legwear. The 3e *Chasseurs* only had scarlet cuffs to the *dolman* or *surtout*, so clearly they needed only a small amount of cloth for these, yet nearly 70m was used. We guess it was used for elite company *culottes hongroise* or even trumpeters' clothing.

Just over a year later, on 12 November 1805, General Pully inspected the regiment again. Clothing and equipment in use comprised:[65]

Item	In Good Repair	In Need of Repair	To be Written Off	Total	Total Made Since 21 October 1804	To be Replaced
Habits						
Dolmans	439			439		
Surtouts	57	386		443	57	
Manteaux	308		100	408	50	
Gilets in broadcloth	450			450	17	
Gilet d'ecuries	404			404	416	
Culottes hongroise	23		420	443	23	
Stable trousers	460			460	492	
Schakos a poil	66			66	12	
Schakos	330		49	399	201	
Bonnets de police	360		100	260	134	

We must ask, how come nearly all the *surtouts* in 1804 were in good condition, and thirteen months later 386 *surtouts* had to be repaired? Given the regiment was not involved in the Austerlitz campaign, what exactly were the men doing to the *surtouts*

The dress of the trumpeters of the 3^{e} *Chasseurs* is well documented.

Firstly, we see a trumpeter of the centre company of the 3^{e} *Chasseurs* in 1803–05 and again *c.*1809 to 1812. The elite company trumpeters no doubt wore a colpack. We have based our reconstruction on the Suhr manuscript and the regiment's archive, which supports trumpeters retaining the *dolman*. In our second image we see the trumpeters wearing scarlet: this is based on both the regiment's archive and an extant garment in the *Musée de l'Armée*. This uniform was in use from *c.*1812 though to 1814. During the First Restoration the trumpeters were ordered to be dressed in Royalist Livery. The habit shown is based on an extant garment in the *Musée de l'Armée*. Lastly, during the Hundred Days, the regiment was ordered to adopt Imperial Livery, which we show.

to as to damage over three quarters of them? Clearly, the clothing authorised to be produced in October 1804 had yet to be delivered, if it was ever ordered. Only 57 of the 404 *surtouts* had been delivered, and just 23 pairs of *culottes hongroise* out of the 808 authorised to be made had been delivered. Yet despite the regiment's tardiness in ordering clothing, the elite company had been decked out in fur-covered *schakos*, the '*schakos a poil*'. Despite hardly any of the 1804 authorised clothing being made, General Pully authorised the production of 90 *manteaux*, 202 new *surtouts* and *gilets*, 404 *gilet d'ecuries*, and yet again 808 pairs of *culottes hongroise* and stable trousers and 17 further *schako a poil* and 177 *schakos*. Cloth and other materials in the *dépôt* comprised:[66]

Centre company troopers of the 3e *Chasseurs* had three distinctive orders of dress after the *dolman* had been removed from use.

Firstly, we see a trooper wearing the regulation *surtout*, adopted from 21 October 1804 and worn through to winter 1807. Secondly, adopted in winter 1807 was the short-tailed *habit* worn with a distinctive red waistcoat. These garments were in use through to 1813 alongside the *kinski*, which was brought into use in 1811. From 1813 the regiment adopted Bardin regulation, which is shown in our third image.

Item	In *Dépôt* 1804	Purchased since 1804	Total	Amount Used	Remaining in *Dépôt*
Green broadcloth for 1st squadron	766m 47	1,673m 39	2,439m 86	761m 99	1,677m 87
Green broadcloth for 2nd squadron	367m 60	619m 11	986m 17	149m 60	836m 57
White broadcloth	271m 76	358m 61	630m 37	14m 17	616m 20
Scarlet broadcloth	14m 60	104m 74	118m 80	66m	52m 80
Scarlet serge		1,072m 54	1,072m 54		1,072m 54
Scarlet tricot		84m 19	84m 19	22m 19	61m 90
White serge	710m 75	2,113m 20	2,823m 95	1,452m 22	1,371m 73
Linen	561m 30	785m	1,346m 30	1,166m 80	179m 23
Large buttons	8 doz	1,441 doz	1,449 doz	701 doz	748 doz
Small buttons	1,738 doz		1738 doz	502 doz	1,236 doz
Bone buttons for pantalons		1,536 doz	1,536 doz	1,536 doz	

The list of cloth, as in 1804, poses interesting questions. Stable trousers seem to have been made out of broadcloth and not *treillis* after October 1804. Seemingly the stable trousers were *pantalons à cheval*, which acted as both campaign dress and undress use in stables. Pully's report also brings another startling comment. In 1804 and 1805 the regiment had not a single *banderole-porte-mousqueton* or *banderole-porte-carabine*, yet 404 infantry muskets were issued to the regiment!

The regiment had been almost completely redressed while in cantonments in Germany in the course of 1806 and 1807, and by June 1807 was wearing *habits*:

Item	In Good Repair	In Need of Repair	To be Replaced	Total	Observations
Habits	606			606	The regiment has no plumes, stable trousers, gauntlets, *pantalons à cheval*. The regiment has totally lost its *petit equipment*.
Surtouts					
Gilets en drap	606			606	
Stable coats	606			606	
Culottes hongroise	606			606	
Pantalons à cheval					
Stable trousers					
Caleçon	606			606	
Manteaux	596			596	
Bonnets de police	606			606	
Schakos	506			506	
Colpacks	100			100	
Schako covers	The regiment has none				
Pompoms					
Plumes					

The regiment was back in France by winter 1807 and General Pully, who had last inspected the regiment in 1805, did so again on 21 January 1808:[67]

Item	In Good Repair	In Need of Repair	To be Written Off	Total	Total Made Since 10 December 1805	To be Replaced
Habits	575	332		907	1,018	
Dolmans						
Pelisses						
Surtouts						
Manteaux	606	121	10	837	606	
Gilets in broadcloth	575	296	36	907	1,149	
Gilet d'ecuries	710	137	60	907	1,269	
Culottes hongroise	724	183		907	1,820	
Stable trousers	594	193	120	907	1,383	
Colpacks	40	69	17	100	43	
Schakos	500	109	198	807	560	
Bonnets de police	710	197		907	43	

Given the stable trousers were six months old or less, it is remarkable how many pairs needed repairs or total replacement in such a short space of time. Cloth and other materials in the *dépôt* comprised:[68]

Item	In *Dépôt* 1805	Purchased since 1805	Total	Amount Used	Remaining in *Dépôt*
Green broadcloth	2,514m 44	6,946m 38	9,460m 82	8,568m 45	1,192m 37
White broadcloth	613m 30	826m 90	1,440m 20	1,251m 32	188m 88
Scarlet broadcloth	52m 80	156m 40	209m 20	142m 32	66m 88
White serge	1,372m 73	5,151m 58	6,523m 36	5,514m 52	1,011m 79
Scarlet serge	1,072m 54	3,023m 34	4,095m 88	3,410m 28	685m 60
Green tricot		700m	700m	700m	
Scarlet tricot	61m 90		61m 90	61m 90	
Treillis	71m 40	3,311m 35	3,382m 75	3,382m 10	0m 65
Linen	179m 23	6,167m 98	6,347m 21	6,072m 10	275m 20
Large buttons	748 doz	1,500 doz	2,248 doz	1,477 doz	771 doz
Small buttons	1,342 doz	2,537 doz	3,879 doz	3,783 doz	96 doz
Bone buttons for stable trousers	The regiment has none				

As in 1805, the scarlet tricot is very much a curious addition to the list of cloth. Tricot was used to make *porte-manteaux* and *culottes hongroise*. Arguably as in 1805, trumpeters and elite company had scarlet breeches and scarlet *porte-manteaux*, and we also assume the trumpeters had scarlet habits. However, Suhr shows blue *dolmans* faced scarlet in use by 1810, but scarlet *surtout* faced in blue were returned to service by 1813. Furthermore, by this date the stable trousers seemingly were no longer closed down the outside leg by bone buttons. Again, as in 1805, the regiment had no *banderole-porte-carabine* to carry the An XI carbine or *mousqueton*. But General Pully commented that on 26 November 1805 the Arsenal at Turin had supplied 272 pistols, 18 carbines, 18 bayonets and 27 sabres. The Arsenal at Milan had provided 100 pistols. On 3 April

The elite company of the 3ᵉ *Chasseurs* wore distinctive uniforms across the First Empire. From 1804 to 1808 it seems the company wore scarlet *culottes hongroise*, based on the regiment's paper archive. The *surtout*, based on two contemporary images, had non-regulation scarlet cuffs. From 1808, the *surtout* was replaced with a *dolman* and from 1811 with a habit, as we show. Colpacks were in service through to winter 1813. In our second image, we present an elite company trooper during the 1814 campaign. Lastly, we show a reconstruction of an elite company trooper of the 3ᵉ *Chasseurs* at the end of the Hundred Days based on the regiment's paper archive.

1806 the Arsenal at Grenoble dispatched 12 carbines with bayonets; 3 December 1806 the Arsenal at Moutou supplied 224 carbines and bayonets along with 69 sabres. Finally, on 18 June 1807 a further 200 carbines with bayonets and 456 sabres were delivered from the Arsenal at Moutou. At the same time, 79 pistols, 146 fusils, 55 bayonets and 126 sabres were taken into the Arsenal at Moutou.[69]

Virtually destroyed in the Russian campaign, the regiment was rebuilt around the 60 sous-officiers and men that had remained in the *dépôt* in June 1812.[70] Everything had to be replaced: a process that carried on into spring 1813.The regiment at this stage adopted Bardin regulation.[71] The 3e *Chasseurs* were disbanded in June 1814. Clothing and equipment then in use comprised:[72]

Item	In Good Repair	In Need of Repair	Need Replacing in 1 Year	To be Replaced	Items Needed
Habits-vestes	178				
Gilet	178				
Veste d'ecurie	178				
Culottes hongroise	178				
Caleçon	93		85		
Pantalons à cheval	178				
Pantalon d'ecurie	178				
Manteaux	178				
Porte-manteaux					
Bonnets de police	178				
Schakos					
Pompom	Nil				

Every man was dressed in kit that was in good condition, having been recently issued to replace clothing that was non-regulation, the inspector noted. The last issue of clothing, the regimental accounts record, was made on 1 March 1813 when 12,102 francs 50 was spent on clothing, and a further 2,626 francs 20 was spent on 109 pairs of *pantalons à cheval* and 27 *gilet d'ecuries*. Clearly, the regiment only adopted 'Bardin' in summer 1814! In addition, the men were issued 528 shirts, 176 black stocks, 157 pairs of linen socks, and 157 pairs of shoes. The regiment's equipment and armament was as follows:[73]

Item	In Good Repair	In Need of Repair	Need Replacing in 1 Year	To be Replaced	Items Needed	Comment
Schako	174					Plus 15 covers in good condition and 163 to be written off
Pompoms	174					
Gibernes	164					

Item	In Good Repair	In Need of Repair	Need Replacing in 1 Year	To be Replaced	Items Needed	Comment
Porte-gibernes	164					
Banderole-porte-carabines	123					
Waistbelts	170					
Sword knots	170					
Pairs of gloves	167					
Pairs of boots	148			26		
Trumpets	11					Also 178 pairs of braces

The regiment was armed with 118 *mousquetons* – yet 123 *banderoles* were in use! – 168 sabres were issued for 170 sabre belts and 157 pistols were issued. The men further had 528 shirts, 176 black stocks, 157 pairs of linen socks, 157 pairs of shoes, 176 *epinglettes* and 171 musket worms. Cloth held in the *dépôt* was as follows:[74]

3m 50 blue broadcloth
7m 22 white broadcloth
0m 58 scarlet broadcloth
0m 15 green broadcloth
95m 36 white serge
0m 60 linen for *caleçon*
66m 36 white worsted lace for *porte-manteaux*
176m 92 worsted lace 8mm wide
231m 70 worsted lace for *culottes hongroise*
94m 14 white serge dyed red

Beige broadcloth is also listed, presumably for making the *manteaux*, but none remained. The presence of blue broadcloth confirms that trumpeters had blue habits: was this for new Royalist Livery items? Arguably no. Partial regimental accounts starting in 1812 offer a great degree of insight into the dress of the regiment. On 21 March 1813 the regiment redressed five trumpeters, buying:[75]

2m 75 blue broadcloth, total 31fr 93
12m 46 scarlet broadcloth, total 197fr 11
174m flat worsted braid for pantalons, total 26fr 70

We guess that, based on the proportion of cloth, the habit was scarlet faced blue, and the pantalons were scarlet perhaps with a blue side stripe. What shade of blue was used? A vivid mid-blue or darker imperial blue? An extant garment in the *Musée de l'Armée* has a mid-blue collar, and in all respects is identical to the garment described by the paper archive: beyond reasonable doubt the trumpeters wore a scarlet *kinski* with blue collar and tail facings. The collar is decorated with a single row of 22mm wide silver lace. It has white loops at the shoulder to take, we assume, white-fringed epaulettes.[76] Five new trumpets were purchased for 129 francs 90 and 12 *aigrettes* for trumpeters: the only *aigrettes* the regiment had. Some 90m of lace was purchased for 217 francs for *bonnets de police*, 7 pairs of shoes for 42 francs, 200 *schakos* costing 13 francs 55 each, and 470 cockades for 70 francs 50.[77] The purchase of lace for the *bonnets de police* confirms the regiment did not adopt Bardin regulation and never wore *pokalems*.

In the *dépôt* were stocks of new clothing, which included 10 *habits*, 134 *bonnets de police*, 23 *manteaux*, 1 *schako de modèle*, 2 pompoms, 26 *gibernes* with belts, 21 sword knots. Needing repair were 17 *gilet d'ecuries*, 14 pairs of stable trousers, 1 *schako* and 6 trumpets, and 42 *gibernes* were awaiting disposal.

The dress of the regiment in 1815 can be inferred from the items the regiment possessed at disbandment on 30 August 1815:[78]

Item	In Good Repair	In Need of Repair	Need to be Replaced
Habits-vestes	140	121	1
Gilets blanc	5	90	
Gilet d'ecuries	191	131	
Culottes Hongroise	86	45	
Pantalons à cheval	176	74	
Stable trousers	142	23	
Caleçon	274	59	
Manteaux-Capote	69	93	
Bonnets de police	289	77	
Porte-manteaux	300	57	
Schako for elite company	31	5	
Schakos	237	40	29
Schako covers	79	62	
Gibernes	255	202	109
Porte-gibernes	118	102	96
Porte-carabines	40	250	10
Waistbelts	205	139	96
Sword knots	152		2
Pairs of gloves	260		
Adjutants' epaulettes	2		
Scarlet epaulettes	38		

The regiment was seemingly dressed as per the February 1815 dress regulations, with the elite company in their own pattern *schakos*, and they were the only members of the regiment with fringed epaulettes, and had adopted Bardin-regulation kit. We are not sure if the *aigrette* was worn or not. These items could have been included with the *schakos*.

The trumpeters appear to have had blue habits with Royalist Livery as the *dépôt* held far more blue broadcloth in September 1815 than a year earlier:[79]

281m 90 green broadcloth
173m 23 white broadcloth
14m 90 scarlet broadcloth
12m 57 blue broadcloth for trumpeters
11m 40 capucine broadcloth inherited from 23e *Chasseurs* in 1814
1,566m 70 green tricot
925m 91 scarlet serge
593m 45 capucine serge inherited from 23e *Chasseurs* in 1814
1,330m 14 flat lace 10mm wide
49m 20 lace for corporals
339 dozen bone buttons

The magazine of the 1e and 2e squadrons on 1 October 1815 comprised, 0m 10 beige broadcloth, 3m 50 *bleu de ciel* broadcloth, 82m 32 white broadcloth, 0m 58 scarlet broadcloth, 430m 15 green broadcloth, 25m 65 capucine broadcloth, 700m 85 white serge and 28m 50 green tricot.[80] Seemingly the beige cloth was used to make the *manteaux-capote*, which in theory was to be green according to the 1812 regulations. No doubt for reasons of cost, the cheaper beige cloth was used. Between October 1814 and September 1815 some of the capucine [a shade of orange] wool cloth was used, which perhaps was used to repair clothing for members of the 23e *Chasseurs* who now served in the 3e *Chasseurs*. The *bleu de ciel* surely must be the same cloth as in *dépôt* in 1814, and further shows that the facings of the trumpeters' *habits* had been this colour. The regiment may have adopted Imperial Livery during the Hundred Days.

4e *Chasseurs à Cheval*

Formed as the *Chasseurs de France Comte* in 1788, the regiment became the 4e *Chasseurs* in 1791. General Pully inspected the 4e *Chasseurs* on 10 December 1805:[81]

Item	In Good Repair	In Need of Repair	To be Written Off	Total	Total Made Since Last Inspection	To be replaced
Habits						
Dolmans						
Surtouts	400		211	611	300	
Manteaux	341	10	165	516	47	
Gilets in broadcloth	400		211	611	400	

Item	In Good Repair	In Need of Repair	To be Written Off	Total	Total Made Since Last Inspection	To be replaced
Gilet d'ecuries	467	27	117	611	277	
Culottes hongroise	611	137		748	748	
Stable trousers	141	46	124	611	701	
Bearskins	70	10	20	100	16	
Schakos	333	47	131	511	118	
Bonnets de police	600		11	611	600	

The elite company we see were wearing colpacks to mark out their status. Cloth and other materials in the *dépôt* comprised:[82]

Item	In *Dépôt* 1804	Purchased since 1804	Total	Amount Used	Remaining in *Dépôt*
Green broadcloth	6m 37	2,449m 73	2,456m 10	1,967m 64	488m 46
White broadcloth	69m 42	195m 64	265m 60	239m 46	25m 60
Yellow broadcloth	3m 97	34m 99	38m 96	38m 96	
Green tricot		90m	90m	90m	
White serge	1,051m 69		1,051m 69	1,051m 69	
Treillis		414m	414m	414m	
Linen	49m 26	2,781m 40	2,830m 66	2,830m 66	
Large buttons	879 ½ doz		879 ½ doz	627 ½ doz	252 doz
Small buttons		810 doz	810 doz	810 doz	
Bone buttons for pantalons	The regiment has none				

It seems the regiments stable trousers did not open on the side seams as no buttons for this purpose existed. The regiment was next inspected on 17 June 1808, when it was wearing:[83]

Item	In Good Repair	In Need of Repair	To be Replaced	Total	Issued since Last Review
Surtouts	583	215	22	820	559
Manteaux	413	88	34	535	379
Gilets en drap blanc	568	148	104	820	613
Gilet d'ecuries	385	122	5	512	805
Culottes hongroise	622	198	820	731	
Stable trousers	869	28	44	941	1,084
Colpacks	80	2		82	
Schakos	607	127	12	746	639
Bonnets de police	701	177	100	978	697

Three contemporary images show the evolution of the regiment's dress very well.

Firstly, we show a trooper of 4e *Chasseurs c.*1804 in a print by Martinet. When General Pully inspected the 4e *Chasseurs* on 10 December 1804, he noted every man was wearing a *kinski*, which shows the regiment had abandoned *dolmans* incredibly early in its history. Secondly, an evocative drawing of the 4e *Chasseurs* by Lieutenant Bregeot of the 16e *Chasseurs* dated 1814, showing the dress of the regiment from 1808 through to 1813. The regiment's archive tells us that the elite company wore this uniform, but with the addition of colpacks. Lastly, a trooper of the 4e *Chasseurs* as depicted in a plate published in Paris by Aaron Martinet in 1814. (*Collection KM*)

Dépôt held an additional 17 colpacks, and the inspector ordered the production of 593 *manteaux*, 615 *surtouts* as well as 73 additional colpacks among other items.

The regiment was rebuilt following the Russian campaign, when we assume it adopted Bardin-regulation clothing and equipment. On 13 December, the War Ministry ordered the regiment was to be expanded to ten squadrons with the addition of six new squadrons, designated as *Éclaireurs* and armed with lances![84]

The clothing of the 4e *Chasseurs* at the close of the 1814 campaign, and despite three months of peace, was in deplorable condition, with the vast majority of the regiment's clothing needing to be replaced:[85]

Item	In Good Repair	In Need of Repair	Need Replacing in 1 Year	To be Replaced	Items Needed
Habits	12	46	42	45	165
Gilet d'ecuries	9	9	16	11	225
Culottes hongroise	20	8	18	3	195
Pantalons à cheval	5	5	42	25	207
Schakos	47	41	30	22	135
Pairs of boots			1	1	223

The men were clearly wearing *habits-vestes* as not one man had a regulation white sleeveless *gilet* to cover the expanse of shirt that would be visible if the men were wearing the cutaway habit. The regiment's equipment and armament were in the same deplorable condition:[86]

Item	In Good Repair	In Need of Repair	Need Replacing in 1 Year	To be Replaced	Items Needed
Gibernes and *porte-gibernes*	21	161	16	35	41
Porte-mousquetons	25	140	12	26	58
Waistbelts	59	52	15	34	112
Porte-mousqueton straps	38		52		
Sword knots	35		44		
Trumpets	None				
Trumpet cords					
Carbines	135	91		5	
Sabres	50	94		16	
Pistols	20	7		4	
Bayonets	None				
Lances	14	6			

Archive sources provide additional information for the appearance of the regiment at the end of the Empire. Firstly, we present an elite company trooper based on the regiment's paper archive and on notes by General Vanson, for the Hundred Days, housed in the *Musée de l'Armée*. In our second image we present a lancer of the scout company of the 4e *Chasseurs*. On 13 December, the War Ministry ordered the regiment was to be expanded to ten squadrons with the addition of six new ones, designated as *Éclaireurs* and armed with lances, twenty of which were in use in summer 1814.

The bulk of the equipment was in poor condition or totally missing. The lances are unexpected. Were these used by the elite company? In 1814 *chasseur* regiments had been ordered to form a company of scouts armed with lances. Here we see that the 4[e] *Chasseurs* had in deed done so. In, addition, the men were wearing 409 shirts, 155 black stocks, 82 pairs of shoes, 66 pairs of grey linen gaiters, 37 handkerchiefs, and 250 white cravats. The gaiters are a surprise in a light cavalry unit, and we note not a single pair of socks were issued, the men wearing their boots and shoes over bare feet. To make replacement clothing the regiment had virtually no stocks of cloth, just 1m 45 of green broadcloth, 13m 95 of '*citron*' broadcloth, 1m 66 of yellow serge, 11m 54 of white tricot,

The dress of the trumpeters is recorded primarily in primary sources.

Firstly, we see a trumpeter of the elite company wearing reversed colours from notes by Rousselot, and surely dates to the years before 1805. Secondly, we show a trumpeter of the 4e *Chasseurs* from 1806 to 1814 based on notes made by Rousselot. Thirdly, a tentative reconstruction of a trumpeter in summer 1814 based on the regiment's paper archive and a note by General Vanson, housed in the *Musée de l'Armée*. Lastly, a reconstruction of a trumpeter based on the regiment's paperwork for 1814. In July 1814 the trumpeters were authorised to adopt Royalist Livery: we do not know if this was in fact carried out, therefore our image is speculative.

4m 14 of lace in white linen and 58m 53 of white braid. The 4e *Chasseurs* totally lacked any stocks of clothing in the *dépôt*.

Of interest the inspector noted that the regiment had not fully adopted the uniform regulations as decreed on 19 January or 7 February 1812, nor had enacted the modifications of 23 April 1814 concerning the colour of trumpeters' *habits* – presumably green with Imperial Livery – and they had not been replaced with blue with Royalist Livery. Indeed, the inspector noted that 'all new items were to be made with the strictest regard to the regulations and to be carried out with utmost vigour'.[87] We assume therefore that the regiment wore *habits a revers* some five years after they were abolished!

Regimental accounts for clothing ten volunteers who had joined the war squadrons in 1815 reports:[88]

25m 90 green broadcloth costing 10fr 50 a metre. Total 271fr 95
10m 25 yellow broadcloth costing 9fr 50 a metre. Total 97fr 37
28m 14 green tricot costing 5fr 27 a metre. Total 148fr 29
10m 1 yellow serge costing 1fr 60 a metre. Total 16fr
Large buttons. Total 25fr 60
Small buttons. Total 24fr 20
27m 25 of linen costing 1fr 35 a metre. Total 36fr 78
2m 64 linen for *caleçon* costing 1fr 50 a metre. Total 3fr 96
25m 54 *treillis* costing 1fr 60 a metre. Total 40fr 86
2m 20 of linen lace costing 30 centimes a metre. Total 66 centimes
Flat braid. Total 3fr 96

Disbanded on 30 August 1815, the *dépôt* held no materials whatsoever, but it did hold stocks of clothing that included 69 *habits-vestes*, 69 *gilets*, 67 pairs of *culottes hongroise*, 78 *gilet d'ecuries*, 78 pairs of *pantalons à cheval* and the same number of pairs of stable trousers and *bonnets de police* and 66 *schakos*. Sent to the central *dépôt* in Pau were 154 '*manteau a manche*', 120 sword knots, 337 *gibernes*, 337 *giberne* belts, 274 *banderole-porte-carabine*, 16 trumpets with 15 sets of cords. Regimental *dépôt* held 55 pairs of boots, 64 pairs of gloves, 65 *porte-manteaux*, 236 sabres, 180 *mousqueton*, 3 muskets, 30 pistols, 1 bayonet and 15 lances.[89] Clearly the regiment was now dressed in Bardin-regulation kit, and the trumpeters wore blue *habits* with Royalist Livery.

5e *Chasseurs à Cheval*

Formed in 1788 as the *Chasseurs du Hainaut*, the regiment became the 5e *Chasseurs* in 1791 and after service with the Grande Armée from 1805 partly escaped the horrors of the Russian campaign as the bulk of the regiment was on active service in Spain through to the close of hostilities in 1814. The 1e and 2e squadrons were in Spain, the 3e and 4e were in Russia and later Germany and the 5e was in the *dépôt* in France.[90]

We have three contemporary images that show the almost complete evolution of the regiment's uniform in 1802 to 1815.

Firstly, there is a representation of a centre company trooper from the Otto manuscript. The dating of the manuscript is problematical, and this image is hard to reconcile to known facts. Otto clearly shows the use of a *dolman*, however at the time the Otto artist was working, the 5e *Chasseurs* had long discarded the uniform shown! One feels the Otto artist never witnessed the 5e Chasseurs first-hand, or if he did, it was not in 1807–08.

Our second image is a representation of a centre company trooper in 1808 by Martinet. It seems that in new year 1808 the regiment 'chucked out' its *surtouts* and went back to wearing *dolmans*. A letter from Colonel de Bonnemain at Chiclana in 1811 attests that the *dolmans* were still worn in the field along with colpacks. According to his correspondence, the colonel seems to have done everything possible to keep *dolmans* in use. Indeed, at the time of the regiment's disbandment, the elite company was wearing 122 *dolmans* but had lost their colpacks.

Lastly, we show a trooper as they appeared from the First Restoration. In 1814 the inspection returns state the regiment had not 'fully adopted' the provisions of the Bardin regulations, and new *habits-vestes* were ordered to be introduced to replace *dolmans* and *habits a la chasseur*. The two *portmanteaux* are an artist's error, as the artist has redrawn a printed line drawing of a *chasseur* from the 1780s to match the Bardin regulations. (*Collection KM*)

Officers

In circumstances unknown, some of the regiment's baggage was lost on campaign on 25 April 1813. A claim for compensation was made, which reveals a great deal about the dress of the regiment. Adjutant-Sous-Officier Gobet lost two pairs of 'Mameluke'-cut nankeen *pantalons* worth 16 francs, Sous-Lieutenant Bernard lost a linen overcoat worth 86 francs: in total linen items valued at 401 francs were lost. Cloth and equipment lost included:

Surgeon-Major Lajoust: 2 pairs of gloves. 4fr; 1 pair of boots, 21fr
Surgeon-Major Dupuir: 1 sabre, 35f
Surgeon-Major Landry: 1 hat, 20fr
Aide-de-Camp Letru: 1 green broadcloth *habit-veste*, 16fr
Veterinarian Vitry: 1 pair of boots, 19fr

Adjutant-Sous-Officier Gobet: 1 *habit-veste* in green broadcloth, 13fr
Squadron-Commander Lombard: 2 pairs of grey broadcloth *pantalons*, 52fr, 1 contre-epaulette 6fr
Captain Mensier: 1 *habit* in green broadcloth, 10fr, 1 silver-braided waistcoat, 6fr
Captain Sibre: 1 pair of *culottes hongroise* with silver lace, 40fr, 2 yellow broadcloth waistcoats, 20fr

The dress of the trumpeters is shown in two period images, and can be reconstructed tentatively from the regiment's archive. Our first image is dated to 1805. We see an elite company trooper wearing a buff *dolman* faced green with green braid. It is reasonable to suppose that thus uniform remained in use, unchanged until summer 1814.

Secondly, we present an incredibly rare portrait of a trumpeter of the regiment wearing a *habit a la chasseur*. We suppose this uniform was worn from 1808 through to summer 1814 and is the basis for our reconstruction. (*Private collection*)

In use with the 5ᵉ or depot squadron of the 5ᵉ *Chasseurs* in late summer 1814, two trumpeters' *habits* adorned with Imperial Livery and white epaulettes. Lastly in 1814, the inspecting general reported that the regiment had not acted on the decree of 19 January or 7 February 1812, nor the instruction of 23 April 1814 concerning the dress of trumpeters, which were to wear blue *habits* adorned with Royalist Livery.

Lieutenant Labat: 1 green broadcloth *schabraque* with silver lace, 70fr, 1 pair of green broadcloth *pantalons* with silver lace, 122fr
Lieutenant Perry: 1 colpack with *flamme* 80fr, sabretache decorated with old silver lace and rings 80fr
Sous-Lieutenant Fortier: 1 *giberne* worth 80fr
Sous-Lieutenant Vianna: 1 green broadcloth capote, 31fr
Sous-Lieutenant Amiel: 1 pair of grey broadcloth *pantalons*, 24fr, 1 pair of boots 24fr,
Sous-Lieutenant Marahce: 1 leather *porte-manteau*, 40fr

Also lost was a grey mule belonging to Captain Sibre worth 320 francs, a bay horse belonging to Captain Nichier worth 80 francs, a bay horse belonging to Lieutenant Perry worth 480 francs, a black horse worth 530 francs belonging to Sous-Lieutenant Marache, and a black charger worth 1,300 francs, the mount of Captain Bougeqnet.

From the effects lost, we see the officers had grey broadcloth *pantalons* for undress, and elaborately laced green broadcloth *pantalons* for parade dress. Yellow broadcloth undress waistcoats were worn, along with silver-laced, braided *hussar* waistcoats. The officers also had green broadcloth *capotes*, we assume cut as *redingotes*. Of interest the elite company officer still had his colpack, despite all the officers wearing, we assume, 1812-cut *habits-vestes*![91]

Other Ranks

Reviewed on 3 August 1805, shortly before it departed for the Austerlitz campaign, the regiment accounts record that 864 francs had been spent buying colpacks for the elite company, 2,546 francs 35 had been spent repairing clothing and 1,167 francs 30 had been spent making new items. The regiment was wearing:[92]

Item	In Good Repair	In Need of Repair	To be written off	Total	Total made since last inspection
Habit					
Dolmans		350	162	512	
Surtouts	276		41	317	276
Manteaux	302	138	57	497	
Gilets in broadcloth	469	102	202	773	212
Gilet d'ecuries	272	97	414	773	167
Culottes hongroise			773	773	128
Stable trousers			773	773	31
Colpack	77	7	16	100	
Schakos	346	150	177	673	89
Bonnets de police	167		606	773	469

Brand new and ready to be issued were 790 pairs of stable trousers, which were hastily issued to ensure the men had at least one pair of legwear in good condition. The inspector ordered *dolmans* suppressing and authorised 202 new *surtouts*, 808 pairs each of *culottes hongroise* and stable trousers, 404 *gilet d'ecuries* and 202 white *gilets* to be made. Reviewed again on 19 January 1808, the regiment was equipped with:[93]

Item	In Good Repair	In Need of Repair	To be written off	Total	Total made since last inspection	Observations
Habits						
Dolmans						
Surtouts	729		250	979	978	
Manteaux	739		110	849	490	
Gilets in broadcloth	729		110	979	399	
Gilet d'ecuries	479		500	979	1,294	
Culottes hongroise			979	979	1,146	
Stable trousers			698	698	802	
Colpack	80		20	100	·	
Schakos	660		219	879	756	
Bonnets de police	303		666	979	1,294	
Pantalons à cheval			979	979	593	

We have to rely on the regiment's archive to bridge gaps in contemporary iconography.

At disbandment in summer 1814, stores held ten *habits a la chasseur* in need of repair, and we also find the regiment was wearing white *gilets*. Presumably these garments had been adopted for the centre companies from 1808. Our second image shows the elite company as they appeared according to the colonel's letters.

The regiment's legwear was in deplorable condition yet *dépôt* held 152 pairs of brand-new *culottes hongroise*, 409 *schakos*, 56 *surtouts*, and 567 pairs of linen *caleçon*. Also in *dépôt* were 65 shirts, and we find a reference to black silk cravats rather than the regulation black stock.

We know nothing else from the regiment's archive until it was inspected on 1 August 1814, when it possessed the following clothing:[94]

Item	In Good Repair	In Need of Repair	Need Replacing	Items Needed
Habit	105	21	20	
Dolmans	64	3	55	
Gilets blanc	100	16	1	
Culottes hongroise	65	29		
Pantalons à cheval	168	40	34	
Stable trousers	61	33	19	
Caleçon	12		2	
Manteaux	209	27	33	
Gilet d'ecuries	99	56	84	
Bonnets de police	206	16	25	
Schakos	194	37	59	
Schakos covers	20		14	
Braces	105			
Pompoms	135		6	

The presence of *dolmans* in 1814 for *chasseurs* is remarkable but not unexpected as in 1811 a letter from Colonel de Bonnemain at Chiclana attests that it was still worn in the field along with colpacks. According to his correspondence, the colonel seems to have done everything possible to keep *dolmans* in use.[95] We can only assume the colpacks were worn by the elite company – we know the officers were wearing them in 1813 – and they had all been lost by summer 1814.

Indeed, the elite company in summer 1814 was told to sell its horses: they were far too large for *chasseurs* and were 'vanity' on behalf of the captain commanding the company in choosing the best horses he could find: the troop horses were sold to the elite company of the 11e *Dragons*, the horses of the officers and sous-officiers were to be sold to *cuirassier* regiments.[96] Buying 'flashy expensive' horses for the company neatly explains why the elite company wore *dolmans* and why the colonel had been desperate to keep colpacks. The best men in the regiment rode the best horses money could buy and were dressed as well as possible, even if it meant flaunting the regulations.

We also note when we look at the equipment list, six men had a *giberne* and non-regulation belt from which to suspend it: did they use improvised belts or did they stow the *giberne* in the *porte-manteaux*? A further 36 men had no sabre belt, and 113 men had no boots, who we assume wore shoes. The regiment was armed with 245 carbines in service and 13 needing repairs to be written off, 306 sabres in use and 41 needing repairs or to be disposed of, 263 pistols in good condition and 20 needing repairs, and 94 bayonets. In addition, the men were wearing 554 shirts, 352 black stocks, 9 pairs of linen stockings, 2 pairs of wool socks, and 129 pairs of shoes. Cloth in the *dépôt* was minimal: 0m 77 of yellow broadcloth, 10m of green tricot, 181m 87 of yellow serge and 9m 50 of trumpeters' lace, which suggests some trumpeters had Imperial Livery.

Clothing in the *dépôt* included stocks of brand-new clothing comprising 154 white *gilet*s, 4 pairs of *culottes hongroise*, 65 pairs of stable trousers, 9 pairs of *caleçon*, 2 *gilet d'ecuries*, 161 pompoms, 81 *gibernes*, 10 waistbelts, 81 *banderole-porte-mousquetons*. Clothing in *dépôt* needing to be repaired included 49 *manteaux*, 10 *chasseur habits*, 2 trumpeters' *habits* – we assume they were green with Imperial Livery, or were they yellow/buff? Alas we cannot tell, arguably the latter – 18 white *gilet*s, 5 pairs *culottes hongroise*, 13 pairs *pantalons à cheval* among others items and 14 *dolmans* to be written off, accompanied by 2 *habits* and 27 *manteaux*. The cross belts and other items were made from buff leather and not whitened. Clearly throughout the regiment's history it wore *dolmans* with buff belts.

The inspecting officer concluded his inspection, noting that the regiment had not acted on the decree of 19 January or 7 February 1812, nor the instruction of 23 April 1814 concerning the dress of trumpeters, which were to wear blue habits adorned with Royalist Livery.[97]

We have been unable to find any disbandment paperwork for the regiment: we would like to think the regiment clung onto *dolmans* until 1815, but we suspect that the unit was redressed prior and during the Hundred Days into *habits-vestes*.

6e *Chasseurs à Cheval*

Formed in 1788 as the *Chasseurs du Languedoc*, it became the 6e *Chasseurs* in 1791. Inspected on 3 November 1804, the inspector noted that the regiment was wearing 600 *dolmans* and the elite company had 60 colpacks. In addition, 659 *surtouts* were issued – one for every man. *Dolmans* were to be discontinued from use and replaced with the *surtout*, with 202 new examples being authorised for production.[98] Reviewed again on 14 August 1805, the regimental accounts record 720 francs was spent on buying 36 colpacks for the elite company, every single *dolman* was scheduled to be replaced. Every man was wearing a *surtout* in good condition, which is not surprising as the 483 items in store had been issued and a further 61 issued.[99] Inspected at the end of the 1805 to 1807 campaigns on 9 July 1808, every man was wearing a *surtout*, and the elite company had lost its colpacks. At no time do we find any archive references to epaulettes or plumes with the regiment.[100] Destroyed in the Russian campaign, the unit was re-formed in winter 1812. An idea of how the regiment was dressed at the end of the 1814 campaign can be discerned from the table below:[101]

The evolution of the regiment's uniform is well documented by period iconography.

Firstly, Martinet presents a trooper of 6e *Chasseurs c.*1805. The regiment was inspected at Lanciano on 3 November 1804, when the inspector ordered that *dolmans* were to be taken from service. By the end of 1807 every man was wearing a *surtout*. Re-formed in 1814 as the *Chasseurs du Berry*, Martinet presents a centre company trooper in an engraving published during 1814. Our last image is an elite company trooper of the *Chasseurs du Berry* in 1815 printed by Chez Basset. The regiment's archive has a remarkable degree of congruity to the period illustration of the company.

Period iconography cannot always answer the finer points of uniform details.

Our first image is a reconstruction of an elite company trooper of the *Chasseurs du Berry* in 1815 based on a naïve drawing from 1814 preserved in the library of the *Musée de l'Armée*. The drawing also shows officers wearing light grey pantalons over boots, the pantalons having a yellow side stripe, and wearing a red plume with white base in the colpack. The second image shows a centre company trooper reconstructed from the regiment's paper archive.

Item	In Good Repair	In Need of Repair	Need Replacing	Items Needed
Habits	290	72	28	350
Veste en drap blanc	254	148	38	366
Gilet d'ecuries	167	48	21	504
Culottes hongroise	162		247	393
Pantalons à cheval	97	54		589
Stable trousers	89	75	77	489
Manteaux Capote	358	69	26	307
Bonnets de police	250	233	4	253
Schako	286	126	2	186
Colpacks for elite company	71			69
Epaulettes	410			328
Plumes	322	18		400
Cordons du schako	385			355
Under wear	109		136	495
Boots and spurs	115	7	97	521
Waistbelts	540	22		178
Gibernes	588	6		
Porte-gibernes	592	6		142
Banderole-porte-carabines	625			13
Sword knots	173			567
Porte-manteaux	625	156	5	261
Trumpets	14			3
Pairs of Gloves	175			565
Sabres	421	7		
Pairs of Pistols	70	16		
Carbines	337	39		

The elite company it seems had clung on tenaciously to its colpacks, despite these being abolished with the Bardin regulations of 1812. These had obviously been purchased post the 1808 inspection, along with the epaulettes and plumes, no doubt at the colonel's discretion! The centre companies also seem to have retained *schako* cords, abolished in 1810! The regiment had not, according to the inspector, strictly followed the regulations, which is certainly the case given every man was wearing epaulettes – red for the elite company with red and green for the centre companies, we wonder? – and every man was dressed in a *habit a revers*. These again were a post-1808 innovation. The men were also issued 1,219 shirts, 377 black stocks and 403 pairs of shoes, worn like the boots over bare feet as not a single pair of socks existed in the regiment. The inspector noted that the clothing was all old and worn, being issued in the course of 1813, and was in desperate need of repair of replacement. To this end finances were

We are totally ignorant of the dress of the trumpeters of the 6e *Chasseurs*.
We present, firstly, a reconstruction of notes by Eugene Fort. In his study of *chasseurs*, without giving any sources he implies a yellow *habit-kinski* with green facings was worn, decorated with scarlet breast loops. The *reverse* colour *habit-kinski* is perfectly plausible and the archive sources do not contradict the existence of such a uniform.
Secondly, Rousselot presents this trumpeter as dating to 1809. Two documents, of different origin, confirm each other in their outlines and show two trumpeters wearing a short, scarlet *habit* with yellow facings, and wearing a *czapka*, but while that coming from the Cottreau Collection seems to have an unlaced second-dress coat, worn on the march with a *czapka* cover, that of the Marckolsheim manuscript has lace at the collar, cuffs and turnbacks, and an uncovered *czapka*. We cannot date the period when this uniform was said to be worn; Rousselot states 1809, but on what grounds we know not. It is possible that the costume existed, but without any sources beyond arguably secondary sources, we cannot confirm what he presents as anything other than a possibility.
Lastly, Rousselot presents here a trumpeter of the 6e that he dates to the end of the Empire based on a painting in the Marckolsheim series – which we remember is a phantom source not seen since the 1940s and may well post-date the period. The image shows a trumpeter dressed in a white *habits-veste* with yellow collar, *revers*, cuffs and tail facings. The collar and cuffs are decorated with white lace. He wears white-fringed epaulettes. He has a yellow *porte-manteau* laced white and a black sheepskin *schabraque*. The most remarkable feature in all three uniforms we present is the use of the *czapka* with yellow pavilion laced in white. The uniform is possible as the regiment had white broadcloth, yellow broadcloth, yet no hint of the regiment having *czapka* can be found. The uniform may date to the First Restoration as a white *habit* on campaign is distinctly not practical. The white uniform has many points in common with the *Chasseurs de la Charente* about 1816 – the successors to the 6e *Chasseurs* – drawn by Lieutenant Colonel Jolly and used by Job in the 'Dress of the Troops of France'. We have no archive evidence to support such a uniform existing as the regiment's archive stops abruptly in 1814. It is more likely that the uniform shown dates from 1816 as Jolly was present at the time, and Rousselot is wrong. We include the image as we cannot rule out the uniform shown existing in 1815. (*Collection KM*)

in hand to make 272 complete set of uniforms, according to the decree of 7 February 1812. The regiment had virtually no stocks of material in 1814; it had some 20m 39 of yellow broadcloth, 9m 31 of white broadcloth, 20m 50 yellow serge and 37cm of green tricot. The inspector comments:

> Many items are missing and the corps is hoping to receive these items shortly … The uniforms have been in service since 1813 and are generally good despite the

> rigours of war; there is shortly to be delivered replacement items, and will without any exceptions, align with the regulations.[102]

The inspector added that government funds had been allocated to enable the regiment to purchase 272 complete sets of kit to the Bardin regulations. We assume away went colpacks, and away went whatever the trumpeters were wearing in favour of, we assume, blue habits. Away went any non-Bardin clothing: we cannot prove this, however, as no paperwork for 1815 has survived to the current time. A period iconograph by Basset and also the memoires of Lieutenant Henckens tell us that elite company had colpacks.[103]

7ᵉ *Chasseurs à Cheval*

Formed in 1788 as the *Chasseurs de Picardie*, it became the 7ᵉ *Chasseurs* in 1791. Reviewed in October 1804, the regiment was ordered to abandon its *dolmans*, and to adopt *surtouts*. By the summer of the following year, the regiment was wearing *surtouts* and the elite company sported colpacks.[104] When inspected in summer 1807 the regiment was wearing:[105]

Item	In Good Repair	In Need of Repair	To be Replaced	Total	Observations
Surtouts	610			610	
Gilets en drap	610			610	
Gilet d'ecuries		128	482	610	
Capotes			30	30	
Culottes hongroise	610			610	
Pantalons à cheval	The regiment has none				
Stable trousers		607	3	610	
Caleçon	610			610	
Manteaux	160	240	132	532	48 needed
Bonnets de police	403		207	610	
Schakos	112	230	248	498	
Colpacks	120			120	
Schako covers	The regiment has none				
Pompoms					
Plumes					

The use of infantry greatcoats and cavalry cloaks comes as something of a surprise. After leaving Germany, the regiment served in Spain until it embarked on the Russian campaign. The regiment's archive is totally silent alas on all matters clothing related.

Inspected on 21 August 1814, the regiment's clothing was a motley collection of rags. For example, 198 *habits* were in good condition, 17 needed repairs and 115 needed

Period artwork shows the evolution of the regiment's uniform.

Firstly, is a trooper of the 7^e^ *Chasseurs* by Martinet. He shows the use of a *dolman*. The image must date from 1805 or earlier as by summer 1807 every man was wearing a *surtout*. Secondly, Lieutenant Bregeot presents us with his eyewitness painting of a trooper from 1812. Lastly, we show a centre company trooper by Martinet published at the end of the Empire, showing the rank and file wearing the single-breasted *kinski*. This image reflects the dress of the regiment from 1808 onwards. In summer 1814, the inspecting officer noted the companies were wearing *habits a la chasseur*, and had not acted upon the decree of 7 February 1812. The inspector ordered that 400 *habits-vestes* be produced immediately. (*Collection KM*)

total replacement, and a further 88 needing replacement were worn by men on leave. Of the white *gilets*, 178 were in good condition, 13 needed repairs and 119 were fit for total and immediate replacement. Not a single pair of *pantalons à cheval* or stable trousers were in use, the men were wearing their parade *culottes hongroise*, of which 178 pairs were in good condition, 18 pairs needed repair and 114 needed total replacement. No men had a *gilet d'ecuries*, 125 had no *manteaux*, 210 *bonnets de police* were in good condition, while 100 needed total replacement.

Furthermore, the 310 men under arms were also issued 542 shirts, 230 pairs of linen *pantalons de route*, 310 black stocks and 310 pompoms. Not a single pair of socks or *caleçon* existed in the regiment. The *dépôt* held no clothing whatsoever, and cloth in the *dépôt* comprised 94m of rose serge and 25m of linen to make caleçon. *Dépôt* did hold 97 sabre belts, 28 sword knots, 112 *giberne*s. These were 114 *giberne* belts and 93 *banderole-porte-mousquetons*: all brand new and ready to be issued, yet note the regiment possessed no carbines. Also in *dépôt* were 43 black stocks, 19 pairs of shoes and 38 pompoms. The inspecting general comments that the regiment had not acted upon the decree of 7 February 1812 and was incredulous that rather than wearing *habits-vestes*, of the 310 men under arms 275 men were wearing *dolmans* and *pelisses* – this had never been a regulation item for *chasseurs*! – the remainder wore *habits a revers*! In response to the regiment's blatant disregard of the regulations, the inspector ordered

The regiment's archive adds nuances to the period artwork.

When reviewed in summer 1814 the inspecting officer was incredulous that the elite company were wearing *dolmans* and *pelisse*! Secondly, we present a reconstruction of an elite company trooper in 1815 based on notes collected by General Vanson and housed in the library of the *Musée de l'Armée*. Thirdly, is a centre company trooper based on the regiment's archive. Our fourth image is a tentative reconstruction of elite company trumpeter. Rousselot in his personal papers housed in the *Musée de l'Armée* notes that a trumpeter from the Marckolsheim manuscript wears a type of *kinski* coat with, in addition to the edging lace, a buttonhole loop of white lace at the collar and cuff. The front of this garment is very short, like that of the second-dress *surtout*, and is accompanied by a braided waistcoat. He comments it was probably a cut-down *surtout* that has been adjusted to the new fashion. However, given the presence of *dolmans* and *pelisses*, such a uniform seems rather at odds to known facts as we suppose the trumpeters wore *dolmans* and *pelisses* in reverse colours, but we are ignorant when these were adopted. Such a uniform may well be that worn at the time of the 1807 inspection.

Lastly, we present a very tentative reconstruction of a trumpeter in late 1814 and another during the Hundred Days. The regimental archive confirms that the regiment was redressed in Bardin regulation clothing during the First Restoration as ordered. At disbandment, 272m 90 of trumpeter's lace was in stores. We cannot be certain as to which pattern of lace this was, so we present both Royalist and Imperial Livery.

that 400 *habits-vestes* be produced. Perhaps surprisingly, the inspector noted that the regiment had not yet adopted blue habits and new Royalist Livery for its trumpeters.[106]

During the First Restoration, regimental accounts record the purchase of 2m of rose broadcloth costing 12 francs a metre, while 570 white cockades were purchased for 142 francs 50 and 4 trumpets costing 103 francs 92.[107]

The war squadrons were disbanded in September 1815, the *dépôt* held 60 *habits-vestes*, and the same number of *gilet d'ecuries*, *bonnets de police*, *schakos*. Sent to the *dépôt* at Strasbourg were 120 *manteaux*, 179 *porte-manteaux*, 60 pairs of *pantalons à cheval*,

42 *schakos*, 309 *banderole-porte-mousquetons*, 234 sabre belts, 289 *gibernes*, 318 *giberne* belts and 208 sabre knots.

When disbanded the *dépôt* held 18m 36 of white broadcloth and 272m 90 of trumpeters' lace, 283 white vestes, 140 pairs of *culottes hongroise*, 148 pairs of gloves, 140 pairs of *caleçon*, 11 pairs of boots, 64 sabre belts, 93 *gibernes*, 193 *giberne* belts, 163 *banderole-porte-mousquetons*, 4 trumpets, 20 sword knots, 223 watering bridles, 250 head collars, 186 *mousqueton*, 99 pistols and 134 sabres. We cannot say what pattern of trumpeters' lace was held: perhaps a mix of Royalist and Imperial. No *aigrettes* or epaulettes existed for the elite company, but the regiment was indeed wearing Bardin-regulation clothing.[108]

8e *Chasseurs à Cheval*

Formed as the *Chasseurs de Guyenne* in 1788, it became the 8e *Chasseurs* in 1791; the regiment served with the Grande Armée and was almost totally destroyed in the Russian campaign. The author has not been able to discover the regiment's 1805 or 1808 inspection returns, therefore we can say very little about its dress. Reviewed on 8 to 11 July 1814, the inspector noted that the regiment's clothing was in moderately good condition, but its pantalons and boots all had to be replaced. Clothing in use was as follows:[109]

Item	In Good Repair	In Need of Repair	Need Replacing in 1 Year	To be Replaced	Items Needed
Dolman	165	2		1	
Habits-vestes	70				
Gilets blanc	165	12	3	4	
Gilet d'ecuries	128	29		4	
Caleçon	2				
Culottes hongroise	40	16	2	5	
Pantalons à cheval	135	16	6	10	
Stable trousers	172				
Bonnets de police	175	16		5	
Porte-manteaux	159	9		1	
Schakos	196	12		3	
Schakos covers	Nil				
Pompoms	172				
Manteaux-capote	251		1	20	26

The men had issued 125 stocks, and not a single pair of socks or *caleçon*, and if the inspector is correct, no shirts either! The *dépôt* held no stocks of cloth and materials, and

The archive for the 8e *Chasseurs* is fragmented. We have to rely on contemporary images to gain a flavour of the regiment's uniform.

Martinet presents a trooper wearing a *dolman*, which we know the regiment wore in 1804, but had abandoned by 1808. In our second image we have a trooper of the *Chasseurs du Bourbon*, the former 8e *Chasseurs*, in early 1815 in a print by Martinet. The buff-coloured leather work is unexpected.

We present alongside the period artwork a reconstruction of the elite company in summer 1814. Inspected on 11 July 1814, the regiment's clothing was in moderately good condition. Remarkably, the regiment was wearing *dolmans*, of which 165 were in good condition, two needed to be repaired and only one was listed for replacement. Lastly, we present a reconstruction of the centre company.

The dress of the trumpeters is recorded by secondary sources and the regiment's archive.

Firstly, we present a tentative reconstruction of a trumpeter of the 8ᵉ *Chasseurs* noted by Rousselot in his personal papers housed in the *Musée de l'Armée*. We have no knowledge of his sources for such an image.

Secondly, is a tentative reconstruction of an elite company trumpeter in 1814. In summer 1814 the elite company trumpeters were wearing *dolmans*: four trumpeters' *dolmans* were in stores in September 1815.

Lastly, we present two tentative reconstructions of a trumpeter in 1814 and 1815. In summer 1814, the inspecting general ordered the trumpeters to be dressed in blue with Royalist Livery. At the same time, he ordered four Imperial Livery *habits* burned. At disbandment, stores held 100m 36 of trumpeter lace, which may be Imperial Livery.

the only clothing was 94 brand-new *chasseur habits-vestes* and 4 brand-new trumpeter *habits-vestes*. The regiment was in the process of redressing, according to the decree of 7 February 1812 and recent instructions for trumpeters and musicians of 23 April 1814, according to the inspector.[110]

At disbandment in December 1815 the *dépôt* held a wide range of materials:[111]

266m 16 green tricot
199m 95 rose serge

Troupes Françaises
(1808)
A Paris chez Martinet, Libraire, rue du Coq N.° 15
Chasseurs à cheval
9e Regiment

Opposite: The 9e *Chasseurs* is one of the regiments of *chasseurs* that was missed by period artwork and thus we have to rely on the regiment's paper archive.

We start with Martinet, showing a trooper wearing full dress in the years before 1805. Secondly, we present a speculative reconstruction of the dress of the trumpeters at the beginning of the Empire based on inspection returns of 8 September 1805 and 16 June 1808, which tell us the trumpeters wore *bleu de ciel* and that trumpeters of the elite company and trumpet major wore colpacks as just four were in use and a further twenty in store. What the trumpeters wore from 1808 is unknown. Lastly, we present tentative reconstructions of a trooper and a trumpeter in summer 1814.

116 leather hides
100m 36 trumpeter lace
50m red worsted lace for service chevrons
626m 40 flat worsted braid

We cannot be certain which pattern of lace was in store: it could be new Imperial Livery, or left over Royalist Livery from 1814. We simply cannot tell. Brand-new clothing in the *dépôt* included 2 *habits-vestes*, 43 *gilet d'ecuries*, 202 white *gilets*, 93 pairs of *culottes hongroise*, 11 pairs of *pantalons à cheval*, 10 *capotes-manteaux*, 195 pairs of *caleçon*, 450 pairs of braces, 310 pompoms, 4 trumpeters' *dolmans*, 1 *gilet*, 64 pairs of wrist gloves, 129 'black and white leather sword knots', and 30 *banderole-porte-mousquetons*. Were the trumpeters' *dolmans* literally brand new, as in made in 1815, or did they date from 1814 and were therefore in reverse colours? Alas we cannot tell but the balance of probability suggests they were new and unused dating from 1813/14 and were rose pink with green facings. In *dépôt* in good condition were 6 white *gilets*, 10 *manteaux-capote*, 2 pairs of *caleçon*, 117 pairs of gauntlets – a luxury item as light cavalry in theory used wrist gloves only – 80 waistbelts, 194 *gibernes*, 195 *giberne* belts and 192 *banderole-porte-mousquetons*. We also find in *dépôt* 1 shirt and 40 black silk cravats, again a luxury, non-regulation item.[112] The regiment had clearly adopted Bardin regulation in summer 1814 into spring 1815.

9e *Chasseurs à Cheval*

Formed as the *Chasseurs du Lorraine* in 1788, the regiment became the 9e *Chasseurs* in 1791 and was with the Army of Naples from 1801. On 14 January 1805 the regiment was inspected by General Regnier. Clothing in use at that time was follows:[113]

Item	In Good Repair	In Need of Repair	To be Written Off	Total	Total Made Since 1803	To be Replaced
Habits						
Dolmans	219	300	39	558	43	
Surtouts	470	123	28	623	506	
Manteaux	119	78	200	397	1	
Gilets in broadcloth	443	116	63	622	467	

Item	In Good Repair	In Need of Repair	To be Written Off	Total	Total Made Since 1803	To be Replaced
Gilet d'ecuries	244	67	257	568	258	
Culottes hongroise	385	236		621	621	
Stable trousers	118		499	617	128	
Schakos	597	16		613	86	
Bonnets de police	600		24	624	87	

The regiment was clearly wearing *dolmans* and *surtouts* side by side. Oddly the regiment did not have enough *manteaux* for every man. Cloth and other materials in the *dépôt* comprised:[114]

Item	In *Dépôt* 1803	Purchased since 1803	Total	Amount Used	Remaining in *Dépôt*
Green broadcloth	1,864m 11	621m 45	2,485m 56	2,290m 83	194m 73
White broadcloth	663m 86		663m 86	533m 12	130m 74
Crimson broadcloth	147m 88	1m 68	149m 56	51m 61	94m 95
Tricot [white?]	732m 25		732m 25	579m 37	152m 88
Serge [green?]	2,969m 12	35m 86	3,004m 98	1,056m 51	1,948m 47
Linen	1m 10	2,310m 96	2,312m 6	2,307m 49	4m 57
Large buttons	614 doz		614 doz	19 doz	594 doz
Small buttons	4,283 doz		4,283 doz	2,137 doz	2,146 doz
Bone buttons for pantalons	The regiment has none				

We assume the crimson broadcloth actually means rose, as the amount of crimson cloth in *dépôt* in January 1805 matches the amount of rose broadcloth present in the *dépôt* six months later. Clearly the stable trousers did not open on the outside seams. In addition, the *dépôt* held new items of clothing, namely 13 *surtouts,* 210 *manteaux,* 9 *gilet*s, 43 *gilet d'ecuries*, 16 pairs *culottes hongroise,* 10 *schakos*, 7 *bonnets de police*, 451 sabre belts, 349 *giberne*s with belt, 83 musket slings, 2 saddles, 2 bridles, 2 head collars, 2 surcingles, 129 saddle blankets, and 72 sheepskin *schabraques.* General Regnier authorised the production of 57 new *manteaux*, 386 *surtouts*, 193 *gilets*, 386 *gilet d'ecuries*, 772 pairs of *culottes hongroise* and stable trousers, 193 *schakos*, 386 *bonnets de police*, 129 sabre belts, 59 *gibernes* with belts, 83 *porte-manteaux* and 386 pairs of boots. Furthermore, Regnier informed the colonel that the war minister had passed orders that dolmans were to be discontinued with no more to be made, and those in service to be replaced as soon as possible.[115]

General of Division Regnier inspected the regiment on 8 September 1805. He reported that since 14 January 109 *habits* had been made, of which 102 had been issued. What were these *habits*? Officially the regiment was to wear the *surtout* and not *habits.* Clearly the regimental colonel, in replacing the *dolman*, wanted to adopt a more fanciful uniform than the sombre *surtout* and adopted the *habit* unofficially. We see more of the colonel's thinking as 41 *dolmans* had been made with 38 issued, which is surprising given none were authorised for production. Were these for sous-officiers and trumpeters? Perhaps. In addition, 43 *manteaux* had been made and issued, likewise 178 *gilets*, 342 *gilet d'ecuries*, 313 pairs *culottes hongroise*, 1,113 pairs of stable trousers, 116 *schakos* and 65 *bonnets de police*. New equipment comprised 7 new *gibernes* with belts and 7 new *banderole-porte-carabine* – bringing the total of these items up to 90, but only 14 were issued – and 55 pairs of boots. Cloth and other materials in the *dépôt* comprised:[116]

Item	In *Dépôt* 1805	Purchased since 1805	Total	Amount Used	Remaining in *Dépôt*
Blue broadcloth		64m 22	64m 22	16m 20	48m 2
Green broadcloth	194m 73	1,170m	1,364m 73	763m 59	601m 14
White broadcloth	130m 74	151m	282m 58	180m 88	101m 70
Rose broadcloth	97m 95	43m 94	141m 89	40m 54	101m 35
Green tricot	152m 28		152m 28	105m 70	47m 18
White serge	1,948m 47		1,948m 47	415m 3	1,533m 44
Rose serge		177m 91	177m 91	47m 36	30m 55
Treillis		2,403m 61	2,403m 61	2,228m 61	175m 25
Linen	1m 39	1,221m 35	1,222m 74	44m 40	1,178m 34
Large buttons	594 doz		594 doz	594 doz	
Small buttons	2,146 doz	16 doz	2,162 doz	1,334 doz	828 doz
Bone buttons for pantalons		4,000 doz	4,000 doz	3,294 doz	703 doz

The small amount of blue broadcloth is a major surprise. This was clearly destined to make trumpeters' clothing. We assume the *habit* or perhaps even a *dolman*, was rose, faced blue as only a small amount of blue was used, or was the *habit* green and faced blue? Either way we cannot tell, other than suggesting the facings were likely to be blue. The regiment clearly had stable trousers made from *treillis* with bone buttons. The lack of any leather hides shows, as with other regiments, that at this stage suggests *pantalons à cheval* did not exist.

On 16 June 1808 the regiment was inspected by General Randon de Pully at Modena. Clothing in use at that time was follows:[117]

Item	In Good Repair	In Need of Repair	To be Written Off	Total	Total Made Since 14 January 1805	To be Replaced
Habit	534	6	42	582	530	
Dolmans						
Surtouts						
Manteaux	269	58	78	405	205	
Gilets in broadcloth	571	6	80	657	551	
Gilet d'ecuries	401	85	110	686	562	
Culottes hongroise	550	34	91	675	675	
Stable trousers	539	113	46	698	698	
Caleçon	205	100		305	305	
Schakos	589	10	85	684	589	
Bonnets de police	407	194	132	733	407	

What is meant by *habit*? We guess at a short-tailed *habit a la chasseur*, because we see from the return that by this date the unit had disposed of all remaining *surtouts* and *dolmans*. Clearly, the *surtouts* authorised for production in summer 1805 were in fact transmuted into showier *habits*. Cloth and other materials in the *dépôt* comprised:[118]

Item	In *Dépôt* 1805	Purchased since 1805	Total	Amount Used	Remaining in *Dépôt*
Blue broadcloth	48m 2	57m 29	105m 31	98m 51	16m 75
Green broadcloth	601m 14	4,879m 78	5,480m 92	4,837m 11	643m 91
White broadcloth	101m 70	885m 10	986m 80	759m 22	227m 58
Rose broadcloth	101m 35	275m 78	377m 13	243m 18	133m 95
White serge	1,533m 44	209m 4	1,742m 48	1,016m 15	726m 33
Rose serge	30m 35	2,382m 55	2,412m 90	1,813m 37	599m 53
Green tricot	47m 18		47m 18	47m 18	
Treillis	175m 25	2,003m 87	2,179m 12	1,841m 49	337m 63
Linen 104/100	79m 47	3,986m 36	4,065m 83	3,339m 49	726m 34
Linen	1,178m 34	2,880m 45	4,058m 79	3,992m 90	65m 89
Large tin buttons		810 doz	810 doz	727 doz	82 doz
Small tin buttons	828 doz	3,790 doz	4,618 doz	4,579 doz	88 doz
Bone buttons for pantalons	703 doz	2,300 doz	3,003 doz	2,904 ½ doz	98 ½ doz

The lack of green tricot for the production of *porte-manteaux* and *culottes hongroise* makes us suppose these were made from green broadcloth. Pully's inspection report tells us a great deal about items produced by the regiment without official sanction. Despite *dolmans* being discontinued in January 1805, nine new ones had been made, bringing the total in use up to 12 – these we suppose were made from blue (we guess sky blue rather than dark imperial blue) with rose facings for the trumpeters, who it also seems wore colpacks, or at least in the elite company and the trumpet major as four were in use and a further 20 in store. Also issued since 1805 were 568 *banderole-porte-carabine* – the first time the regiment had a major issue of these in its history. Some 533 were issued, 109 in store and 34 placed into *dépôt* for repairs. The *dépôt* held large numbers of items waiting to be repaired, namely 1 *manteaux*, 22 sabre belts, 34 *gibernes* with belts, 35 *porte-manteaux*, 48 pairs of boots, 25 saddles, 25 bridles, 25 head collars, 25 surcingles, 49 saddle blankets and 35 sheepskin *schabraques*. New items in the *dépôt* comprised 40 *gilets*, 1 *gilet d'ecurie*, 6 pairs of *culottes hongroise*, 14 pairs of stable trousers, 20 colpacks, 56 *schakos*, 8 *bonnets de police*, 48 pairs of boots, 119 saddles, 119 bridles, 119 head collars, 119 surcingles, 162 saddle blankets and 117 sheepskin *schabraques*. General Pully furthermore authorised the production of 235 *habits*, 100 *manteaux*, 235 *gilets*, 470 *gilet d'ecuries*, 940 pairs of *culottes hongroise*, linen *caleçon* and pairs of stable trousers, 235 *schakos*, 470 *bonnets de police*, 156 sabre belts, 47 *gibernes* with belts, 104 *porte-manteaux* and 470 pairs of boots.[119]

Almost wiped out in the Russian campaign, 146 other ranks with 26 officers returned from Russia, where they joined 193 men with 148 horses that had 'sat out' the campaign in the remount *dépôt* at Hanover.[120] The re-formed regiment joined the Grande Armée for the 1813 campaign. We know nothing of how these men were dressed. The regiment underwent a shake-down inspection on 8 June 1814, and the clothing then in use was as follows:[121]

Item	In Good Repair	In Need of Repair	Need Replacing in 1 Year	To be Replaced	Items Needed
Habits	265				9
Gilets en drap blanc	240				27
Gilet d'ecuries	252		10	1	14
Culottes Hongroise	237		6	6	9
Pantalons à cheval	214	12	4	29	11
Stable trousers	252				17
Caleçon	239				31
Bonnets de police	263	4	2		10
Braces	268				9
Schakos	258				11
Schako covers	249				15
Pairs of gloves	216				34
Pompoms	258				8
Manteaux-capote	251		1	20	26

Equipment was as follows:[122]

Item	In Good Repair	In Need of Repair	Need Replacing in 1 Year	To be Replaced	Items Needed
Gibernes	257	1			15
Porte-gibernes	257	1			145
Porte-mousquetons	196				18
Waistbelts	259				17
Sword knots	247				27
Pairs of boots	256	4	6		13
Trumpets	16				1
Trumpet cords	16				1

The *dépôt* held the following items clothing and equipment:[123]

Item	New	Good condition	To be repaired	To be written off	Total
Habits			20	4	24
Gilets du parade	62				62
Gilet d'ecuries	33			28	61
Bonnets de police	1			13	14
Stable trousers	20				20
Manteaux	10	10	21	31	72
Porte-manteaux	70	100	31	26	227
Schakos	156		85	30	271
Schako cover			3		3
Waistbelts	43	40	55	43	141
Gibernes	32	150	42	18	242
Porte-gibernes	50	147	38	7	242
Porte-carabines	31	200	3	14	248
Porte-crosses			Nil		
Pairs of boots	17		14	3	34
Pair of gloves	23				23
Sword slings					
Trumpet cords	4			1	5
Pompoms	130	30	10	10	180
Sword knots	347		17	29	393

The existence of parade waistcoats suggests that they were intended to be seen, implying that the *habit* in *dépôt* and in use were not closed to the waist and therefore not of 1812-style cut. These waistcoats were, we suggest, made from facing colour broadcloth, and perhaps braided like *hussar dolmans*. Indeed, the inspector notes that the regiment had not fully adopted the provisions of the decree of 19 January and 7 February 1812, nor of the instructions of 23 April 1814 to dress the trumpeters in blue with Royalist Livery. The inspector noted the modifications were to be carried out with great urgency and that in the future 'the master workmen were to pay better attention to the regulations'. He noted that good progress had been made on replacing the regiments *habits*. Stocks of cloth in the magazine was as follows:[124]

29m 39 white broadcloth
8m 36 green broadcloth
196m 77 rose serge
0m 50 green tricot
477m 95 linen for lining
0m 34 linen for *caleçon*
73.5 dozen large buttons
577dozen small buttons
91m 24 trumpeters' lace
37m 55 lace for chevrons
287m 10 flat wool lace 10mm wide

We assume that some trumpeters in 1814 had Imperial Livery, and that the trumpeters were redressed in Royalist Livery in 1815. We have been unable to find any disbandment records for the regiment, and we assume that by Waterloo it had been reclothed in Bardin-regulation *habits-vestes*.

10e *Chasseurs à Cheval*

Created in 1788 as the *Chasseurs de Bretagne*, the regiment became the 10e *Chasseurs* in 1791. Inspected in October 1804, *dépôt* held 24 brand-new *dolmans* and 535 *habit-surtouts*, 579 *manteaux* and 72 *pantalons d'ecurie en drap vert* i.e., green *pantalons à cheval*. In use were 580 *dolmans*, of which 506 were to be replaced by the new *surtouts*. In addition, the men had stable trousers, *culottes hongroise* and *pantalons à cheval*.[125] Inspected on 10 August 1805, the elite company had 60 colpacks and 512 *dolmans* were in use, all to be replaced, alongside 532 brand-new *habit-surtouts*. The inspector ordered the *dolmans* to be removed from use, and authorised 404 *habit-surtouts* made as a matter of urgency. These garments we assume were *habits a la chasseur*.[126] The regiment was dressed in *habits* in summer 1807.[127]

The regiment fought in Spain from 1808 to 1813, seeing action at Leipzig, and then returned to Spain to fight at Orthez, Viella and Toulouse. Inspected on 1 September 1814, the regiment's clothing was in shreds:[128]

The regiment archive is useful in allowing us to reconstruct how it was dressed. Our first image is a reconstruction of a centre company trooper of the 10[e] *Chasseurs* in summer 1814. Secondly, we show a trooper of the 5[e] or depot company in summer 1814: we depict one of the few men who had been dressed in Bardin regulation kit in spring 1814. Thirdly, we show a trooper wearing a dolman. The regiment's archive reports that in summer 1814 the stores of the 10[e] *Chasseurs* held two brand-new *dolmans* – suggesting that until recently *dolmans* had been worn as late as 1812, if not into 1813! Second to last is a reconstruction of a member of the elite company in summer 1814. Lastly is the elite company during the Hundred Days.

Item	In Good Repair	In Need of Repair	Need Replacing in 1 Year	To be Replaced Total	Items Needed Effective Strength
Habits-vestes	168	125	9	30	7
Gilets en drap	51	16	8	8	256
Culottes hongroise	26	10	53	28	222
Pantalons à cheval	59	134	11	19	116
Stable trousers	58	61		1	219
Caleçon	10	1	30		298
Manteaux	191	81	15	52	
Bonnets de police	94	2	163	13	67
Gilet d'ecuries	66	87	38	34	114
Schako	184	95	6	9	
Colpacks	34	10	1		
Pompoms	284				51
Schako covers	105			100	134
Braces	56		283		

When it comes to the dress of the trumpeters, we have to rely on the regiment's archive.

Firstly, the regimental stores of the 10ᵉ *Chasseurs* in summer 1814 held one *habit de trompette* adorned with Imperial Livery, which we show here, while another pair were issued to the depot company. Secondly, there is a trumpeter of the elite company in 1814 based on the regiment's paper archive and also noted by Rousselot in his personal papers housed in the *Musée de l'Armée*.

The men without *gilets* were clearly wearing Bardin-regulation *habits-vestes*. Given that the regiment had served in Spain almost continuously since 1808, we are inclined to think that a mix of *habit* styles were in use side by side, the cutaway *habit* and the *habit-veste*, the presence of colpacks showing that Bardin regulation was not rigorously enforced in the regiment. Furthermore, it is clear that legwear was an ad hoc mix of *culottes hongroise*, stable trousers and *pantalons à cheval*. Indeed, seven men were on parade wearing their *gilet d'ecuries* for lack of a *habit*! Remarkably, the 45 men in the elite company had clung on to their colpacks! No man had his regulation pair of gloves, 44 men had no *porte-manteau*, and 36 men were wearing their shoes and stable trousers for lack of boots! In the *dépôt* were 963 shirts, 30 pairs of linen overalls, 300 black stocks, 104 white stocks, and 237 pairs of shoes for stable duties.

The *dépôt* had limited stocks of cloth and materials, holding 41m 35 of crimson broadcloth, 162m 10 crimson milled serge and 2m 38 of treillis to make stable trousers. Clothing in the *dépôt* included 2 brand-new *dolmans* – suggesting that *dolmans* had been worn as late as 1813! – 2 *habits-vestes de modèle* – presumably trumpeter and *chasseurs* – 1 *gilet blanc de modèle*, 1 *manteau de modèle*, 1 pair of *pantalons à cheval de modèle*, and 1 *schako de modèle*, 32 shirts, 12 *habit* brushes, 8 dandy brushes, 32 pairs of woollen socks, 16 pairs of shoes and 32 pairs of grey gaiters. The inspector noted that the regiment was badly dressed: the *habits* were of differing cuts and lacked any form of uniformity, adding that the differing colour of equipment made a bad impression: the regiment clearly used blackened cow hide equipment and whitened buff. The 10ᵉ had a very eclectic mix of weapons: in use were 395 *mousqueton*, 339 sabres and 339 pistols. In store were 194 French *mousquetons* – presumably the *hussar* model – in good condition with a further 44 needing repairs side by side with 70 'foreign' *mousqueton*, 96 non-

Firstly, we have a trooper of the 10e wearing a *dolman* by Martinet, purportedly in 1808. The date is clearly wrong, as *dolmans* were taken from service by summer 1805. Secondly, we present Lieutenant Bregeot's eyewitness drawing of the 10e *Chasseurs* in 1812. We assume he is wearing the *habit-surtout*. Lastly, is a print by Martinet published in 1814. (*Collection KM*)

French sabres, and 28 non-French pistols. In addition, 56 French carbines were in store! Sent to the regiment from the 32e *regiment de Ligne* were 349 sets of braces, *schako* covers and white *houpettes* for the *schako*![129] The presence of *items de modèle* suggests that these had been recently been delivered, and were Royalist pattern, or the regiment had received Bardin issue and simply ignored the decree! We suspect the former instance.

In a separate letter of 12 September 1814, the inspector the noted the regiment needed new uniforms as they were worn out, badly made, made from low-quality materials and not uniform in cut, i.e., a mix of *habit à revers* and *habits-vestes*. He also notes he ordered the regiment to change trumpeters dress to blue. About the elite company, he comments that they were wearing *contre-epaulettes* made from copper scales that were to be replaced with scarlet-fringed epaulettes. Furthermore, he ordered that the elite company were to abandon their colpack for *schako du grenadier*. He noted that the *sous-officiers* were wearing officer-quality uniforms made from super-fine broadcloth with elaborate silver lace rank stripes and wore extravagant epaulettes: due to these embellishments he complained that the sous-officiers were almost indistinguishable from officers. The inspector concluded his report by noting that the cut of the *habits* was non-regulation, noting that they had 'slashed collars', and that in lieu of the regulation stock, regiment's stocks were actually black silk cravats.[130]

We have been unable to locate any disbandment paperwork for the regiment, but we can be sure the regiment was reclothed almost as new into Bardin-regulation kit as between 1 September 1814 and 7 June 1815 the colossal sum of 205,844 francs was spent on clothing.[131]

11e *Chasseurs à Cheval*

Formed in 1788 as the *Chasseurs du Normandie*, the regiment was numbered 11e in 1791. The unit was inspected on 28 May 1803 and had the following items of clothing in use:[132]

Item	In Good Repair	In Need of Repair	To be written off	Total	Total made since 20 February 1802
Habits					
Dolmans	600	91		691	34
Pelisses					
Surtouts	685			685	125
Manteaux	308	148	58	514	108
Gilets in broadcloth	402	180	89	691	402
Gilet d'ecuries	308	120	200	628	33
Culottes hongroise	659			659	672
Stable trousers	308	350		658	69
Chapeaux					
Schakos	301	300	51	652	301
Bonnets de police	312	280	60	652	171

Contemporary iconography helps show the evolution of the regiment's uniform.

Firstly, a trooper of the 11^e^ *Chasseurs* by Martinet clearly shows the regiment as it was before summer 1805, by which time *dolmans* had been taken from use. Secondly, we present a trooper again by Martinet published in 1815. No archive sources can be found to confirm or deny this image.

Archive records add more details to the dress of the regiment.

Firstly, a reconstruction of a trumpeter of the 11e *Chasseurs* as they appeared in summer 1814 according to Lucien Rousselot in his personal papers housed in the *Musée de l'Armée*. We have no knowledge of his sources for such an image.

Secondly, a tentative reconstruction of a sapeur of the 11e *Chasseurs* based on the regiment's archive, which lists aprons, axe cases and belts. We have added the lance as these are commonly shown in period iconography as the weapon of choice for *sapeurs*.

Lastly, a trooper as they appeared in 1814 to 1815 based on the regiment's archive.

The *dolman* we suppose was used for parade dress, and the *surtout* for everyday use, but clearly not every man had *surtouts*; perhaps they were reserved for sous-officiers only? Accounts show the regiment had no bone buttons or *treillis*, and therefore it seems the stable trousers were made from linen and were literally overalls. Furthermore, the inspector noted that the *dépôt* held 1 new *habit*, 2 *surtouts*, 4 *manteaux*, 18 *gilets*, 45 *gilet d'ecuries*, 1 pair of *culottes hongroise*, 67 pairs of stable trousers, 45 *bonnets de police*, 90 waistbelts, 90 *gibernes* with belts, 4 *porte-manteaux* and 236 pairs of boots with spurs. The *habit* is unexpected at this date: was it used by the adjutant or trumpeters? To be marked out as not a *surtout*, we assume it had *revers*. The inspecting general authorised the production of 193 *dolmans*, 58 *manteaux*, 386 *surtouts*, 193 *gilets* and *gilet d'ecuries*, and 772 pairs each of *culottes hongroise* and stable trousers.

The regiment was inspected on 8 October 1804 and had the following items of clothing in use:[133]

Item	In Good Repair	In Need of Repair	To be written off	Total	Total made since 28 May 1803
Habits					
Dolmans		690	23	713	6
Pelisses					
Surtouts	2	48	644	694	168
Manteaux	100	204	168	472	15
Gilets in broadcloth	107	246	360	713	343
Gilet d'ecuries	479	158	60	697	922

Item	In Good Repair	In Need of Repair	To be written off	Total	Total made since 28 May 1803
Culottes hongroise	493	204	16	713	1,265
Stable trousers	594	105	14	713	900
Kolpacks	74			74	74
Schakos	348	390	1	639	148
Bonnets de police	462	142	109	713	651

Following the inspection, the inspector passed orders that no more *dolmans* were to be authorised for production and that they were to be replaced by *surtouts*: 404 being made in the next year and a further 404 in the following year. Cloth and other materials in the *dépôt* comprised:[134]

Item	In *Dépôt* 1803	Purchased since 1803	Total	Amount Used	Remaining in *Dépôt*
Green broadcloth	498m 30	1,950m 2	2,448m 32	2,445m 77	2m 55
White broadcloth	395m 92	425m 30	621m 12	621m 12	
Crimson broadcloth	32m 40	104m 91	137m 31	63m 62	73m 69
White serge	378m 95	1,965m 51	2,344m 46	2,214m 66	129m 80
Crimson serge		886m 80	886m 80	870m 75	16m 50
Green tricot	1,408m 87	1,390m 42	2,799m 29	2,664m 10	135m 28
Crimson tricot	30m 98		30m 98		30m 98
Linen		6,168m 99	6,168m 99	5,687m 36	481m 63
Treillis		1,982m 86	1,982m 86	1,986m 92	25m 94
Large buttons					
Small buttons	1,095 doz	3,072 doz	4,167 doz	3,582 doz	585 doz
Bone buttons for stable trousers	6,257 doz	2,196 doz	2,823 doz	2,799 doz	24 doz
Flat worsted braid	471m 94	4,431m 30	4,903m 24	4,094m 81	808m 43

The crimson tricot was clearly destined to make trumpeters' *culottes hongroise* and *porte-manteaux*. Indeed, we suggest the trumpeters wore crimson *habits* or *dolmans* along with the crimson legwear. The *dépôt* held 399 new unissued *surtouts*, 53 *manteaux*, 305 *gilets*, 36 *gilet d'ecuries*, 100 pairs of *culottes hongroise*, 90 pairs of stable trousers, 36 colpacks, 100 *bonnets de police*, 174 waistbelts and 62 *gibernes* with belts, as well as 34 saddle blankets and 26 sheepskin *schabraques*.

The regiment was inspected again on 17 August 1805 and had the following items of clothing in use:[135]

Item	In Good Repair	In Need of Repair	To be written off	Total	Total made since 8 October 1804
Habits	684			684	684
Dolmans					
Pelisses					
Surtouts					
Manteaux	234	199	58	491	111
Gilets in broadcloth	417	107	160	684	417
Gilet d'ecuries	36		648	684	36
Culottes hongroise	190		494	684	190
Stable trousers	162		282	684	102
Kolpacks	75			75	
Schakos	338	142	129	609	225
Bonnets de police		453	231	684	

The *dolman* and *surtout* had been clearly phased out, and habits introduced contrary to regulations, perhaps because the colonel felt they 'looked better'. Another innovation was the issuing of 666 *banderole-porte-carabine* and the equivalent number of carbines.

The regiment was given a shake-down inspection on 1 June 1807:[136]

Item	In Good Repair	In Need of Repair	To be Replaced	Total	Observations
Habits	The regiment has none				
Surtouts					
Gilets en drap	751			751	
Gilet d'ecuries	749			749	
Culottes hongroise	The regiment has none				
Pantalons à cheval	743			743	
Stable trousers	The regiment has none				
Caleçon					
Manteaux	730			730	
Bonnets de police	744			744	
Schakos	663			663	
Colpacks	85			85	
Schako covers	The regiment has none				
Pompoms					
Plumes					

The regiment's sole upper body garment was the *gilet d'ecurie*, which the report noted had short tails: presumably a *kinski*-type garment. What is interesting is that, despite being non-regulation, pantalons *à cheval* are consistently listed on the 1807 inspection returns: clearly the regulations 'caught up' with what was actually happening the field retrospectively. The regiment served with the Grande Armée until 1809, when it became part of ill-fated Army of Portugal, and undertook the Russian campaign soon after. The regiment served in the campaigns of 1813 and 1814, and on 1 August 1814, the rump of the 11e *Chasseurs à Cheval* mustered 53 officers and 261 men and had the following items of clothing:[137]

<table>
<tr><th>Item</th><th>In Good Repair</th><th>In Need of Repair</th><th>Need Replacing in 1 Year</th><th>To be Replaced Total</th><th>Items Needed Effective Strength</th></tr>
<tr><td>Habits</td><td>60</td><td>45</td><td>20</td><td></td><td></td></tr>
<tr><td>Gilets en drap cramoisie</td><td>60</td><td>45</td><td>22</td><td></td><td></td></tr>
<tr><td>Gilet d'ecuries</td><td>54</td><td>49</td><td></td><td></td><td></td></tr>
<tr><td>Culottes hongroise</td><td></td><td></td><td>32</td><td></td><td></td></tr>
<tr><td>Caleçon</td><td colspan="5">Nil</td></tr>
<tr><td>Pantalons à cheval</td><td>70</td><td>21</td><td>10</td><td></td><td></td></tr>
<tr><td>Stable trousers</td><td colspan="5">Nil</td></tr>
<tr><td>Treillis pantalons</td><td>94</td><td></td><td>34</td><td></td><td></td></tr>
<tr><td>Manteaux</td><td>100</td><td>24</td><td></td><td></td><td></td></tr>
<tr><td>Porte-manteaux</td><td>90</td><td>22</td><td>14</td><td></td><td></td></tr>
<tr><td>Bonnets de police</td><td>60</td><td>10</td><td>26</td><td></td><td></td></tr>
<tr><td>Schakos</td><td>104</td><td>16</td><td>52</td><td></td><td></td></tr>
</table>

The existence of crimson waistcoats suggests that they were intended to be seen, implying that the *habit* were not closed to the waist and therefore not of 1812-style cut. The regiment was short of a large number of items of clothing to equip all the men lacking basic items of uniform, and an even larger quantity to replace all the items listed as worn out and needing replacement. The regiment's equipment and armament were in the same deplorable condition as the clothing:[138]

<table>
<tr><th>Item</th><th>In Good Repair</th><th>In Need of Repair</th><th>Need Replacing</th><th>Total</th><th>Effective strength</th></tr>
<tr><td>Waistbelts</td><td>120</td><td>10</td><td></td><td></td><td></td></tr>
<tr><td>Gibernes</td><td>100</td><td>29</td><td></td><td></td><td></td></tr>
<tr><td>Porte-gibernes</td><td>129</td><td></td><td></td><td></td><td></td></tr>
<tr><td>Banderole-porte-carabine</td><td colspan="5">Nil</td></tr>
<tr><td>Pairs of boots with spurs</td><td>80</td><td>22</td><td></td><td></td><td></td></tr>
<tr><td>Pairs of gauntlets</td><td colspan="5">Nil</td></tr>
<tr><td>Sword knots</td><td>120</td><td>10</td><td></td><td></td><td></td></tr>
</table>

Despite having no shoulder belts to carry the carbine, 94 were in use: we can only assume they were carried slung over the troopers' back. In addition, the men had between them 399 shirts, 183 black stocks and had not a single pair of shoes or socks. The *dépôt* held 30m 42 of crimson broadcloth. The inspector notes that the regiment was to changes its *habits* to conform to the regulations.[139] We have been unable to locate any disbandment records for the regiment, but we assume the regiment adopted Bardin-regulation clothing and the trumpeters were adorned in blue *habits* with Royalist Livery.

12e *Chasseurs à Cheval*

Raised in 1788 as the *Chasseurs du Champagne*, the regiment became the 12e *Chasseurs* in 1791 and served with the Grande Armée until 1808. Reviewed on 24 September 1804, the regiment had 41 officers and 760 other ranks. The clothing and equipment in use was as follows:[140]

Item	In Good Repair	In Need of Repair	To be written off	Total	Total made since 1802
Habits			Nil		
Dolmans	1	266	236	503	10
Pelisses			Nil		
Surtouts	484	2		486	387
Manteaux	271	67	54	392	1
Gilets in broadcloth	450	36	11	497	490
Gilet d'ecuries	47	227	13	287	105
Culottes hongroise	148			148	130
Stable trousers in broadcloth	240	245		495	466
Stable trousers in *treillis*	37	175	25	237	839
Kolpacks	100			100	
Schakos	216	268	138	622	246
Bonnets de police	394	69	272	735	

The inspector remarked that the regiment had adopted 'a type of stable trousers, made from broadcloth, with leather reinforcement, the leg closed by buttons' without sanction of the War Ministry. Clearly the regiment had made *pantalons à cheval* on their own initiative as they were far more practicable than *culottes hongroise*. The inspector desired they be removed from service. The *dépôt* held stocks of materials, notably:[141]

0m 28 blue broadcloth, 25m 62 being used since 1803
796m 10 green broadcloth

Firstly, we present a trooper of the 12e *Chasseurs* depicted by Martinet. This image must date to 1805 or earlier as by summer 1805 the regiment was dressed in *kinski*. Secondly, we present an officer of the elite company dressed in a *kinski* and sporting the colpack. Lastly, is Martinet's depiction of a *chasseur* of the 12e wearing a *kinski* in a print published in 1815.

17m 80 white broadcloth
97m 35 crimson broadcloth
14m 2 green and crimson tricot
1,636m 86 white milled serge
90m linen

The blue broadcloth is totally unexpected, yet when we study the regiment in later years the trumpeters were dressed in *bleu celeste* – clearly the tradition began in the consular period. Was this garment a *dolman* or a *surtout*? We suppose a *bleu celeste dolman* with crimson collar and cuffs.

Reviewed again on 28 July 1805, the inspector noted that equipment and clothing had been repaired and the weapons were in good condition. In the previous six months 413 *surtouts* had been issued, 4 *manteaux*, 258 *gilets*, 22 *vestes*, 489 pairs of *culottes hongroise*, 458 pairs of stable trousers and 206 pairs of *pantalons à cheval*. Some 19m 28 of *bleu celeste* broadcloth had been used to make new trumpeters' clothing. Just 36 plumes had been issued.[142]

At the end of the 1805–07 campaign, the regiment was inspected on 1 January 1808. The regiment was still dressed in the *surtout*, which now sported short tails: 1,086 had been made and issued after July 1805. Of these, 1,071 were in use and 168 needed repairs. The *kinskis* were worn with white *gilets*, of which 784 had been made since 1805, with 1,028 in use and of which 228 needed repairs. The regiment had not a single pair of *pantalons à cheval* in use – all the pairs in existence in 1804 and 1805 had either been worn out, or less likely taken out of service. As in 1804 the elite company

Lucien Rousselot's papers in the *Musée de l'Armée* present several depictions of the regiment that cannot be supported by archive papers.

Firstly, is a trooper of the 12e *Chasseurs* recorded by a German artist in 1812.

Secondly, a trumpeter of the 12e *Chasseurs*. From 1800 to perhaps 1806 the regiment's trumpeters wore *bleu celeste* – at first a *dolman* and then a *surtout*. By 1808 the trumpeters were dressed in crimson-faced green *surtouts*. A water colour in the De Ridder Collection (Bibliotheque Nationales, Est Oa 475) – arguably that copied by Rousselot and dating to 1825! – shows a corporal and a trumpeter of the centre companies, and an officer of the elite company in 1812; this last figure and the trumpeter are in a short *habit*, while the brigadier is in a long *habit* with lapels. The trumpeter is dressed in sky-blue-faced crimson. His headdress is more curious; he wears a crimson *czapka*, decorated on the front by a crowned eagle in the Polish form, of which the spread wings cover the full width of two faces of the upper part, or pavilion. As the image is made post-epoch, it may be fiction but we know the regiment had trumpeters in *bleu de ciel* at the end of the Empire.

wore colpacks. One major change was that the trumpeters no longer wore *bleu celeste*, and were instead dressed in crimson-faced green.[143]

We know nothing more until the regiment was inspected in summer 1814, when it possessed the following items of clothing in use:[144]

Item	In Good Repair	In Need of Repair	Need Replacing in 1 Year	To be Replaced	Items Needed
Habits	146	83	11		
Surtouts	117	8	1		
Gilets en drap blanc	161	23	5		
Gilet d'ecuries	72	43	8		
Culottes hongroise	63	14	12		
Caleçon	Nil				
Pantalons à cheval	75	100	15		
Manteaux	98	56	1		
Bonnets de police	204	6	12		
Stable trousers	Nil				
Schakos	248	46	4		

The regiment's own paper archive adds dimensions to the dress of the regiment. Firstly, we present a trooper of the 12e *Chasseurs* as they appeared in summer 1814, reconstructed from the regiment's paper archive. We also present a reconstruction of a trumpeter of the 12e *Chasseurs*. The regiment's archive notes that on 26 September 1814 two trumpeters' *dolmans* were in store. The Musée l'Empéri preserves a *dolman* for the 12e *Chasseurs*' trumpeters. Thirdly, is a reconstruction of a centre company trooper of the 12e *Chasseurs* as they appeared at Waterloo based on the regiment's paper archive. Lastly, is a tentative reconstruction of a *sapeur* based on an inspection report from 1811.

Presumably a mix of *kinski* and *habits a la chasseur* were in use. The men were also issued 500 shirts, 256 pairs of linen *pantalons*, 229 pairs of back gaiters and 100 pairs of ankle boots. The regiment's equipment was as follows:[145]

Item	In Good Repair	In Need of Repair	Need Replacing in 1 Year	To be Replaced	Items Needed
Waistbelt	211	26	1		
Giberne	205	50			
Porte-gibernes	222	29			
Banderole-porte-carabines	135	20	1		
Pairs of boots with spurs	50	89	41		
Sword knots	68	1			

The regimental *dépôt* held the following minimal amounts of cloth, just 50m of white serge and 100m of green tricot, but it did hold a substantial amount of clothing and equipment:[146]

Item	New	Good repair	Need repair	To be written off	Total
Habits	Nil				
Surtouts	350				350
Trumpeters' *dolmans*	1	1			2
Gilets en drap cramoisie	270				270
Gilet d'ecuries	1				1
Manteaux	7				7
Porte-manteaux	13		1		14
Bonnets de police	37				37
Waistbelts	8				8
Gibernes	64				64
Porte-gibernes	64				64
Banderole-porte-carabines	88				88

The existence of crimson waistcoats suggests that they were intended to be seen, implying that the *habit* was not closed to the waist and therefore not of 1812-style cut. What is a surprise is the fact that trumpeters wore *dolmans* and not habits, but again this is paralleled with the 8e *Chasseurs*.

At the time of the regiment's disbandment following Waterloo, the following stocks of materials existed in the *dépôt* on 21 December 1815:[147]

2,259m 33 green broadcloth
58m 55 white broadcloth
47m 65 *bleu de ciel* broadcloth
95m 95 crimson amaranth broadcloth
46m 23 *garance* broadcloth
115m 75 green tricot
73m white serge
247m 55 crimson serge
769m 83 linen for linings
182 dozen medium-sized buttons
1,978 dozen small buttons
87 dozen bone buttons
13m 75 silver lace for rank stripes
79m 12 wool lace for service chevrons

105m lace for corporals
125m lace for *porte-manteau*
0m lace silver lace
1,300m white worsted lace 12mm for *culottes hongroise*

The *bleu de ciel* cloth was seemingly used to make trumpeters' clothing in imitation of the *Garde Imperiale*, and remarkably the Musée l'Empéri preserves a *dolman* for the 12e *Chasseurs*' trumpeters. It is mid-blue, with amaranth collar and white lace and braid. Is it possible therefore that the trumpeters sported these garments at Waterloo? Indeed, and we note the *dépôt* held two such garments in 1814.

We know from the regiment's own records, that rather than a sheepskin *schabraque*, the trumpeters had their own pattern made from *garance* broadcloth, cut to be 'swallow tailed' like those used by the lancers of the *Garde Imperiale*, and had a crimson broadcloth edging. Troopers had white sheepskins, and of this regulation type, 219 were in the *dépôt* and 279 issued to troop horses. Stocks of clothing in the *dépôt* was as follows:[148]

16 *habits-vestes*
127 *gilets en drap blanc*
18 *manteaux-capote*
27 *caleçon*
32 *schakos*
50 pairs of braces
117 sets of *cordon du schako*
19 pairs of stable trousers
260 pairs of gloves
316 waistbelts
1 sword knot
543 *gibernes*
260 *porte-gibernes*
392 *porte-carabine*
21 *schako* covers
22 *porte-manteaux*
214 pompoms
37 plumes with covers

The *schako* cords are likely to date from the First Restoration or Hundred Days as none were deposited into the magazine or in use in October 1814. These items could have been issued to the elite company, along with the plumes. By Waterloo the regiment was, we assume, uniformly dressed in Bardin-regulation clothing.

13e *Chasseurs à Cheval*

Formed in 1792 from the *Legion des Americains* and the *Legion des Midi* as the 13e *Chasseurs*. With the Grande Armée from 1805–07, it fought at Essling and Wagram. Reviewed on 29 July 1805, we note that 664 *surtout*s were in service, and the elite company had 80 colpacks.[149] In summer 1807 the regiment was wearing:[150]

Item	In Good Repair	In Need of Repair	To be Replaced	Total	Observations
Habits	223	262	113	598	
Gilets en drap	189	309	64	562	
Gilet d'ecuries	76	87	20	183	
Culottes hongroise	99	48	206	353	
Pantalons à cheval	814	98	235	434	
Stable trousers	The regiment has none, *pantalons à cheval* are used in their place				
Caleçon	132		309	441	
Manteaux	172	173	260	607	
Bonnets de police	112	224	185	517	
Schakos	1,914	98	308	297	
Colpacks	The regiment has none				
Schako covers					
Pompoms					
Plumes	4	42		46	

We assume the plumes were issued to the elite company to mark their status. Inspected again on 7 February 1808, we note from the report that 905 *surtouts* were in use, along with 95 colpacks for the elite company.[151]

The regiment's archive tells us that in 1813 the 4e, 5e and 6e squadrons were with the army in Germany, and were in action at Dennewitz, as well as the Campaign of France. The 1e, 2e and 3e squadrons remained in Spain from 1809 to 1814. Given the dispersed deployment of the regiment, it had two regimental *dépôt*, which were given a shake-down review in spring 1813.

For the 1e, 2e and 3e squadrons, the *dépôt* was at Niort, which held:[152]

4m 80 orange broadcloth
1,160m 42 *treillis*
533 leather hides
8 new *habits-vestes*
120 *habits-vestes* in the process of being made by the tailor
31 *habit-longues*
31 *veste en drap orange*
93 *gilets en drap blanc*

Representations of the 13ᵉ *Chasseurs* from the epoch, provide a timeline of the regiment's dress.

Firstly, is Martinet's print showing the regiment in *dolmans*, which we know were abolished by summer 1805. Secondly, drawn by Lieutenant Bregeot of the 16ᵉ *Chasseurs*, we see a back view of a *fourrier* of the 13ᵉ. Alas we cannot tell the form of uniform coat he is wearing. (Collection KM) Thirdly, Martinet again offers us a trooper of the regiment in 1814, who is seemingly wearing a *kinski*-type garment. Lastly, is an *officier* of the 13ᵉ *Chasseurs*, seemingly wearing a *habits-veste*. (*Photograph and Collection of Bertrand Malvaux*)

The regiment's archive adds nuances to the impression gained from contemporary artwork.
Up first is a trooper of the 13e *Chasseurs* reconstructed from an inspection report dated 1 April 1813. Secondly, a trooper of the 13e *Chasseurs* reconstructed from a review undertaken on 1 August 1813. Thirdly, we present a reconstruction of an elite company trooper of the 13e *Chasseurs* based on the regimental inspections of 1 April and 1 August 1813. Fourthly, is a reconstruction of a centre company trumpeter noted by Rousselot in his personal papers housed in the *Musée de l'Armée*. Reversed colours would accord with army tradition. Second to last is a reconstruction of an elite company trumpeter as they appeared in late 1813 noted by Rousselot. Last of all is a trumpeter as they appeared at the time of disbandment in summer 1814.

71 pairs *culottes hongroise*
877 pairs of *caleçon*
71 pairs of stable trousers
27 new colpacks
13 old colpacks
78 *capotes-manteaux*
39 *porte-manteaux*

Materials held in the *dépôt* were:[153]

2,296m 21 green broadcloth
41m orange broadcloth
115m 40 white broadcloth
137m 60 orange serge
162 *peau de mouton* (sheepskins) to make *schabraques*

28 *manteaux*
4 sets of clothing for the condemned
199 pairs of pistols

Lodged in the stables we find, among other items:[154]

172 saddles with the same number of surcingles, curb bridles, snaffle bridles and headcollars
156 saddle blankets and parade head collars
150 *schabraques*
107 pairs of linen overalls
329 shirts
25 pairs of grey linen gaiters
462 black stocks
11 pairs of epaulettes
63 pairs of gloves
10 plumes
2 red pompoms
5 grenades in copper

Found in a box in the back of the store rooms were 51 pairs of *pantalons hongroise*, 1 *habit-longue*, 177 pairs of stable trousers, 75 pairs of *caleçon*, 28 life-expired *gilet d'ecuries* and 12 new *giberne* covers. It seems that elite company troopers had copper grenades on their *giberne*s, protected with a linen cover. In a report made later that year we notice the 31 *habit-longues* were to be 're-made' – one suspects the tails cropped short – and 1 *habit* for *chevau-leger-lancier* was in *dépôt* along with 51 lancer-pattern pairs of *culottes hongroise*, 68 pairs of *caleçon*, and 125 pairs of stable trousers, again all lancer pattern. The regiment was clearly in the process of adopting Bardin regulations in spring 1813.[155] We assume the lancer-pattern habit was serving as model for the regiment in adopting Bardin regulation. What the report does do is demonstrate that regiments on active service in Spain did re-equip with the latest regulation in some cases. The report also shows that long-tailed *habits* remained in use into 1813, when if we restricted ourselves to the regulations, these garments were said to have had disappeared by 1806, so too *dolmans*: but as the primary sources show, *dolmans* were used into 1814, long-tailed *habits* into 1813, and also the *habit a revers* into 1814 with braided waistcoats. The regulations are meaningless, and regimental archives are the primary source of information.

Reviewed on 1 August 1814, the regiment was wearing:[156]

Item	In Good Repair	In Need of Repair	Need Replacing in 1 Year	To be Replaced	Items Needed	Effective Strength
Habits-vestes	371	119	54	21	324	789
Gilets en drap blanc	308	39	60	31	351	789
Culottes hongroise	392	12	108	10	267	789
Veste d'ecurie	362	60	144	7	216	789
Pantalons de treillis	407	1	38	28	315	789
Pantalons à cheval	146	54	72	17	500	789
Manteaux	372	45	70	26	272	789
Caleçon	228		78	8	475	789
Bonnets de police	514	24	61	57	133	789
Schakos	563	38	22	10	156	789

When we look at equipment in use, 310 men we wearing shoes, as they lacked a regulation pair of boots, 95 men had no *giberne* and belt and, rather shockingly, 117 men lacked a sabre and belt! In addition, 597 *banderole-porte-carabine* were in use for 499 carbines, for which just 12 bayonets were issued. In terms of *petit-equipement* in use on 1 August, the men had between them 1,984 shirts – more than two per man, we assume sous-officiers had three – 617 black stocks, and 476 pairs of shoes with 275 pairs of grey linen gaiters. Cloth in the *dépôt* was 6m 23 orange broadcloth, 16m 48 orange serge, 112m 10 trumpeters' lace, 306m 88 worsted braid for *culottes hongroise*, 13m of white worsted lace for *porte-manteaux* and 3,738 dozen bone buttons. Clothing in store comprised 28 *habits-vestes*, 125 *gilets en drap blanc*, 123 pairs of *culottes hongroise*, 112 *veste d'ecurie*, 22 pairs of stable trousers, 27 pairs of braces and 3 colpacks. Clearly, the elite company were wearing colpacks, and we know their *giberne*s were ornamented with copper grenades as 6 of these were in store, along with 3 scarlet plumes, and 11 pairs of scarlet epaulettes. We also assume the trumpeters wore Imperial Livery. The regiment was ordered to adopt blue trumpeters' clothing with Royalist Livery. The inspector noted that the regiment was in the process of adopting the provisions of the decrees of 12 January and 8 February 1812.

In September 1815 the *dépôt* at Belfort held 178 *habits-vestes*, 208 white *gilets*, 130 *gilet d'ecuries*, 230 *bonnets de police*, 72 *manteaux*, 94 pairs of *pantalons à cheval*, 180 pairs of *culottes hongroise*, 93 new *schako*s and 45 needing repairs, 147 pompoms and 23 pairs of scarlet epaulettes. We also find 146 pairs of linen gaiters, 90 nose bags made from linen with leather straps, 2 handkerchiefs, 197 nights caps and 118 pairs of clogs for stable duties. Some men were issued capotes rather than *manteaux*, 5 being in use at disbandment, and 21 pairs of scarlet epaulettes.[157]

14e *Chasseurs à Cheval*

The regiment was created in 1793 from four squadrons of the *Hussards des Alpes* and a company each of the *Hussards de l'Egalities* and the *Hussards de la Mort*. Reviewed on 6 October 1805, General Pully remarked that the regiment was in chaos, and that the 'clothing, equipment and armament was all non-regulation and had to be replaced'.[158] From 1805 the regiment was with the Army of Italy. It took part in the Siege of Stralsund in 1807, thence Essling and Wagram. Inspected on 25 September 1809, the men were wearing *surtouts* that had had their tails cropped short, which were ordered to be replaced with *habits*.[159] From 1810 to 1813 the regiment was in Span, and marched to Germany in summer 1813. The regiment charged at Saint-Dizier, Brienne and other actions in the Campaign of France. Reviewed on 1 October 1814, the regiment had 120 men on parade. Their clothing was in tatters:[160]

Item	In Good Repair	In Need of Repair	Need Replacing in 1 Year	To be Replaced	Items Needed
Habits-vestes	111	4	10	40	44
Gilets en drap blanc	30		4	7	169
Gilet d'ecuries	138	5	34	8	25
Caleçon	13		13	1	133
Culottes hongroise	29	1	63	3	114
Pantalons à cheval	129	5	34	6	36
Stable trousers	17		12	4	177
Bonnets de police	135	1	34	12	28
Schakos	128	5	9	11	57
Schako covers	24			1	185
Pompoms	157				53
Manteaux	103	13	3	27	28

Dépôt held no stocks of clothing, no stocks of equipment or weapons and no materials. The inspector noted that the regiment had been clothed from the *dépôt*, but several men were still wearing clothing that did not accord to the regulation of 8 February 1812. Ergo, the regiment only adopted the Bardin regulation in summer 1814 into spring 1815.

When disbanded in 1815, the *dépôt* held some stocks of materials:[161]

316m 80 green broadcloth
53m white broadcloth
13m 61 orange broadcloth
48m 81 orange serge
238m 59 linen for linings
247m 52 linen for *caleçon*
97m flat white wool braid 10mm wide

Martinet shows us a trooper of the regiment *c.*1805, before the *surtout* was adopted in summer of that year to replace the *dolman*. Secondly, Martinet presents us a trooper from 1814. Thirdly, we present a trooper of the 14e *Chasseurs* reconstructed from the regiment's paper archive from 1814. Lastly, we show an elite company trooper of the 14e *Chasseurs* based on notes made by Eugene Forte from papers of Colonel Vanson housed in the library of the *Musée de l'Armée*. This is not supported by the regiment's archive, but we cannot dismiss the source.

Dépôt also held 1 *habit-veste*, 18 *gilet d'ecuries*, 87 pairs of *culottes hongroise*, 11 *manteau a manche* (sleeved cloak), 10 *bonnets de police*, 13 *porte-manteaux*, 627 *schako* covers, 177 pompoms, 52 waistbelts, 79 *giberne*s with belts, 60 *banderole-porte-mousquetons* with just 44 carbines, 280 pairs of braces, 596 pairs of wrist gloves and 3 trumpets. Also in *dépôt* was a complete 'Bardin start-up kit' comprising *items de modèle:* 1 *habit-veste de trompette* and 1 *habit-veste de chasseur*, 1 *gilet blanc*, 1 *veste d'ecurie*, 1 pair *pantalons à cheval*, 1 *manteau a manche* and 1 *bonnet de police*. Was the trumpeter's *habit* blue with Royalist Livery or green with Imperial Livery? Alas we cannot tell, but on balance of probability it was blue with Royalist Livery. We know the model items were used as 11 *manteau a manche* were in *dépôt*, as we noted earlier. Also in *dépôt* were 260 black stocks and 22 nose bags for the horses.[162]

15e *Chasseurs à Cheval*

Formed in 1793 from the *Chasseurs de Beysser*, the regiment was with the Army of Italy from 1805, joined the Grande Armée in 1807, and fought in Spain from 1808 to 1814. Three squadrons were detached in summer 1813 and these fought at Leipzig and the Campaign of France. We are fortunate that some of the regiment's standing orders exist and were collated by Lucien Rousselot in the 1940s.[163]

Officers

15 April 1812 the officers of the regiment were allowed to wear their *bonnet de police* up to 10 am. The lace was to be silver, 42mm wide for senior officers, 30mm for captains

Martinet presents the uniform of the regiment at the beginning of the Empire, before *dolmans* had been replaced in 1805 with *surtouts*, and again in 1814. The *schako* cords and plumes are unexpected at this date.

Regimental papers in the in the library of the *Musée de l'Armée* allow us to present the following images.

Firstly, reconstruction of a trooper of the 15ᵉ *Chasseurs* during 1811–13, and secondly, his colleague in the elite company.

Thirdly, is a trumpeter of a centre company after 26 September 1813, the dress of the trumpet major, and trumpeter of the elite company.

Lastly, we present a tentative reconstruction of a *sapeur* based on notes made by Rousselot housed in the library of the *Musée de l'Armée*. We do not know the origin of his information. Certainly, the regimental standing orders make no mention whatsoever of *sapeurs*.

and 24mm for lieutenants and sous-lieutenants. The same order outlined in minute detail the officers clothing. The *habit-surtout* was worn over an orange waistcoat laced and braided in silver, green *culottes hongroise* with lace according to rank in silver, boots with silver lace and tassel, bronze spurs, *giberne* and belt, wrist gloves in doe hide, sword knot and *schako* cords. In undress the men wore the *schako* with no ornamentation, a *habit-veste* with orange patches surmounted with a button to the retroussis, *culottes hongroise* with no lace, made from broadcloth or casimir, *pantalons à cheval* in grey broadcloth with lateral bands in orange broadcloth, black boots, bronze spurs, chamois leather gloves and a black silk sword knot.

On 30 September 1812 officers in full dress were expected to wear their *habits-vestes* and grey *culottes hongroise*, which were worn on a full-dress parade on 26 September 1813.

On 6 August 1814 the colonel decreed that for town dress officers were to wear:

> Chapeau of the model, black pleated stock, with the collar of the shirt visible. *Habit* and *veste*, nankeen *pantalons*, boots with black lace and bronzed iron spurs, regimental sabre until épées are received, sword knot in white linen, gloves in yellow leather or nankeen.

For full dress the officers were to wear:

> *Schakos* with silver pompom, cravat with the knot not visible, green broadcloth *culottes hongroise* with lacing appropriate for rank, habit, boots with black lace and silver tassels, regimental sabre and silver sword knot, *giberne* and belt.

The colonel also allowed officers to wear a green *redingote* in barracks before 11 am, along with the *bonnet de police* and grey broadcloth *pantalons à cheval*, as well as on manoeuvres. On 8 August 1814 the colonel reminded the adjutants, lieutenants and sous-lieutenants that they had to wear on their epaulettes marks of their rank – one suspects that they had got away with wearing extravagant epaulettes not dissimilar from captains as the colonel remarked that the current rank distinctives were not sufficiently obvious.

An order of 23 October 1814 notes that the officers' sabre belt was to be in black Moroccan leather with two rows of silver embroidery, with a simple S-clasp fastening, two silvered buckles, studs and sabre hook – one gets the feeling that officers were wearing sabre belts that did not match the colonel's ideals. On 27 April 1815 officers were allowed to wear around town a '*habit frac*', the front closed by a row of 12 large buttons, with distinctive colour piping and facing. The *redingote* was still tolerated to be worn in morning dress; we know from the same order that it was double breasted, had a standing collar that was now decorated with a small patch of orange cloth.

The order of 11 May 1815 tells us that in full dress officers wore *chapeau* and épées at dismounted duties and were ordered to buy new cockades for their *schakos* and *chapeau*, and to remove the *fleur-de-lys* badge from the shield of the épée and replace it with an 'N'.

Other ranks

Reviewed on 11 October 1804, the regiment was decked out in 591 *dolmans*, of which 84 were in good condition, 454 needed repairs and the remainder were headed for the dustbin. In addition, 620 *habits* were in use: 3,789 being in good condition, 202 needed repairs and 139 immediate replacement. Elite company had 81 colpacks. The inspector ordered all the *dolmans* to be removed from service.[164] When inspected again on 16 November 1805, 639 *habits* were in use alongside 579 *dolmans*. The *habits* were worn with white *gilets*. In addition, *pantalons à cheval* were in unofficial use, some 510 pairs, and the elite company had 87 colpacks. Stores had made 267 *surtouts* – 202 had been ordered in 1804 – but were as yet unissued. A further 202 *surtouts* were ordered to be produced, and the *dolmans* and *habits* to be replaced.[165] Moving on to 16 January 1808, stores had made 958 *surtouts* and 1,125 pairs of *pantalons à cheval*.[166]

The order of 17 April 1812 dealt with the stable dress of the regiment, viz: *bonnet de police*, *gilet d'ecurie*, linen pantalons. The regiment's colonel stressed that once stable duties had been completed, the men must clean and wax their boots, thoroughly beat and brush their *gilet d'ecurie* and clean the *bonnet de police*. It was forbidden for the men to take off their *gilet d'ecurie* and *bonnet de police* until stable duties had been completed. In full dress the men were to wear the *schakos*, *surtout*, white broadcloth *gilet* and *culotte hongroise*.

On 28 April 1812 company commanders were ordered to buy green *schako* covers for the sous-officiers of their companies. In undress the *schakos* was to be covered and decorated with a pompom only. The captains were to ensure that their men placed their *sacs a distribution* beneath the *porte-manteaux* and not to stow them beneath the seat of the saddle, and they were to be carried at all times other than parades and inspections. It was to contain the *habit* and *bonnet de police*. A few days later, on 30 April, company commanders were to obtain oil cloth *schako* covers for the trumpeters, who like the sous-officiers were to have the *schakos* covered at all times bar parades. On 2 May 1812 the colonel ordered that sous-officiers and men were forbidden from cutting their hair, and the order of 28 December 1812 confirms that the men were still wearing the *queue* by this date. Indeed, the order of 1 February 1813 stressed the men were to keep their hair brushed, to do so each morning, and not to wear their 'hair long' i.e., it had to be kept in the *queue*.

The order of 5 October 1812 tells us that, for lack of green cloth, the regiment's *pantalons à cheval* were made from locally sourced brown broadcloth with black leather reinforcement. Company officers were to ensure that any *pantalons à cheval* in cloth other than brown were replaced as speedily as possible. On 26 September 1813 the colonel reported that blue *schabraques* were in use – these were clearly for trumpeters as they were to be swapped for items made from black sheepskin. We wonder as to the colour scheme of the trumpeter's uniform. The regiments facings were orange, which could have clashed appallingly with the blue. We lack sufficient detail to reconstruct the uniform sadly. Rousselot in his study of *chasseurs* states the *habit* was *bleu de ciel* with blue collar, laced white and orange cuffs, and orange piping to the collar, front opening, turnbacks and soubise pockets, all set off with brown *pantalons à cheval*! The elite company did not have *aigrettes*, and the order of 17 August 1814 reinforced that fact that 'the elite company will continue to wear red pompoms'.

The 329 other ranks of the regiment were inspected on 1 August 1814, and their clothing was found to be in tatters. No man had every item of clothing, and what was in use was mostly '*hors de service*', i.e. needed repairs or total replacement:[167]

Item	In Good Repair	In Need of Repair	Need Replacing in 1 Year	To be Replaced	Items Needed
Habits-vestes	120	95	6	111	2
Giles en drap	22	27	2	67	216
Culottes hongroise					327
Pantalons à cheval	42	16	7	233	37
Stable trousers	13		7	17	297
Caleçon				20	314
Manteaux	76	127	7	89	35
Bonnets de police	64	18	7	102	143
Gilet d'ecuries	36	36	7	239	16
Schakos	126	25	1	175	7

Cloth in stores included 50m of white broadcloth and 29m of *brun-marron* broadcloth for making legwear. Also in stores were twenty-three *aigrettes* for the elite company and twenty pompoms for trumpeters. We have been unable to locate any further records for the regiment, so we cannot say what was worn during the Hundred Days.

16e *Chasseurs à Cheval*

The regiment was created in 1793 from the *Chasseurs Normands de Labreteche.*

Inspected on 23 September 1804, the regiment's clothing, even in a time of peace, was in very poor condition. The regiment had 671 *dolmans,* all of which were scheduled for replacement. Likewise, the regiment had 590 *surtouts* in use, 440 being scheduled for replacement as '*hors de service*'. Indeed, most of the clothing was listed as '*hors de service*': 302 out of 456 *manteaux,* 547 out of 647 white *gilet*s, every single one of the 500 *gilet d'ecuries* and pairs of *caleçon*, 585 pairs of stable trousers the 695 pairs of *culottes hongroise.* Also, 511 of the 623 *schakos a flamme* were on the list for replacement. The clothing must have been in tatters! Yet sat in the *dépôt*, brand new and unissued, were 201 *dolmans*, 89 *manteaux*, 628 new white *gilet*s, 544 *gilet d'ecuries*, 16 pairs of *caleçon*, 24 pairs of *culottes hongroise*, 626 pairs of stable trousers, 34 '*cordons du fil*' with 42 sets in use that we assume to be *schako* cords, 5 plumes were in store with 192 in service, which we assume were the regulation black, 142 *schakos* and 450 *bonnets de police.* One wonders why all this new kit was not issued to make up for the acute issues facing the rank and file's clothing?[168]

The regiment was with the Grande Armée from 1805 and fought at Austerlitz and Jena. Regimental accounts for the purchase of cloth and clothing from 1806 report that the following items were made:[169]

62 *manteaux* at 3fr 86 each
600 pairs of *culottes hongroise* at 89 centimes each
312 pairs of stable trousers, total 84fr 14

Period iconography presents a cross spectrum of the dress of the regiment.

Firstly, Martinet presents a trooper before the abolition of the *dolman* in summer 1805 and after the replacement of the *schako a flamme* in use in October 1804. The regimental archive supports the presence of plumes and *schako* cords. Martinet then presents an officer of the elite company in undress, and Weiland gives us an officer of elite company in parade dress. A print by Chez Bassett published in 1814 shows the use of the *kinski* and also a sunray plate. Lastly, is a print by Martinet from 1814, confirming the use of the *kinski*.

The papers of Rousselot offer us other depictions of the regiment. Firstly, is a trooper of the 16e *Chasseurs* as witnessed by Albrecht Adam. Secondly, is a trumpeter also witnessed by Albrecht Adam. Lastly, is a trooper based on the regiment's archive documents from summer 1814.

150 *bonnets de police*, total 40fr 50
16 pairs of *pantalons for trumpeters*, total 15fr
60 *habits*, total 48 francs
396 *gilet d'ecuries* total 133fr 67
624 pairs of *pantalons* at 1fr 50 each, total 686fr
603 *vestes* at 29 centimes each, total 66fr

Cloth usage was:[170]

2,369m 35 green broadcloth, costing 10ftr 85 a metre for *manteaux*, total 2,596fr 62
24m 96 green broadcloth costing 10fr 85 a metre, total 278fr 82 for *culottes hongroise*
84m 14 green broadcloth, costing 10fr 58 for 62 pairs of *pantalons à cheval,* total 912fr 91
40m 50 green broadcloth for *bonnets de police*, total 439fr 2
15m green broadcloth for 16 pairs trumpeters' *pantalons*, total 162fr 75
686m 40 green broadcloth for 624 pairs of *pantalons à cheval,* total 926f 64
30m linen, costing 1fr 50 a metre to line 150 *bonnets de police*, total 40fr 50
48m 8 *bleu celeste* broadcloth costing 10fr a metre for *surtouts*
7m *bleu celeste broadcloth* costing 7fr a metre for *bonnets de police*

We know from the accounts that the 624 pairs of *pantalons* ordered had a blue side stripe, the *vestes* had blue collars as it seems did the *gilet d'ecuries*, the *bonnets de police* had blue turbans, and the *habits* had blue piping, all of which required an additional 52m 4 of *bleu celeste* broad cloth.[171] Regiment records report that in 1807 779 *habits* were made, 821 pairs of *pantalons à cheval*, which were made from green broadcloth with blue side stripe, 809 pairs of stable trousers and 623 white *vestes*.[172]

The regiment was given a shake-down inspection on 25 January 1808 and had 1,103 *surtouts* in service and 504 brand-new examples in store ready to be issued; 668

manteaux were in use. The report also tells us 956 new-model *schakos* had been bought, of which 755 had been issued. The inspecting general authorised the regiment to adopt *habits* in lieu of *surtouts*, and agreed 808 be purchased, 222 in 1808, the rest as the remainder of the *surtouts* came out of use over the next two years.[173]

In action at Essling and Wagram, as well as at Smolensk and Borodino, the regiment was re-formed in 1813. The 3e, 4e and 5e squadrons were reviewed on 19 March 1813. The men who had been taken into the *dépôt* in summer 1812 were all clothed and equipped, the new entrants were wearing civilian clothing: the *dépôt* was waiting for the delivery of cloth before they could start making uniforms. The squadron's 393 men present that day had no weapons or equipment.[174] By the 22nd of the month, the major reported that the cloth had not arrived, but the *dépôt* had taken delivery 112 carbines, 112 sabres and 112 pistols as well as 30 horses for nearly 400 men.[175] By the end of the month, the major reported that 112 men, all of whom had been in *dépôt* since 1812 had been dispatched to the 1e squadron, and was still waiting for cloth and materials to arrive.[176] It was not until the end of May that the *dépôt* was able to dispatch three squadrons to the field, by which time the *dépôt* had no stocks of cloth or materials, the major asking for more funds to buy materials.[177]

Inspected on 1 August 1814, the regiment's clothing was in shreds:[178]

Item	In Good Repair	In Need of Repair	Need Replacing in 1 Year	To be Replaced	Items Needed
Habits-vestes	55	14	106		
Gilet sans manche	23	21	33		
Veste d'ecurie	35	21	81		
Culottes hongroise	16	27	16		
Caleçon	Nil				
Pantalons à cheval	25	24	57		
Stable trousers	6		15		
Manteaux	8	104	26		
Porte-manteaux	24	82	71		
Bonnets de police	65	119			
Schakos	59	10	112		
Pompom	Nil				

The men were issued 166 *banderole-porte-carabine*, yet were issued 183 carbines! The men were also issued 2,690 shirts, 114 black stocks – many men used black linen scarves to pad out the collar of the habit the inspector noted – and had not a single pair of *caleçon* or socks. The *dépôt* held 40 new sleeveless *gilet*s, and 9 *gilet d'ecuries*, 98 waistbelts, 29 *giberne*s, 26 *porte-giberne*s and 23 sword knots. Of interest, the inspector noted that the regiment had not adopted the uniform regulations as decreed on 19 January or 7 February 1812, nor had enacted the modifications of 23 April 1814 concerning the colour of trumpeters' *habits*. Little wonder as the regiment was disbanded soon after the review.[179]

17e *Chasseurs à Cheval*

Formed on 25 May 1793 from the *Chevau Légère Belge de Westflandres*, the regiment was disbanded on 23 September 1803. No regiment of this designation existed during the Empire.[180]

18e *Chasseurs à Cheval*

Formed as the *Chasseurs Belge* in May 1793, it was disbanded on 23 September 1803. No regiment of this designation existed during the Empire.[181]

19e *Chasseurs à Cheval*

Formed on 10 June 1793 for the *Chasseurs de la Legion de Rosenthal*, the regiment was with the Army of Italy from 1805. The regiment standing orders from 1808 to 1809 have survived, which adds a tremendous amount of detail to the dress of the regiment.

Standing Orders

On 4 January 1809 in *petit tenue*, linen *pantalons* were to be made for *sous-officiers* and men. Officers were to follow likewise. Twelve days later, an order was given for the men to wear at stable duty, linen *pantalons*, shoes, *surtouts* and *bonnets de police*. The riding boots were prohibited from being worn in the stables.

The colonel issued orders regarding the dress of the regiment on 24 February 1809. Sous-officiers were allowed a *surtout* made from super fine broadcloth, lined and piped in aurore broadcloth, and a *habit* again made from superfine green broadcloth, piped in aurore broadcloth and lined in aurore serge to cost 6 francs 50. The *revers* had fourteen medium buttons, six worn on the cuff, two at the collar and six on the back. Under the *habit* was worn a white *gilet*, which fastened with nine small buttons. They were also allowed *culottes hongroise*, and *pantalons à cheval,* a double-breasted *capote*, the front fastening with eighteen buttons and two buttons to the rear, and a *bonnet de police* decorated with 148mm of silver lace, tassel and embroidered hunting horn. Troopers wore a habit made from 'common broadcloth' a white *gilet*, a pair of broadcloth *pantalons* decorated with 5m of white braid, a *bonnet de police* decorated with 148mm of white worsted lace, a white hunting horn and tassel and 3m of white braid for the *flamme* and tassel cut from strips of white cloth. Like the *sous-officiers*, the *pantalons à cheval* were broadcloth reinforced with leather and were worn for campaign dress and stable duties. For stable duties, the men wore *habits-vestes*, which cost 1 franc 40 to make, and it seems also a *gilet d'ecurie*, the cuffs being closed by two buttons, a button

The 19ᵉ are particularly well documented by period iconography. Firstly, we have a trooper by Martinet dating to before summer 1805, when the regiment had not yet adopted the *surtout*. Secondly, Martinet gives us an officer of the elite company wearing a campaign dress *kinksi*. Thirdly, Berka presents us a trooper in a long-tailed *habit*. Left to right we have a trooper of the 12ᵉ *Chasseurs* wearing a *kinski*, a trooper of the 19ᵉ *Chasseurs* and thence a trooper of the 27ᵉ, dated to roughly 1808. Lieutenant Bregeot presents for us a sous-officier as he remembers them during the Russian campaign. Martinet then presents a trooper in 1814 wearing a *kinski*. Lastly, we have a dated portrait of Lieutenant Mournier of the elite company wearing a Bardin *habits-veste* and colpack. (*Collection KM*).

at the shoulder and the front closed by six buttons. *Sous-officiers* and troopers had a tricot *porte-manteau* lined with *treillis* and a *manteau*.

Officers were ordered on 26 February 1809 to wear colpacks and grey pantalons tucked into the riding boots, and officers of the centre companies green pantalons laced in silver, tucked into their boots. *Sous-officiers* were allowed to wear *culottes hongroise* decorated with silver soutache decoration. For stable duties the men were allowed a *gilet* made from linen with sleeves from 28 February. New plumes were issued on 20 March 1809, and on the march plumes were to be stowed in the *porte-manteaux*, as were the *flammes* from the colpacks.

Inspections

When given a shake-down inspection on 1 June 1807, the regiment was wearing:[182]

Item	In Good Repair	In Need of Repair	To be Replaced	Total	Observations
Surtouts	201	160	148		
Gilets en drap blanc	320	21	168		
Culottes hongroise	240	60	209		
Pantalons à cheval	270	69	170		
Gilet d'ecuries	209	110	1490		
Stable trousers	The regiment has none, *pantalons à cheval* are used in their place				
Schakos	410	31	68		
Bonnets de police	359		150		
Manteaux	219	40	250		
Colpacks	The regiment has none				
Schako covers					
Pompoms					
Plumes					

The elite company was devoid of any special distinction, yet colpacks existed by the end of 1808 according to the standing orders. The regiment was part of the Army of Germany in 1809 when it charged at Essling and Wagram and charged at Borodino. The regiment was re-formed and fought in the German campaign of 1813 before joining the Army of Italy for the 1814 campaign, seeing action at Caldiero, Mincio and

The regiment's paper archive confirms the use of Bardin regulation clothing. Our first reconstruction is based on the regiment's tailoring accounts dated December 1813 and the regiment's disbandment records of summer 1814. The second image confirms the officer's portrait about the use of the colpack in 1814.

Taro. Over winter 1813 the regiment replaced a lot of worn-out and missing clothing. Some 100 *schakos* for the war squadrons in Germany were purchased for 3,503 francs, and 60 pairs of *pantalons à cheval* costing 252 francs were obtained, along with 70 pairs of boots for the sum of 1,470 francs. For 321 men arriving into the *dépôt* in December 1813, some 12,340 francs was spent on their basic clothing needs, and some 538 francs was expended on the regimental tailor to make the garments according to the decree of 19 January and 7 February 1812.[183] Clearly the regiment only started to adopt Bardin regulation in winter 1813.

Inspected on 1 September 1814, the regiment's clothing was mostly missing or worn out:[184]

Item	In Good Repair	In Need of Repair	Need Replacing in 1 Year	To be Replaced Total	Items Needed
Habits-vestes	113	105	3	23	8
Gilets en drap	21	15		1	215
Culottes hongroise	32	5	5	8	202
Pantalons à cheval	64	51	3		134
Stable trousers	11	2			239
Caleçon	15	2		23	212
Manteaux	145	10			97
Bonnets de police	229	2			21
Gilet d'ecuries	50	31	3	15	153
Schakos	187	1		3	12
Colpacks	49				
Pompoms					252
Covers					252
Braces					252

Equipment wise, 3 men had no sabre belt, 14 men no *giberne*, 26 lacked a *giberne* belt – so how was the *giberne* carried? On a piece of string or tucked in the *porte-manteaux*? – just 6 sous-officiers had gloves, 246 men had none, 8 trumpets were issued, so too 220 sword knots, 205 *banderole-porte-carabine* and 205 *boucletaux* – the leather strap that fastens the carbine to the carbine clip. Yet we note 218 *mousquetons* were issued: how were these carried? Across the back on the musket sling? Two hundred and forty-nine sabres were in use and 160 pistols. Between them, the 252 men had 571 shirts – roughly 2 each for the men and 3 for the *sous-officiers* and trumpeters – 43 pairs of linen overalls, 192 black stocks – clearly men used improvised neck cloths – 224 white stocks, just 2 pairs of linen ankle socks, and 89 pairs of shoes.

Dépôt held little in the way cloth, holding 31m 94 of white broadcloth, 29m 50 of aurore broadcloth, 186m of linen, 96m 80 of white lace. Ironically the *dépôt* held a lot of brand-new clothing that could have gone a long way to make up for chronic shortages, viz 48 *habits-vestes*, 112 white *gilets*, 8 new *manteaux*. *Dépôt* also had 10 *manteaux* in good condition and 8 needing repairs, as well as 26 life expired *habits*, 4 *manteaux* and 49 *schakos*.[185]

Arriving with the regiment in 1815 long after it had been disbanded were 50 pairs of gloves, 50 sabre knots and 50 *schakos* covers. The regiment owed 3,505 francs to regimental workmen for 100 *schakos* and 100 complete sets of leather equipment, 252 francs for 50 pairs of stable trousers, 1,470 francs for 70 pairs of boots. In addition, 595 francs was owed to the regimental tailor for making 50 uniforms.[186] We know nothing about the dress of the trumpeters. We cannot assume they were Imperial Livery, although it would be an educated suggestion!

20e *Chasseurs à Cheval*

Created in 1793 from the *Legion du Centre*, the regiment was with the Grande Armée from 1806 and was given a shake-down inspection on 1 June 1807:[187]

Item	In Good Repair	In Need of Repair	To be Replaced	Total	Observations
Surtouts	589			589	
Gilets en drap	589			589	
Gilet d'ecuries		589			
Culottes hongroise	589			589	
Pantalons à cheval	589			589	
Stable trousers		589		589	
Caleçon	The regiment has none				
Manteaux	91	300	108	499	90 needed
Bonnets de police	91	220	218	529	60 needed
Schakos	100	311	50	461	
Colpacks	128			128	
Schako covers	The regiment has none				
Pompoms					
Plumes					659 needed

The regiment fought at Wagram in 1809, served in Spain from 1810 and was back with the Grande Armée in 1812. The regiment's paperwork is particularly complete for the process of clothing and equipping men as they joined the *dépôt* at Bonn. Reviewed on 9 July 1812, the regiment's major was awaiting cloth and materials to begin production of the replacement clothing needed for the year 1812 as well as newly admitted conscripts. Delivery was expected for 72 new *schakos* with covers, *schako* plates and chinscales, and orders had been placed for equipment. The 120 men in the *dépôt* had been issued shirts, *caleçon*, linen *pantalons de route* and night caps.[188] The *dépôt* of the regiment was reviewed 19 July 1812, the inspector reporting that the regimental tailors

Martinet presents a trooper of the regiment in 1814. It is one of the few period images of the regiment.

had clothed 87 conscripts completely, only 72 men had been issued a *schako* and no man had sabre, waistbelt or *giberne* and belt.[189] By 30 July 1812 the *dépôt* held 189 men: the major reported that 30 men had arrived on 20–21 July and had been equipped, 38 men had arrived on 28 July from the 10ᵉ *Chasseurs* and had been partially clothed and equipped, and 24 men had arrived that day destined for the 31ᵉ *Chasseurs* and were provided with a *gilet d'ecurie* and stable trousers. Orders had been placed for more *schakos*, as well as the men's equipment and *porte-manteaux*. The regiment needed money and materials, the major noted, if the men were not to be uselessly tied down in the *dépôt*.[190]

By 9 February 1813 the *dépôt* held 119 other ranks with 107 troop horses. The major reported that the conscripts and enrolled volunteers had been completely clothed, and the tailor and workmen were making clothing for the men that were scheduled to arrive with the regiment: the work could proceed faster if the *dépôt* had sufficient resources: money was needed to buy broadcloth, serge and tricot. Delivery from Strasbourg was expected for *gibernes*, *porte-gibernes*, *banderole-porte-mousquetons*, waistbelts, braces and *schakos*. Contracts had been passed to obtain items that the *dépôt* could not produce.[191]

A week later the *dépôt* mustered 253 other ranks with 240 horses. Major Barbe reported that 131 men had clothed and equipped, but the *dépôt* had yet to receive the cloth and materials from the merchants so the tailors could make more uniforms.[192] By 4 March 1813 the regiment mustered 27 officers and 504 other ranks, lacking 44 corporals, 1 corporal-trumpeter and 4 trumpeters. Some 211 men were awaiting equipment and to complete their clothing.[193]

Disbanded in summer 1814 into the 2ᵉ *regiment des Chevaux-Legere-Lanciers* the regiment possessed 101 *habits-vestes* in good condition and 23 needing repairs, just 32 men had a *gilet*, 82 *filet d'ecuries* were in good condition and 22 needed repairs, 114 pairs of *culottes hongroise* were in good repair and 10 were life expired, only 14 pairs of *caleçon* were in use, not every man had a pair of *pantalons à cheval*, 94 pairs were in good condition, 26 needed repairs and 4 men had none. Likewise, only 109 *manteaux*, all in good condition, were in service, only 78 men had *schakos*, and 110 had a *bonnet de police*. Cloth and materials in the *dépôt* included 55m 53 of white broadcloth, 6m 57 aurore broadcloth, 715m of green broadcloth, 1,279m 70 white serge, 167m 95 green tricot, 163m 18 linen for lining, 181m 33 linen for *caleçon*, 607m 92 *treillis*, 2m 70 of

Speculative reconstruction of a centre company trooper of the 20e *Chasseurs* in 1813 based on notes made by Rousselot housed in the library of the *Musée de l'Armée*. We do not know the basis of his observations. Secondly, we present a reconstruction of a trooper based on the regiment's disbandment paperwork. Thirdly, we present a *sapeur* reconstructed from the regiment's archive papers for 1811. Lastly, is a speculative reconstruction of a trumpeter in 1814 based on notes made by Rousselot housed in the library of the *Musée de l'Armée*.

white worsted lace 22mm wide for corporals' stripes, 507m 8 aurore serge and 2m 40 red worsted lace for service chevrons. Brand-new clothing in the *dépôt* included 140 *gilet drap blanc*, 71 *gilet d'ecuries*, 87 pairs of *culottes hongroise*, 143 *manteaux*, 167 *porte-manteaux*, 49 *bonnets de police*, 76 pairs of stable trousers, 197 *schakos*, 372 *schako* covers and 168 pompoms. No epaulettes or *schakos* existed for the elite company, nor any *aigrettes*, so we assume the elite company was dressed in the same manner as the centre companies.[194]

21e *Chasseurs à Cheval*

Formed in 1793 from the *Hussards de Braconnier*, the regiment was with the Grande Armée from 1806. It fought in Spain for two years to 1812, and took part in the 1812 campaign in Russia, the Germany campaign of 1813 as well as the Campaign of France.

Officers

A standing order for the regiment dated 13 May 1809 tells us that the officers were to provide a set of harness and head collar, a *schabraque* with lace, a *kinski* for undress, a pair of boots with silver lace and tassel, a *giberne* of the regimental model, a pompom, a black plume with aurore tip for company officers and a white plume for officers on the staff and senior officers. In addition, officers were to have a pair of epaulettes and sword knot appropriate to their rank, a pair of gauntlets and a pair of white wrist gloves. In full dress officers were ordered to wear their *habit*, *pantalons* in broadcloth with lace, plume and *giberne*, sabre with sword knot, epaulettes, laced boots, gloves for dismounted duty and gauntlets for mounted. In undress or small clothes, officers wore the *kinski*, green broadcloth pantalons, no plume in the *schako*s and wrist gloves, sabre with steel fittings and boots with black lace and tassel. Nankeen (yellow-hued cotton) *pantalons* were allowed to be worn walking in town in undress, and in the summer. The officers on the march were ordered to carry the *porte-manteau*, which was to contain the *surtout*, a pair of *pantalons* in broadcloth, a pair of boots, the laced *schabraque*, gauntlets, plume in cover, five or six shirts, several handkerchiefs and two or three pairs of nankeen *pantalons*. The *pantalons* for undress were to be cut from grey broadcloth; any other colour was strictly forbidden. On the march officers were to wear green *pantalons*. Officers had two *porte-manteaux*, one made from broadcloth in the form of 'a sausage' with aurore piping and silver lace to the ends, and the other to be of leather and carried in the regimental waggon.[195]

Other Ranks

Inspected on 26 August 1805, the regiment was wearing 503 *surtouts* along with 498 white *gilets* and 547 braided aurore waistcoats! The white *gilets* we assume were for everyday wear and the aurore-braided examples for full dress parade. The elite company boasted 88 colpacks, with 12 more brand-new examples in the *dépôt*.[196] We have no further inspection reports for the regiment; the 1807–08 report is missing from the regiment's archive.

Disbanded in summer 1814, the 1e squadron had the following clothing:[197]

Period iconography shows us neatly the evolution of the dress of the regiment. Firstly, Martinet gives us a trooper sometime before August 1805 when the regiment abandoned the *dolman* for the *kinski*. The dress of the regiment once the *dolman* had been removed is captured by Zimmerman in 1808, our second image. Martinet gives us an elite company officer wearing the *kinski* and colpack dated also to 1808. Lastly, Martinet gives us a trooper in 1814.

Item	In Good Repair	In Need of Repair	Need Replacing in 1 Year	To be Replaced	Items Needed
Habits	128				
Gilets en drap blanc	89				
Gilet d'ecuries	89				
Culottes hongroise	126				
Caleçon	89				
Pantalons à cheval	89				
Manteaux a manches	117				
Porte-manteaux	89				
Bonnets de police	89				
Schakos	89				

The 128 men on parade were wearing 140 shirts and had 60 pairs of linen *pantalons* and 85 stocks. Just 70 men had socks, and 40 men were wearing shoes for lack of boots. The *dépôt* had no clothing or materials what so ever.[198] The 2ᵉ, 3ᵉ, 4ᵉ and 5ᵉ squadrons were wound up into the 5ᵉ *Chasseurs*, who were wearing at disbandment:[199]

Item	In Good Repair	In Need of Repair	Need Replacing	Items Needed
Habits	91	3	95	
Gilets en drap blanc	25		1	
Culottes hongroise	17	1		
Pantalons à cheval	70	5	67	
Stable trousers	48		29	
Manteaux	178	18	1	
Gilet d'ecuries	85	52	33	
Bonnets de police	89	6	23	
Schakos	200	6	16	
Schako covers	222			
Pompoms	189			

The 249 men on parade lacked 26 *gibernes*, 21 *giberne* belts – from this we see that some men had *giberne* belts and no *gibernes*! – 25 sabre belts, 34 sword knots, 46 *banderole-porte-mousquetons*, and no man had a pair of gloves. The men were issued 545 shirts, 80 pairs of linen *pantalons de route*, 196 black stocks – more than 50 men had improvised neck wear – and not a single pair of socks or shoes for stable duties were in use. The regimental *dépôt* held some stocks of cloth and materials:[200]

1,100m 33 blue broadcloth
346m 40 white broadcloth
38m 5 scarlet broadcloth

242m white serge
1,504m 33 aurore serge
161 dozen large copper buttons
934 dozen small copper buttons
137 dozen bone buttons

Reconstruction of a trooper of the 21^{e} *Chasseurs* in 1813 based on the regiment's paper archive. At the time of disbandment, brand-new, ready to be issued clothing included 39 *dolmans* with a further 20 needing repairs. The *dolmans* are unexpected, but it seems had been worn recently given the regiment had been busy making new examples in 1813 or even as late as 1814.

Secondly, we present a reconstruction of a trooper of the 21^{e} *Chasseurs* in 1813 to 1814 based on the regiment's paper archive and an illustration by Martinet: the regiment's archive lists 15 brand-new black plumes in store, which Martinet also shows in his print dated 1814. Again, another commonality between both the archive and the illustration are copper buttons and not white metal.

The most surprising aspect of the 21^{e} *Chasseurs'* paper archive is that it records *chasseurs* dressed as line infantry. The inspecting general noted that the regiment possessed 5 infantry *capotes*, 126 infantry *habits-veste*, 96 *bonnets de police* and 7 infantry *gibernes* with belts! Due to shortages, it seems the men were given whatever could be found, regardless if it was cavalry kit or not. This explains why some troopers of the 21^{e} *Chasseurs* wore infantry greatcoat.

The dress of the regiment's trumpeters is open to some debate. Up first is a speculative reconstruction of a trumpeter of the 21e *Chasseurs* based on notes made by Rousselot housed in the library of the *Musée de l'Armée*. We cannot confirm or deny Rousselot's observations.

Secondly, is a tentative reconstruction of elite company trumpeter based on the regiment's paper archive. The inspecting officer who reviewed the regiment prior to its disbandment noted that the regiment had not acted fully on the decree of 19 January or 7 February 1812, nor the instruction of 23 April 1814 concerning the dress of trumpeters, which were to wear blue *habits* adorned with Royalist Livery. The inference here is that the trumpeters may have been dressed in Imperial Livery.

The contents of the *dépôt* are hugely surprising. Brand-new, ready to be issued clothing included 2 *manteaux*, 39 *dolmans* with a further 20 needing repairs – which implies that these items had been worn until fairly recently – 7 white *gilets*, 300 pairs of *caleçon*, 45 *schako* covers, 149 pompoms, 52 *gibernes*, 64 *giberne* belts, 65 sabre belts, 75 *banderole-porte-carabines* and 83 sword knots. The *dolmans* are unexpected, but not as surprising as the presence of 5 infantry *capotes*, 126 infantry *habits-vestes*, 96 *bonnets de police* and 7 infantry *gibernes* with belts! The presence of infantry *habits* – clearly made in the regiment, hence the blue and scarlet broadcloth – is remarkable. Due to the lack of green broadcloth – more likely the cost and a good yellow dye – the regiment were dressed either in *dolmans* or as line infantry! Other items in the *dépôt* included 15 brand-new plumes – in theory abolished in 1810! – 98 sabre belt hooks, 69 buckles for the *porte-gibernes*, 15 slides, buckles and tips for *banderole-porte-mousquetons*, 18 slides and tips for the *porte-gibernes*, 133 *giberne* plates (?) and 2 carbine clips. Clothing and items of *petit equipment* in *dépôt* included 31 pairs of *pantalons de route*, 19 black stocks, 202 pairs of linen socks, 299 pairs of black gaiters, 3 pairs of grey linen gaiters and 1 *haversac*.[201]

The inspecting officer continued, noting that the regiment had not acted on the decree of 19 January or 7 February 1812, nor the instruction of 23 April 1814 concerning the dress of trumpeters, which were to wear blue habits adorned with Royalist Livery.[202]

22e *Chasseurs à Cheval*

Created in March 1793 from the *Legion des Pyrenees Orientales*, the regiment served with the Grande Armée until 1808, when it marched into Spain, where it remained until the First Restoration. When reviewed on 31 July 1805, 391 *dolmans* were in use, 508 *surtouts*, and the elite company had 100 colpacks. The inspector ordered the *dolmans* removed from service and authorised 202 more *surtouts* to be made.[203] When

Martinet presents three figures from the regiment: a trooper from August 1805 or earlier, a trooper in 1814 and an officer of the elite company wearing campaign dress.

Reconstruction of a trooper of the 22e *Chasseurs* as they appeared in summer 1814 prior to incorporation to the 3e *Lanciers*.

Secondly, we present a speculative reconstruction of an elite company trumpeter of the 22e *Chasseurs* based on notes made by Rousselot housed in the library of the *Musée de l'Armée*. We cannot confirm or deny Rousselot's observations.

Lastly, we present a tentative reconstruction of an elite company trumpeter. The inspecting officer who reviewed the regiment prior to its disbandment noted that the regiment had not acted fully on the decree of 19 January or 7 February 1812, nor the instruction of 23 April 1814 concerning the dress of trumpeters, which were to wear blue *habits* adorned with Royalist Livery. The inference here, is that the trumpeters may have been dressed in Imperial Livery.

Composite mannequin of a trooper of the 22e *Chasseurs*. The *schako* is from the 23e *Chasseurs*. The habit and legwear are original to the 22e: the *habit* with its facing colour *revers* is a unique distinction. The silver stripes at the cuff mark the garment out as belonging to a sergeant. The waistcoat is added to complete the image. (*Musée de l'Empéri, Collections du Musée de l'armée, Anciennes collections Jean et Raoul Brunon*)

Portrait of a sous-lieutenant of the 22e *Chasseurs* painted shortly before the regiment was disbanded. (*Private collection France*)

reviewed on 29 December 1807, the regiment was well dressed, in new *surtouts* and needed 493 pairs of pistols, 179 musketoons, 541 bayonets and 279 sabres.[204] We have no other details. Disbanded in summer 1814, the men were taken into the 3e regiment des *Chevaux-Legere-Lanciers*. Of the 369 men on parade, their clothing was in tatters. For example, 32 *habits* were in good condition, 10 needed repairs, 55 total replacement and 258 men had no *habit*! Of the *gilet*s, 9 men had one in good condition, 60 needed immediate replacement and 291 men had no *gilet*, 263 men had no *gilet d'ecurie*, 270 no *bonnet de police*, and of those in use 151 were life expired. Some 213 men had no *manteaux* or *culottes hongroise*, no man had a pair of *pantalons à cheval*, and the shortage of legwear was made up with the use of 200 pairs of life-expired stable trousers. Further, 191 men had no *giberne* and belt, 283 men were on parade in shoes as they had no boots, and 201 men had no *schakos*. The regiment's clothing and equipment was in dreadful condition and in essence everything had to be replaced. The *dépôt* held nothing other than 77m of green tricot, 70 brand-new *gibernes*, *porte-gibernes* and *porte-carabines* and 8 waistbelts. No *aigrettes*, grenadiers' *schakos* or epaulettes existed for the elite company in use or *dépôt*, so we assume the regiment had none of these. The inspection returns state the regiment had not 'fully adopted' the provisions of the Bardin regulations. Nothing is said in the paper archive about trumpeters.[205]

23e *Chasseurs à Cheval*

Created from the *Hussards de la Legion des Ardennes*, the regiment was part of the *Armee du Rhine* in 1799, thence the Army of Italy until 1809, when it fought at Essling and Wagram. Given a shake-down inspection on 1 June 1807, the regiment was wearing:[206]

Item	In Good Repair	In Need of Repair	To be Replaced	Total	Observations
Surtouts	462	20	26	508	
Gilets en drap blanc	503		17	520	
Gilet d'ecuries	360	156	48	565	
Manteaux	494	9	23	526	
Culottes hongroise	475		8	483	
Stable trousers	347	170	32	561	
Schakos	495	30	36	531	
Bonnets de police	325	70	159	454	
Colpacks	The regiment has none				
Schako covers					
Pompoms					
Plumes					

The regiment remained in Germany and marched to Russia in 1812. The paperwork for the regiment at the end of the Empire is remarkable for its completeness.

Reviewed on 30 April 1812, the *dépôt* held 134 *surtouts*, 141 *gilets d'ordonnance* i.e., white sleeveless waistcoats, 166 *gilet d'ecuries*, 483 pairs of *culottes hongroise*, 487

Martinet presents us the uniform of the regiment as it was before summer 1805 and shortly before disbandment in 1814. We also present the elite company of the 23e *Chasseurs* as witnessed by the Suhr brothers in 1808–12. Of interest are the white metal scales to the shoulder boards of the epaulettes.

The regiment's archive adds more details to the overall evolution of the regiment's uniform.

Firstly, is a reconstruction of a trooper of the 23^{e} *Chasseurs* as they appeared on 8 April 1807. Secondly, is a reconstruction of a trooper as they appeared on 30 April 1812. Thirdly, a reconstruction of a trooper as they appeared on 5 April 1813. Fourthly, we present a tentative reconstruction of an elite company trooper as they may have appeared on the same day.

pairs of stable trousers, 220 pairs of *caleçon*, 115m of green broadcloth, 187m capucine broadcloth and 120m white broadcloth. Weapons in *dépôt* comprised 12 carbines, 6 sabres and 46 pairs of pistols. Other items in the *dépôt* included 64 *manteaux*, 51 *porte-manteaux*, 61 *schakos*, 61 waistbelts, 87 *gibernes*, 54 *banderole-porte-mousquetons*, 223 pairs of boots, 185 sword knots, 9m of silver lace and 33m 80 white and red worsted lace.[207] The *surtouts* are without a doubt *kinski*.

The *dépôt* on 1 January 1813 held 10 *gilet*s in white broadcloth, 77 *gilet d'ecuries*, 170 pairs of *culottes hongroise*, 195 pairs of *caleçon*, 244 pairs of stable trousers, 57 pairs of *pantalons à cheval*, 82 *bonnets de police*, 87 *manteaux* and 4 centre company *schakos*. Materials in the *dépôt* included 827m 74 green broadcloth, 85m 23 white broadcloth,

The dress of the trumpeters of the regiment is recorded by the regiment's archive and period iconography. Firstly, Suhr presents the trumpeters of the 14ᵉ, 23ᵉ and 24ᵉ *Chasseurs* painted between 1808 and 1812. Secondly, we present a speculative reconstruction of an elite company trumpeter of the 23ᵉ *Chasseurs* based on notes made by Rousselot housed in the library of the *Musée de l'Armée*. We cannot confirm or deny Rousselot's observations. Arguably, reverse colours were worn by the trumpeters of the regiment, as the archive suggests that these garments were indeed made. The archive does not list colpacks, however, so we know *schakos* were in use in 1813–14. Lastly, is a reconstruction of elite company trumpeter from the regiment's paper archive.

11m 38 capucine broadcloth, 858m 56 green tricot, 523m 90 capucine serge, 60m 40 *treillis*, 110m 34 of linen, 88m of worsted lace for rank service chevrons and 16m 40 white braid for *culottes hongroise*.[208] In a letter of 5 April 1813 from the regiment's major to the War Ministry, he reported that the *dépôt* had clothed and equipped 420 sous-officiers and men, while a further 130 men were needed to bring the regiment to operational strength. He notes 70 men had been equipped with *surtouts* and 320 men had been dressed with *habits* taken from the reserve.[209]

The remarkably complete regimental administration paperwork reveals that in 1813 just 30 *schakos* were purchased for the elite company, along with 55 scarlet *aigrettes* and 120 pairs of scarlet-fringed epaulettes. We assume some grenadier *schako* and *aigrettes* already existed to bring the numbers up to 120 of each. We note 10 pairs of epaulettes went to men in the *dépôt* and 110 pairs were issued over the course of 1813 to the elite company of the war squadrons. Centre companies had 1,523 pompoms, with 820 being issued, 703 remaining in *dépôt* in January 1814. Trumpeters had 13 *habits* made, for which 172m 60 of trumpeters' lace was purchased:

93m 10 on 15 May 1813
67m 79 on 1 April 1814
12m 1 April 1814

Just 159m of trumpeters' lace was used. Of the 13 *habits* made, just 2 were issued to conscripts, 11 being issued to long-serving soldiers in the *dépôt* and none going to the war squadrons! The specification for the trumpeters' habits was as follows:

1m 63 green broadcloth
0m 20 capucine broadcloth
1m 3 capucine serge
1m 44 linen for lining
9 large buttons
4 medium buttons
8 small buttons
13m 30 trumpeters' lace
3 hooks and eyes

From this detailed specification, the *habit* clearly was single breasted, the front closed by nine large buttons. The eight small buttons were presumably distributed with two at the collar and three at each cuff, and four medium buttons at the back of the habit. Bardin gives exactly this *habit*, but notes such a garment required 12m of No. 1 Lace, which is listed as horizontal, and 3m of Lace No. 2, the vertical pattern.[210] Clearly some differences existed between reality and the regulations!

From January 1813 to 1 January 1814 the regiment made 1,022 *habits*. Each required:

1m 36 green broadcloth
0m 20 capucine broadcloth
1m 3 capucine serge
1m 44 linen for lining
4 medium buttons
22 small buttons

These garments do not seem to be Bardin *habit*s, as officially they required 1m 49 of green broadcloth and required 20 small and 8 large buttons.[211] We suspect therefore that we are dealing with a variation of a *habits-veste*. Indeed, Martinet in his print of the regiment shows a *habit-veste* but with exceptionally small tails with no pockets as on a *kinksi*. Further, the *schako* has a large central cockade and no plate, white cords and a capucine over green plume. This image must date to 1814 and earlier.

Other items made in the course of 1813 were 968 white *gilet*s, 1,247 *gilet d'ecuries*, 756 pairs of *culottes hongroise*, 870 pairs of *caleçon*, 1,093 pairs of stable trousers, 1,159 pairs of *pantalons à cheval*, 1,175 *bonnets de police*, 967 *manteaux* and 974 *porte-manteaux*.[212] Cloth used throughout 1813 was as follows:[213]

7,304m 7 green broadcloth
484m white broadcloth
287m 89 capucine broadcloth
5,885m green tricot
1,066m 5 capucine and white serge
3,367m *treillis*

1,162m 70 white worsted lace for *porte-manteaux*
2,192m 10 13mm wide white worsted lace for *culottes hongroise*
172m 90 Imperial Livery for trumpeters

The *dépôt* held on 1 January 1814:[214]

68m green broadcloth
7m 73 white broadcloth
178m 42 green tricot
608m 44 capucine and white serge
315m 18 *treillis*
63m 70 white worsted lace for *porte-manteaux*
1,245m 34 13mm wide white worsted lace for *culottes hongroise*
94 *habits*
71 *gilets*
184 *gilet d'ecuries*
109 pairs *culottes hongroise*
64 pairs of *caleçon*
65 pairs stable trousers
204 pairs *pantalons à cheval*
2 *bonnets de police*
50 *manteaux*

At the time of disbandment, the regiment had purchased a huge quantity of cloth, so that it held in May 1814 565m 62 green broadcloth, 102m 72 white broadcloth and 48m 95 capucine broadcloth. We also learn from the paper archive that the regiment had purchased 654m of green tricot but only 9m 97 remained after the production of 109 pairs of *culottes hongroise* in January 1814. We also find that 97m 35 of serge was used to repair habits, while 14m 40 of lace for *porte-manteaux* was used. The trumpeters' lace obtained on 1 April 1814 was burned the following month.[215]

24e *Chasseurs à Cheval*

Raised in 1793 from volunteers, the regiment was with the Army of Italy from 1796 to 1807, when it fought at Friedland. Sent to Spain in 1808, it was at Essling and Wagram in 1809 before returning to Spain. Reviewed on 6 September 1805, the men were wearing *dolmans* and not a single colpack existed. General Pully ordered all the *dolmans* to be replaced with *surtouts* as a matter of urgency.[216] Was this carried out? The next review of the 24e was in May 1807, by which time they were wearing stable coats. No colpacks existed, nor plumes or epaulettes. The inspector ordered 500 pairs of '*pantalons d'ecuire en drap garnie en peau de veau*' to replace life-expired *culottes hongroise*, 400 *schakos*, 600 *habits*, 500 pairs of boots and 600 plumes as a matter of urgency.[217]

Period iconography has recorded the regiment very well indeed.

Up first is a trooper before summer 1805, when still adorned in *dolmans*. Both Martinet and Otto agree that officers of the elite company wore colpacks and *surtouts*, as does the regimental archive.

Otto also presents a centre company trooper and trooper of the elite company. Most importantly, Otto shows an elite company trumpeter. Otto is working in new year 1808. Working almost contemporaneously, the Suhr brothers' plates show a remarkable ensemble for the trumpeter. He wears, we assume, a light orange *schako* with white plume lace and cords. His *kinski* is shown as brick red – we assume capucine as Suhr shows an officer of the regiment with brick red facings on two occasions – with a green collar with capucine patches. The shoulder straps are light orange piped white. The cuffs and tail lining and facings are also light orange. The nine buttons to the front of the *kinski* are decorated with white lace Brandenburgs that end in a rosette and tassel! He wears white pantalons. The difference between the elite and centre company trumpeter's ensemble is remarkable, and makes us question the identification of the trumpeter of the 24e by Suhr. (*Collection KM*)

Trooper of the 24e *Chasseurs* at the end of the Empire in a print by Aaron Martinet. He is wearing a single-breasted *kinski*, and still has cords and plume to his *schako.* The inspector in summer noted that the four war squadrons had not adopted the Bardin regulation, which is what Martinet clearly shows. Secondly, is a reconstruction of a trooper of the 5e squadron as they appeared in summer 1814, according to the regiment's paper archive. Lastly, we show the *sapeurs* of the regiment as rendered by Suhr. Of note the epaulettes had copper fish scale boards. The regiment's paper archive for 1811 by and large confirms the presence of *sapeurs* and this uniform.

However, as history tell us, the Friedland campaign rather got in the way of the 24e being reclothed. On returning to depot in November 1807, the regiment's archive tells us that of the 911 other ranks in the regiment, the depot squadron was wearing 285 *surtouts*, 243 of which had been made since 1805. The remaining men under arms were wearing stable coats. A total of 108 colpacks had been issued to the elite company since November 1807, and the inspector ordered every man to be dressed in *surtouts* and the life-expired stable coats 'in use since the campaign of 1805' to be replaced.[218] Clearly, the hoped for distribution of *habits-vestes* had not happened. Reviewed again on 1 March 1808, the regiment needed absolutely everything; it was either missing or worn out.[219]

We know nothing about the regiment's dress until the 1e to 4e squadrons were taken into the 13e *Chasseurs* on 1 August 1814 and were wearing:

Item	In Good Repair	In Need of Repair	Need Replacing in 1 Year	To be Replaced	Items Needed
Habits	69	6			2
Gilets en drap blanc	69	6			2
Gilet d'ecuries	21	44		11	1
Bonnets de police	61			15	1
Culottes hongroise	75				2
Caleçon		75			2
Pantalons à cheval	10	31		17	19
Stable trousers	40	31	5		1
Manteaux	32	18			27
Porte-manteaux			Nil		
Braces	76				1
Schakos		23		15	39

The 5e squadron of the 24e *Chasseurs* were given a shake-down inspection on 8 June 1814. The clothing then in use was as follows when the men passed to the 9e *Chasseurs*:[220]

Item	In Good Repair	In Need of Repair	Need Replacing in 1 Year	To be Replaced	Items Needed
Habits-vestes	69	6			2
Gilets en drap blanc	69	6			2
Gilet d'ecuries	21	44		11	1
Bonnets de police	61			15	1
Culottes hongroise	75				2
Caleçon		75			2
Pantalons à cheval	10	31		17	19
Stable trousers	40	31	5		1
Manteaux	32	18			27
Porte-manteaux			Nil		
Braces	76				1
Schakos		23		15	39

Of the 77 men on parade, they were issued 201 shirts, 80 black stocks, 77 pairs of shoes and 75 pairs of grey linen gaiters, yet despite not having an elite company in the 5e squadron, 38 men had scarlet-fringed epaulettes! No cloth or materials were in *dépôt,* but the *dépôt* did hold stocks of brand-new clothing namely 90 *habits*, 121 *gilet tresses* – i.e., braided waistcoats, which means the *habits* were *habits a la chasseur* to show the costly and non-regulation waistcoat – 32 *gilet d'ecuries*, 69 *bonnets de police*, 823 pairs of *culottes hongroise*, 12 pairs of stable trousers, 19 pairs of braces, 270 waistbelts, 201 *gibernes* and belts, 184 *banderole-porte-mousquetons*, 184 *porte-crosses* and 5 pairs of boots. Also in *dépôt* were 196 black stocks. The inspector notes that the regiment had not fully adopted the provisions of the decree of 19 January and 7 February 1812, nor of the instructions of 23 April 1814 to dress the trumpeters in blue with Royalist Livery.[221] Sadly we do not know what the trumpeters were wearing.

25e *Chasseurs à Cheval*

Formed in 1795 from the *Legion des Montagnes*, the regiment was led by Pierre Soult from 1802. It was part of the Army of Italy from 1796 until 1812, when the regiment took part in the Russian campaign, and thence the campaigns of 1813 and 1814, elements being besieged at Magdebourg and Hambourg. Inspected on 21 July 1814, the clothing in use was as follows:[222]

Item	In Good Repair	In Need of Repair	Need Replacing in 1 Year	To be Replaced	Items Needed
Habits-vestes	194	34	2	34	
Gilets en drap blanc	223	12	2	11	
Gilet d'ecuries	178	35	4	52	
Culottes hongroise	229		8		
Pantalons à cheval	185	12	12	50	
Stable trousers	147		26	32	
Caleçon	67		11	17	
Manteaux	201	27		5	
Bonnets de police	238	8		14	
Schakos	253	6		5	
Schako covers	206			6	
Pompoms	226			16	

The *dépôt* held 111 brand-new *chasseur habits-vestes*, 1 new trumpeter's *habit*, 22 pairs of stable trousers, 50 white *gilets*, 41 *gilet d'ecuries* and 96 pairs of *caleçon*. Cloth in the *dépôt* included 0m 87 of green broadcloth, 0m 70 *garance* broadcloth for facings, 0m 46 green tricot, 329m 14 of linen, 81m 42 of *garance* serge, 537 dozen bone buttons, 81m 95 of lace for the *porte-manteaux*, 54m 34 lace for corporals' stripes, 61m 65 lace

Firstly, we have a trooper of the 25e *Chasseurs* in 1808. The yellow braiding to the *dolman* and legwear is unexpected Secondly, is an eyewitness drawing of a trooper by Lieutenant Bregeot of the 16e *Chasseurs* from the end of the First Empire. Lastly, Martinet shows a trooper at the end of the Empire: the cords and sunray plate are unexpected and not matched by the regiment's paper archive. (*Collection KM*)

for service chevrons, 236m 40 flat worsted lace for *culottes hongroise* and 100m 36 of trumpeters' livery.[223] Given that one *habit* existed in *dépôt* for trumpeters, we assume it, like other garments, was adorned with Imperial Livery, with over 460m of lace being used from the 560m, which was the standard unit of purchase.[224] According to the inspector, the regiment had not acted upon the decree of 19 January 1812, 7 February 1812 or the instruction of 23 April 1814. Therefore, we have to imagine the regiment did not wear *habits-vestes*, yet had adopted Imperial Livery.[225]

Trumpeter of the 25e *Chasseurs* as they appeared in summer 1814. Secondly, we present a trooper as they appeared in summer 1814 based on the regiment's paper archive. Lastly is the trumpet major of 1812–13 tentatively reconstructed from notes made by Rousselot housed in the library of the *Musée de l'Armée*. We cannot confirm or deny Rousselot's observations. Arguably, reverse colours were worn by the trumpeters of the regiment, as the archive suggests that these garments were indeed made.

26e *Chasseurs à Cheval*

The regiment was raised in 1802 from the *Piedmontese Chasseurs à Cheval*. Reviewed on 31 July 1805, every one of the 554 men on parade was wearing a *surtout*, and the elite company was wearing 100 colpacks. We assume only the elite company troopers carried carbines as only 80 *banderole-porte-mousquetons* were issued for 481 firearms![226] The regiment fought at Austerlitz and Stralsund in 1807. Reclothed at the end of 1807, the *dépôt* issued 613 *habits*, 33 carbines, 85 pairs of pistols and 47 sabres, as well as 638 white *gilets*. We are ignorant of the dress of the elite company.[227] Having been reclothed, the regiment was in action at Rolica and Vimeiro in 1808. The regiment remained in Spain until it marched to Germany in spring 1813 to fight at Dresden and Leipzig, and thence the campaign of France. It was disbanded in June 1814. The clothing in use by the men of the 1e squadron was as follows:[228]

Item	In Good Repair	In Need of Repair	Need Replacing in 1 Year	To be Replaced	Items Needed
Habits	2	18	14	22	41
Gilet d'ecuries		1	8		50
Culottes hongroise			2		61
Pantalons à cheval		1	4	3	60
Kolpacks			5	6	
Schako	4	13	8	8	44
Pairs of boots			1		61

Given the lack of white *gilet*s, we assume the *habits* closed to the waist and could either be long cut *kinski* or *habits-vestes*. The men were also issued 45 shirts – not enough for every one of the 87 men on parade to have a shirt, 55 black stocks, 21 pairs of shoes, 24 pairs of grey linen gaiters, and surprisingly 96 white linen cravats! Of interest, the inspector noted that the regiment had not adopted the uniform regulations as decreed on 19 January or 7 February 1812, nor had it enacted the modifications of 23 April 1814 concerning the colour of trumpeters' *habits*, which were clearly green with Imperial Livery.[229]

The 1e squadron's equipment and armament was in the same deplorable condition:[230]

Item	In Good Repair	In Need of Repair	Need Replacing in 1 Year	To be Replaced	Items Needed
Gibernes and porte-gibernes	16	56	14	29	
Porte-mousquetons	18	50	14	12	
Waistbelts	20	57	8	13	
Boucletaux	12		10		49
Sword knots	10		16		51

Period artwork shows something of the evolution of the regiment's uniform. Firstly, we present an elite company trooper of the 26e *Chasseurs* from the Otto manuscript dating to 1808. Secondly, a centre company trooper of the 26e *Chasseurs* as depicted by Martinet in 1814. The 1e squadron of the regiment, according to the paper archive, did indeed have white waistcoats and single-breasted *kinksi* as Martinet shows, but the archives are silent on plumes, cords and the nature of the *schako* plate. Lastly, we show an elite company officer in a print by Martinet from the end of the 1st Empire. The colpack and plume is most conspicuous, yet despite what Bardin regulation stated, the elite company did indeed have colpacks. (*Collection KM*)

In comparison, the clothing of 3e squadron was as follows:[231]

Item	In Good Repair	In Need of Repair	Need Replacing in 1 Year	To be Replaced	Items Needed
Habits	38	5	4		
Gilets en drap blanc	29	14	4		
Gilet d'ecuries	28	7			
Culottes hongroise	12	7			
Caleçon	47				
Bonnets de police	27	7			
Schakos	47				
Manteaux	7				
Pantalons à cheval		4			
Treillis pantaloons	5				
Pompoms	47				
Porte-manteaux	27				

The 3e squadron's equipment was as follows:[232]

Item	In Good Repair	In Need of Repair	Need Replacing in 1 Year	To be Replaced	Items Needed
Gibernes and *porte-Gibernes*	47				
Porte-mousquetons	43				
Waistbelts	47				
Boucletaux	The squadron has none				
Sword knots					
Pairs of boots	8				
Trumpets with cords			1		

The regiment's archive sheds some light on how the regiment looked.

Firstly, a reconstruction of an elite company trooper in summer 1814. Secondly, a tentative reconstruction of a centre company trumpeter of 1812–14 from notes made by Rousselot housed in the library of the *Musée de l'Armée*. Thirdly, another tentative reconstruction of a trumpeter of the elite company, again from notes made by Rousselot housed in the library of the *Musée de l'Armée*. In both cases, we cannot confirm or deny Rousselot's observations. Arguably, reverse colours were worn by the trumpeters of the regiment, if we read between the lines of the disbandment paperwork, which tells us that trumpeters had not adopted Royalist colours and colpacks certainly existed. Second to last, a tentative reconstruction of a *sapeur* of the 26e *Chasseurs* of 1812–14 from notes made by Rousselot housed in the library of the *Musée de l'Armée*. Finally, a trooper of the regiment as they appeared at the time of disbandment. The archive is silent on the form of the *schako* plate in use, as well as cords and plumes shown by Martinet, so we have omitted these.

The regimental *dépôt* held the following amounts of cloth:[233]

27m scarlet broadcloth
84m 51 red serge
26m 10 green tricot
119m *treillis*
142 dozen large buttons
1,413 dozen small buttons
2,401m 32 white lace 8mm wide
466m 70 white lace 22mm wide

Not an inch of Imperial Livery existed, so we assume the trumpeters did not have this lace. Yet we also note the regiment in theory had capucine facings and not scarlet! The inspection returns state the regiment had not 'fully adopted' the provisions of the Bardin regulations.

27e *Chasseurs à Cheval dit Chevau-Legers Belges du Duc d'Arenberg*

The regiment had been formed on 30 September 1806 as the *Chevau-Legers Belges du Duc d'Arenberg*, becoming on 29 May 1808 the 27e *Chasseurs à Cheval*. Inspected at Liege on 19 December 1807, the materials and clothing used since 19 October 1806 were as follows:[234]

Item		In *Dépôt* 1806	Purchased since 1806	Total	Amount Used	Remaining in *Dépôt*
Broadcloth	Green		4,541m 94	4,541m94	4,338m 94	203m
	Amaranth		190m 10	190m 10	173m	17m
Tricot	Green		6,338m 35	6,338m 35	3,159m 35	199m 60
	Amaranth		92m 92	92m 32	92m 32	
Serge	White		4,893m 96	4,893m 96	4,893m 96	
	Amaranth		3,097m 72	3,097m 72	3,097m 72	
Linen			1,754m 82	1,754m 82	1,754m 82	
Treillis			3,635m 10	3,635m 10	3,635m 10	
Buttons	large		1,154 doz	1,154 doz	1,154doz	
	medium		5,000 doz	5,000 doz	5,000 doz	
	small		961 doz	961 doz	961 doz	
	bone		2,692 doz	2,692 doz	2,692d oz	
Leather hides			1,154	1,154	1,154	

The Suhr brothers have left us a legacy of the regiment as they witnessed it sometime between 1808 and 1812. In the first image we see men in campaign dress and parade dress. The image cannot date any earlier, as the unit possessed not a single item of *hussar* kit in winter 1807. The use of the *surtout* is recorded by the regiment's paper archive. Secondly, we present an elite company trooper and officer. Lastly, is a trumpeter of the regiment.

Item		In *Dépôt* 1806	Purchased since 1806	Total	Amount Used	Remaining in *Dépôt*
Clothing	*Habits-vestes*		1,154	1,154	1,154	
	Gilet a manche		1,159	1,159	1,154	5
	Surtouts		1,170	1,170	1,154	16
	Capote-Manteaux		1,165	1,165	1,154	11
	Gilet d'ecuries		1,167	1,167	1,154	13
	Pantalons de treillis		1,154	1,154	1,154	
	Schakos		1,112	1,112	1,074	38
	Bonnets de police		1,154	1,154	1,154	
	Bonnets d'oursin		80	80	80	
Equipment	Waistbelts		1,154	1,154	1,154	
	Gibernes		1,156	1,156	1,154	2
	Porte-carabines		1,084	1,084	1,084	
	Pair of boots		1,167	1,167	1,154	13

The inspecting officer noted all the clothing was in perfect condition, and that for the coming year 300 *surtouts* were authorised for production and 300 pairs of stable trousers made from *treillis*. We assume the *bonnets d'oursin* were in fact colpacks.

The regiment was disbanded in summer 1814. Of the men of the regiment taken into the 7^e^ *Chasseurs*, the former 1^e^ and 2^e^ squadrons, we find that thirty-one men in the old elite company were wearing *dolmans* and *pelisses*, as well as the colpacks. The reviewing officer commented that the squadrons had not acted upon the decree of 7 February 1812, nor had not yet adopted blue *habits* and new Royalist Livery for its trumpeters:[235]

Item	In Good Repair	In Need of Repair	Need Replacing in 1 Year	To be Replaced	Items Needed	Observations
Habits	7	6	31		39	31 of these are in fact *dolmans*
Vestes	4	1			78	
Pantalons à cheval	1	7	16	6	53	
Culottes hongroise	3				80	
Bonnets de police	63	1			19	
Gilets	4	4	25	4	50	
Manteaux	28				84	
Schakos	83					31 of these are colpacks

Portrait of Justin Antoine de Tessères. Born at Vallereuil in the Dordogne on 13 April 1788, he joined the 27e *Chasseurs* in 1808. We see him wearing his *pelisse* edged in grey astrakhan over his amaranth braided waistcoat in a portrait executed in 1809. He died in Paris on 14 November 1876.

The men were also issued 92 shirts, 18 pairs of linen pantalons, 57 black stocks, 90 white stocks and not a single pair of socks. The 5[e] squadron was disbanded on 8 June 1814 and mustered 29 officers and 168 men. Clothing in use at disbandment was as follows:[236]

The regiment's archive is very complete and allows us to present the following reconstructions.

Firstly, a reconstruction of a trooper *c*.1807 based on the regiment's archive. This order of dress seems to have been worn again towards the middle years of the Empire. Second is a reconstruction of a trooper based on a review dated 5 March 1813, which lists every item shown in the image. The sunray plate is taken from notes made by Rousselot housed in the library of the *Musée de l'Armée*. Third is a reconstruction of the elite company as they appeared in summer 1814. Fourth is a reconstruction of 1e, 2e, 3e and 4e squadrons as they appeared at the time of disbandment in summer 1814. Lastly, is a reconstruction of a trooper of the 5e squadron as they appeared in summer 1814.

The dress of the trumpeters is largely based on notes made by Rousselot housed in the library of the *Musée de l'Armée*. Up first is a reconstruction of a trumpeter of the 27e *Chasseurs* of 1810–13, which we assume is based on Suhr. Secondly, a trumpeter of the elite company as they appeared in summer 1814 based on the regiment's archive. Thirdly, we present a speculative reconstruction of a trumpeter of the 1^{e}, 2^{e}, 3^{e} and 4^{e} squadrons as they seem to have appeared in summer 1814. Lastly, a trumpeter of the 5e squadron as he appeared on 5 June 1814.

Item	In Good Repair	In Need of Repair	Need Replacing in 1 Year	To be Replaced	Items Needed
Habits-vestes	2	3	3	1	29
Gilet d'ecuries	1		4	2	33
Culottes hongroise	1	1	2		32
Pantalons à cheval		1	2	1	33
Schakos	2	4	2	2	28
Pairs of boots			1		34

The 168 men were wearing mostly civilian clothing, the inspector noted. Those that had been equipped were dressed as for the decree of 19 January and 8 February 1812. The squadron's equipment and armament were in the same deplorable condition:[237]

Item	In Good Repair	In Need of Repair	Need Replacing in 1 Year	To be Replaced	Items Needed
Gibernes and *porte-gibernes*		36	6	15	
Porte-mousquetons		35	6	7	
Waistbelts	15	22	3	9	
Boucletaux	6		8		38
Sword knots	4		11		20
Trumpets	2			1	
Trumpet cords	2				

The *dépôt* held minimal amounts of cloth and materials, namely 13m 5 beige broadcloth for *manteaux*, 179 dozen large tin buttons, 166m 15 Imperial Livery for trumpeters, 332 dozen bone buttons for stable trousers, 65m of white 22mm wide lace for *porte-manteaux*, 424m of amaranth serge to line the regiment's *habits*, 1,000m of white worsted lace for *culottes hongroise*, 500m 8mm wide worsted lace and 308 dozen copper buttons for *pantalons à cheval*. In addition, the *dépôt* held the following stocks of clothing and equipment:[238]

Item	New	Need repair	To be written off	Total
Habits	30		6	36
Culottes hongroise	32	13		43
Pantalons à cheval	20			20
Pantalons de treillis	15			15
Manteaux	48	11		52
Schakos	174		59	233
Caleçon	15			15
Porte-manteaux	35			35
Bonnets de police	207			207
Kolpacks	32			32
Gibernes and belts	30	62	25	117
Porte-mousquetons	27	54	62	143
Black leather sword knots			25	25
Trumpets			4	4
Trumpet cords			3	3

The presence of black leather sword knots is something of a surprise, likewise the colpacks as these in theory had been abandoned since 1813. The inspector further noted that the 30 new *habits* were 'non-regulation', and further comments that 440 old *schakos* and 100 brand-new plumes, as well as 24 *mousquetons*, 60 sabres and 37 bayonets, had been 'lost' at Philippeville. Cloth in the *dépôt* and other items included:[239]

Martinet gives us two figures from the regiment. A trooper dated 1814 with yellow ochre leather work tallies with an eyewitness watercolour made in 1813 or 1814, which we present alongside. Martinet shows a *kinski* and our eyewitness a *habit-veste*. Both images may be correct, as in the chaos of the end of the Empire, as long as men had a uniform, I suspect no one cared too greatly if differences existed between companies and squadrons of the same regiment. Martinet also presents an officer of the elite company. His gold lace embellishments were unique for a *chasseur* regiment, which traditionally had silver.

0m 96 green broadcloth costing 11fr 45 a metre
0m 83 amaranth broadcloth costing 10fr a metre
0m 25 green tricot
26m amaranth tricot
139m 17 linen for *caleçon*
29m 55 linen for lining
16m 43 *treillis*
38 dozen large buttons
271 dozen small buttons
273m 12 white worsted lace
4m 10 lace for corporals' stripes
1,273m 3 round wool cording

Presumably the amaranth tricot was for the trumpeters' *gilet d'ecuries* and *porte-manteaux*? In theory the regiment did not have amaranth facings if we go by the Bardin regulation, but clearly never adopted the *garance* facings. This shows the value of archive research as we cannot always be certain that regulation theory became practice. The inspector added that the amaranth broadcloth and the yellow braid and lace and copper buttons were to be distributed to regiments that had these distinctions. The regimental accounts note that the regiment was in debt for materials and equipment yet to be delivered:

807fr 50 had been spent on broadcloth
1,877fr 50 for 50 pairs of boots costing 18fr a pair
6,912fr 89 for broadcloth and serges
2,975fr for harness

Did these various orders arrive with the regiment? The lack of paperwork precludes any definite answer.

Of interest, the inspector further noted that the regiment had not adopted the uniform regulations as decreed on 19 January or 7 February 1812, nor had it enacted the modifications of 23 April 1814 concerning the colour of trumpeters' *habits*. He ordered that all new items were to be made with the strictest regard to the regulations and to be carried out with utmost vigour, which seems rather pointless as the regiment was disbanded the same day it was reviewed![240] We are left to wonder as to the appearance of the trumpeters, and presumably the regiment wore both the old-style cutaway *habits* alongside with *kinskis* and *dolmans* in the elite company with colpacks.

28e *Chasseurs à Cheval*

The 28e *Chasseurs* was created with the decree of 7 January 1808, with manpower being drawn from the Tuscan Dragoons. It was fully organised by 29 May 1808, but only became the 28e *Chasseurs* with the decree of 1 July 1809. The regiment was disbanded on 8 June 1814 and mustered 34 officers and 733 men. The regiment had the following items of clothing:[241]

Item	In Good Repair	In Need of Repair	Need Replacing in 1 Year	To be Replaced	Items Needed	Effective Strength
Habits	75	50	10	3	44	182
Gilets en drap blanc	52	7	2		122	182
Culottes hongroise	10			1	171	182
Veste d'ecuries	60	26	21	2	73	182
Caleçon						182
Pantalons de treillis	2	1			179	182
Pantalons à cheval	36	47	10	5	84	182
Manteaux	123	33		1	25	182
Porte-manteaux	80	51	35	5	11	182
Bonnets de police	78	8	39	5	52	182
Schakos	128	30	6	10	8	182

The regiment's equipment and armament was as follows:[242]

Three contemporary images show the 28ᵉ. Martinet gives a trooper in 1814, and an officer of the elite company, perhaps as they appeared in 1805 to 1813. Lastly, an eyewitness watercolour of a trooper of the 28ᵉ *Chasseurs* by Lieutenant Bregeot of the 16ᵉ *Chasseurs*. (*Collection KM*)

Item	In Good Repair	In Need of Repair	Need Replacing	Total	Effective strength
Waistbelts	226				
Gibernes	226				
Porte-gibernes	226				
Porte-carabines	188				
Pairs of boots with spurs	226				
Pairs of gauntlets	125				
Sword knots	226				

The *dépôt* in Hamburg held the following amounts of cloth and other materials:[243]

2,634m 32 green broadcloth
58m 40 crimson broadcloth
823m 38 green tricot
80m linen for lining
308m 40 crimson serge
531m 30 *treillis*
20m wool lace for corporals
60m Imperial Livery for trumpeters
271m lace for *porte-manteaux*
288m braid for *culottes hongroise*
29m lace for service chevrons

We present first a trooper of the 28e *Chasseurs* based on the regiment's disbandment paper work, and a print from the epoch by Martinet. Second is a reconstruction of a trumpeter of 1812–14 based on notes made by Rousselot housed in the library of the *Musée de l'Armée* and the regiment's paperwork. We know at disbandment the regiment had not adopted Bardin regulations, so seemingly the trumpeters wore reversed colours. Rousselot's hypothesis is perfectly plausible. The presence of Imperial Livery suggests some trumpeters wore this lace on their clothing. Did they have reversed colours with lace to collar and cuff, or the Bardin *habits-veste*? We cannot tell.

The squadron of the 28e *Chasseurs* based at Hamburg also had in store 61 pairs of shoes and 91 pairs of gaiters, a further 107 *gilet d'ecuries* and 57 pairs of gloves. The 28e in theory had amaranth facing, but crimson cloth is listed. The black cloth was seemingly for gaiters worn by the men in Hamburg. Stores also held:[244]

Item	New	Good Repair	Need Repair
Habits	389	189	111
Gilets manche	835		29
Veste d'ecuries	346		3
Culottes hongroise	810	138	
Caleçon	394		
Pantalons à cheval			
Treillis pantalons	583		
Manteaux-capote	290	117	116
Porte-manteaux	382	138	
Bonnets de police	582		
Schakos	489	157	218
Manteaux		18	81
Waistbelts	429	500	100
Gibernes	330	500	132
Porte-gibernes	690	200	198
Porte-carabines	805	400	103
Pairs of boots with spurs	30		
Pairs of gauntlets	307		
Sword knots	620	200	80

The use of sleeved and non-sleeved *manteaux* is interesting to note. The *dépôt* at Orleans held 510 shirts, 200 black stocks, 61 pairs of shoes, 94 pairs of grey gaiters, 59 *sacs a distribution*, 107 *gilet d'ecuries* and 57 pairs of gauntlets. We know nothing more of the dress of the regiment.[245]

28e *Chasseurs à Cheval Bis*

In 1813, the 1e, 2e and 3e squadrons of the regiment were based in Spain and baptised the 28e *Chasseurs à Cheval Bis*, or the additional 28e *Chasseurs*, as they were administratively a separate regiment. Disbanded in summer 1814, the *dépôt* at Orleans held the following cloth:[246]

2m yellow broadcloth
3m 50 black broadcloth
883m 39 white broadcloth
410m 33 green broadcloth
12m 30 crimson broadcloth
166m 28 white serge
175m green tricot
2,851m 72 linen for linings
60m linen for *caleçon*
910 dozen buttons
2,185m 99 crimson serge
90m *treillis*
207m lace for *porte-manteaux*
1,518m 66 white lace for *culottes hongroise*

Trooper of the 28e *Bis Chasseurs* at the time of the unit's disbandment in summer 1814 based on the regiment's paper archive. Grey or black gaiters were worn for stable and dismounted duties. Secondly, is a trumpeter reconstructed from the regiment's paper archive, which reports an unknown quantity of Imperial Livery had been burned.

The only possible use of the yellow broadcloth was somewhere on the trumpeters' kit. We are at a loss to imagine how this uniform could have looked. Conceivably the black broadcloth was for gaiters. The *dépôt* also held stocks of clothing:[247]

Item	Good Condition
Habits-vestes	77
Gilets en drap blanc	115
Veste d'ecuries	115
Culottes hongroise	42
Caleçon	34
Pantalons à cheval	166
Stable trousers	30
Manteaux	7
Porte-manteaux	114
Bonnets de police	74
Schakos	166
Manteaux-capote	87
Waistbelts	72
Pairs of boots with spurs	50

In addition, the *dépôt* at Orleans held 510 shirts, 200 black stocks, 61 pairs of shoes, 94 pairs of grey gaiters, 59 *sacs a distribution*, 107 *gilet d'ecuries* and 57 pairs of gauntlets. We know nothing more of the dress of the regiment.[248]

29e *Chasseurs à Cheval*

Formed in 1808 from the 3e *regiment de Provisoire de Chasseurs à Cheval*, the regiment served in Spain until it marched into Germany in 1813 to fight at Leipzig. The regiment was disbanded in 1814. The 1e squadron passed to the 15e *Chasseurs*. The men were wearing *habits-vestes*, and remarkably the elite company swaggered in 87 colpacks with a further 26 being in stores.[249] The 2^e^ and 3^e^ squadrons passed to the 1^e^ *regiment Chevau-Legere-Lanciers*. The 157 men who remained with the regiment at the end of the 1814 campaign were wearing:

Item	In Good Repair	In Need of Repair	Need Replacing in 1 Year	To be Replaced	Items Needed
Habit	55	17		57	28
Gilets en drap blanc	55	9		24	69
Gilet d'ecuries	44	4	1	33	75
Culottes hongroise	57	7		18	75
Pantalons à cheval	30	18		20	89

Item	In Good Repair	In Need of Repair	Need Replacing in 1 Year	To be Replaced	Items Needed
Stable trousers	57			10	90
Caleçon	51			10	96
Garricks	47	14	1	20	75
Bonnets de police	66	5	3	39	50
Schakos	65		3	69	20

Not enough clothing was in use for every man to have one of each item: it was very much a case of 'make do and mend'. We assume 'garricks' are the regulation sleeved *manteaux-capote* with shoulder cape, called in English Garricks. Equipment was in the same condition:[250]

Item	In Good Repair	In Need of Repair	Need Replacing in 1 Year	To be Replaced	Items Needed
Waistbelts	105			25	27
Gibernes	65	29		46	17
Banderolle de gibernes	65	29		46	17
Banderolle-porte-mousquetons	79			46	32
Sword knots					157
Pairs of boots	40	35	19	9	54
Pairs of gloves	42				115
Trumpets with cords	4				

For the 79 good-condition *banderolle-porte-mousquetons*, just 58 *mousquetons* existed in good condition and 6 needed repairs. Clearly men were on parade with the shoulder belt but no weapon for which it was designed to carry! For the 157 men on parade, 98 sabres were in good condition, 20 needed repairs and 15 were to be written off: the regiment had 133 sabres for 157 men, and just 63 pistols. In addition, the 157 men had between them 363 shirts, 131 black stocks, 205 white stocks, 52 pairs of shoes, not a single pair of socks or stockings, and 103 *sacs a distribution*.

Trooper of the 29e *Chasseurs* by Martinet published in 1814.

Cloth in the *dépôt* comprised 19m 55 of amaranth broadcloth, 2m 50 white broadcloth, 420m 96 of green broadcloth, 224m 10 green tricot, 283m 93 line for lining, 96m 77 of lace for *culottes hongroise* and 50 leather hides. *Dépôt* held some brand-new clothing and equipment, which included 4 habits, 71 white *gilets*, 56

With limited iconography, the regiment's archive helps in reconstructing how the regiment appeared. Firstly, a trooper of the centre companies as they appeared in summer 1814. Secondly, we present an elite company trooper of the 29e *Chasseurs* reconstructed from a watercolour by Colonel Jolly of the 6e *Lanciers*. Thirdly, is a centre company trooper reconstructed from a watercolour again by Colonel Jolly. No plumes are recorded in the regiment's paper archive, but are almost universally shown by Martinet as in use in 1814, so we suppose these items did exist and were counted with the *schako*. Lastly, is a tentative reconstruction of a trumpeter in 1814.

pairs of *culottes hongroise*, 1 pair of *pantalons à cheval de modèle*, 1 garrick i.e., *capote-manteau,* 39 *bonnets de police*, 64 *giberne*s and 74 *porte-gibernes*, 5 *porte-carabines*, 100 waistbelts, 90 sword knots and 18 pairs of boots. No epaulettes or elite company *schako*s existed in use or in *dépôt,* so we assume all ranks were dressed the same. Waiting to be repaired in *dépôt* was 1 *habit*, 1 *veste d'ecurie*, 15 *bonnets de police*, and ready for selling to the rag merchant were 4 *habits,* 2 pairs *culottes hongroise*, 25 *veste d'ecurie*, 4 pairs *pantalons à cheval,* 1 *bonnet de police*, 25 garricks and 102 *schakos*. Remarkably, *dépôt* in 1814 held a *dolman* for the trumpet major, and 1 *dolman* for a trumpeter.[251] We find nothing more of the dress of the regiment when we consult the regiment's paper archive prior to disbandment.[252]

30e *Chasseurs à Cheval*

The regiment was formed on 3 February 1811 and was formed around the nucleus of the disbanded Hanoverian Legion as the 30e *Chasseurs à Cheval*. On 5 July 1811 the regiment possessed 31 officers and 776 other ranks, and its clothing was as follows:[253]

Habits: 402 good, 6 needing repairs, 27 *hors de service*
Gilets: 406 good, 3 needing repairs, 7 *hors de service*
Pantalons in broadcloth: 0 good, 34 needing repairs, 16 *hors de service*
Culottes hongroise: 319 good, 11 needing repairs, 64 *hors de service*
Gilet d'ecuries: 107 good, 47 needing repairs, 252 *hors de service*
Pantalons de toile: 0 good, 18 needing repairs, 276 *hors de service*
Bonnets de police: 8 good condition, 19 needing repairs, 257 *hors de service*
Schakos: 217 good condition, 3 needing repairs, 2 *hors de service*
Boots: 253 pairs good condition, 109 pairs needing repairs, 24 pairs *hors de service*
Manteaux: 24 good condition, 3 needing repairs, 2 *hors de service*
Porte-Manteaux: 421 good condition, 1 needing repairs, 7 *hors de service*
Ceinturon: 109
Gibernes: 159
Banderole: 126
Sword knots: 69
Sabres: 219
Carbines: 216
Bayonets: 201
Plumes: 80

Trooper of the 30e *Chasseurs* as they appeared at the close of 1811 by Martinet. It is worth comparing Martinet to our reconstruction based on the regiment's paper archive.

The unit officially had amaranth facings and was dressed as a standard *chasseur* regiment. The *culottes hongroise* were made from green tricot, as were the *gilet d'ecuries* and *porte-manteaux*. We also note sheepskin *schabraques* were in use, but just four examples existed. Indeed, the regiment possessed just four horses, and was never considered operational. None of the men who arrived with the regiment were issued new clothing. Most of it was life expired and was in desperate need of being replaced or repaired. To 'knock the regiment into shape' senior NCOs were transferred from the *Garde Imperiale*.[254] On 18 June a new colonel, Gobrecht, was appointed and the regiment became the 30e *Regiment de Chasseurs Lanciers*.[255]

31e *Chasseurs à Cheval*

The regiment was raised in 1811 from elements of the 1e and 2e Provisional Light Cavalry Regiments. The 1e provisional regiment was organised on 18 September 1810 following a decision dated 10 August 1810 issued by the Minister of War, General Clarke. It was raised from using the 4e squadrons of the 11e and 24e *Chasseurs à Cheval.*

During the organisational review, the inspector in charge noted that for the squadron of the 11e regiment 'eighty-two *surtouts* are in bad condition, as well as thirty-eight *manteaux*. Thirteen *vestes* are missing, twenty-two sets of equipment are in bad condition, as well as forty-nine harnesses. Finally, ten muskets and sixteen pistols are missing.' As for the squadron of the 24e *Chasseurs*: 'there is no complete uniform for a volunteer which is currently on his way to join the unit, a large part of the *vestes*, stable trousers and boots are generally in poor condition. Harness needs great repairs. The pistols are almost all due for repair. One musket, two sabres and one hundred and

Martinet offers us a trooper and officer of the elite company in 1811. We also present a portrait of an officer of the 31e *Chasseurs c.*1812. (*Musée de l'Empéri, Collections du Musée de l'armée, Anciennes collections Jean et Raoul Brunon*)

nineteen pistols are missing. The strength of the 4e squadron of the 11e *Chasseurs* stood at 262 officers and men and that of the 24e *Chasseurs* at 253 officers and men.'[256]

The 2e provisional regiment was formed on 20 September 20 and was composed of the 4e squadron of the 12e *Chasseurs* (259 officers and men) and the 4e squadron of the 5e *Hussar* (258 officers and men). For the squadron of the 12e *Chasseurs*, the inspector noted the uniforms were new, but missing were 'twelve *habits*, forty-five pairs of *culottes hongroise* and five *manteaux*.' For the 5e *Hussar*, the inspector noted that 'all the effects are complete, except the *culottes hongroise*, none exist. *Gilet d'ecuries* and *bonnets de police* are old and in poor condition.'[257]

The imperial decree of 7 September 1811 consolidated the disparate squadrons into a single regiment within the army of the north of Spain. Reviewed on 23 October 1811 in the town of Penaranda by Charles Crosse, 'sous-inspecteur aux revues' (junior review inspector). On that date, the 1e provisional regiment had as 'present under arms', 13 officers, 301 men and the 2e, 12 officers and 279 men. Crosse's report confirms a great inconsistency in clothing and equipment. Each man had in fact kept his original uniform and armament, and Crosse was furthermore astonished by the poor state of clothing, equipment and armament. The officers of both regiments explained that, indeed, during the formation of the provisional regiments, the parent units had ensured that any man who was to join the newly formed regiments would leave with only the poorest available kit. The clothing in use was:[258]

Regiment	*Habits* or *pelisses*		*Surtouts* or *Dolmans*		*Gilets*		*Gilet d'ecuries*		*Culottes hongroise*		*Schakos*	
	In service	To be replaced	In service	To be replaced	In service	To be replaced	In service	To be replaced	In Service	To be replaced	In service	To be replaced
11e *Chasseur*	132	102		234	220	14		234		234	230	4
12e *Chasseur*	151	77		228	151	77	177	51		228	127	101
24e *Chasseur*		209	8	201		209	54	155		209	200	9
5e *Hussars*	158	59	152	65		212	99	118	1	216	218	
TOTAL	441	447	160	728	371	517	330	558	1	887	724	114

The new regiment must have presented a very mixed look, with some men wearing *habits* and others from the 5e *Hussar* decked in *pelisses* and *dolmans*! Of note, the inventory of items of equipment includes *sapeurs*' axes and aprons, of which no such men existed. Does this therefore indicate the presence at some stage of *sapeurs* in any of these four regiments? Indeed, it seems to imply this. It is the only reference we have found in archive paperwork for *sapeurs* in light cavalry regiments.

On 7 September 1811, the Emperor wrote from Compiegne to General Lacuee, Comte de Cessac, Minister Director of the Administration of War, in Paris:

Trooper of the 31e *Chasseurs* as they appeared in 1811 based on the regiment's archive and a print by Aaron Martinet. Our second reconstruction is a trooper as they appeared 1813, again recreated from the regiment's paper archive. Lastly, is a trooper in parade dress based on the regiment's paper archive in summer 1814.

> Monsieur le Comte de Cessac, send on the field 600 pairs of boots, 600 pairs of stable trousers, 600 shirts, stocks and other effects of linen and shoe in the same proportion to the brigade of General Wattier. Make these effects of Bayonne and make the restraint on the mass of linen and shoe … Make sure that the dépôt passes to this new regiment the effects which belong to it as a matter of urgency.[259]

The intention of the Emperor was however, to make the new 31e *Chasseurs* into a unit of good standing. The existing colonel, Houssin de Saint-Laurent, was transferred to be colonel of the 10e *Chasseurs* and was replaced by Colonel Louis-Alexis Desmichels, who took effective command by December of 1811. He had previously been *chef d'escadron* (squadron leader) in the *chasseurs à cheval* and also *grenadiers à cheval* of the Imperial Guard.

To standardise the dress of the regiment, it was to wear the single-breasted *habit kinski* in green with chamois facings and piping. Under Bardin they received the *habit-veste,* retaining the chamois facings. This is what Martinet shows us in his 'generic' plates. The 4e and 5e squadrons based in Germany were reclothed at the end of 1813 into Bardin regulation with the production of:[260]

1,572 pairs of *culottes hongroise*
1,572 pairs of *pantalons à cheval*
389 *bonnets de police*
1,189 *vestes*
610 capotes-*manteaux*
401 pairs of *caleçon*
213 *habits-vestes*

Materials purchased in the same quarter of the 13 included 600 dozen medium buttons, 400 dozen small buttons, 462m flat worsted braid, 230m worsted lace and 72 leather hides to make *pantalons à cheval.*[261]

Disbanded in 1814, the *dépôt* of the 4e and 5e squadrons held very little in way of materials, notably 0m 25 white broadcloth, 0m 55 green broadcloth, 0m 87 chamois serge and 276m 26 silver lace. In *dépôt* were 50 brand-new *schakos*. The remaining 456 men under arms were wearing:[262]

Item	In Good Repair	In Need of Repair	Need Replacing in 1 Year	To be Replaced	Items Needed
Habits-vestes	127	251	2	68	8
Gilets blanc		27	2	92	335
Culottes hongroise	5	18	1	8	424
Gilet d'ecuries	26	153	52	40	125
Pantalons à cheval	86	131	38	15	186
Caleçon	3				453
Manteaux	195	155	3	8	75
Bonnets de police	172	163	37	16	68
Schakos	316	118		11	11
Schako covers					456
Pompoms	456				

About the regiment's equipment, the inspector noted the four master workmen did not carry a *giberne* and belt and the 73 *sous-officiers* and trumpeters did not carry a carbine and *banderole-porte-carabine*. We do not know how the trumpeters were dressed.

31e *Chasseurs à Cheval Bis*

In 1813, the 4e and 5e squadrons headed to Germany, while the 1e, 2e and 3e squadrons under Colonel Desmichels were assigned to the Army of Italy. The dress of these squadrons is detailed by an officer, Hypolite d'Espinchal:

> The uniform of the 31e Chasseurs was of the highest elegance; it consisted of a green Polish jacket; with chamois collar, facings and piping, red pantalons with chamois band. For senior officers, gold and silver giberne as well as the baudrier and belt, gold and silver lace belt with two large twist and gold finials, the Polish schako, embroidered in silver, topped by a white aigret. Officers and *chasseurs*: a red girdle for the elite company; green and chamois for the lancers, and chamois for the centre companies, who also had green and chamois swallow nests instead of shoulder straps on their shoulders.
>
> For weapons, the light cavalry sabre, carbine, and pistols; the squadron of lanciers, carried lances.[263]

We have no definite archive sources to shed further light on the dress of the regiment. Not a single document exists that informs us about the regiment's uniforms.

We present a centre company trooper of the 31e *Bis Chasseurs*, secondly an elite company trooper of a lancer company trooper and finally a trumpeter based on notes made by Rousselot housed in the library of the *Musée de l'Armée*.

Chasseurs d'Elite

The *Chasseur d'Elite* were formed 23 April 1814 and raised from Royalist volunteers. They were in reality poorly dressed as the bulk of the clothing listed is described as in need to replacement, as follows:[264]

Item	In Service, but Due to Expire in the next Year	In Need of Repair	To be Replaced in the Next Year	To be Replaced	Items Short	Observations
Habits-vestes	15	93	106	101	135	
Gilets en drap blanc	Nil				450	
Gilet d'ecuries	9	56	42	60	283	
Culottes hongroise	10	20	82		332	

Item	In Service, but Due to Expire in the next Year	In Need of Repair	To be Replaced in the Next Year	To be Replaced	Items Short	Observations
Stable trousers				10	440	
Caleçon	Nil				450	
Bonnets de police	15	56	140	131	110	
Schakos	60	120	180	10	80	
Pantalons à cheval	4	44	52	69	281	
Trumpets	Nil					

Equipment was as follows:[265]

Item	In Service, but Due to Expire in the Next Year	In Need of Repair	To be Replaced in the Next Year	To be Replaced	Items Short	Observations
Manteaux	30	108	20	206	86	
Pair of boots	3	30	140	152	125	
Pairs of gloves	Nil				450	
Plumes	Nil				450	
Aiguilettes	Nil				450	
Waistbelts	60	112	60	105	113	
Gibernes	112	113	20	95	110	
Porte-gibernes	249	9		80	112	
Porte-mousquetons	164				286	
Sword knots	141				309	

A trooper of the Chasseurs d'Elite as they appeared at the time of the regiment's disbandment in October 1814, having been formed from Royalist Volunteers in April 1814. Secondly, we present a trumpeter as they appeared in summer 1814 based on the regiment's paper archive and a print by Bassett.

The regiment was armed with 28 muskets in good condition, 76 needing repairs and 38 to be written off, and also had 326 sabres and 232 pistols. We know nothing further about the regiment as it lasted for a matter of weeks: 23 April to 11 October 1814. The regiment's history has therefore gone unremarked until now.

Chasseurs du Roi

Formed from the 1e and 26e *Chasseurs à Cheval* as well as the *Chasseurs d'Elite* on 11 October 1814, the regiment was officered and manned by ardent Royalists. Part of the process of reclothing the men was the production of 68 *habits-vestes*, 400 *gilets*, 306 pairs of *culottes hongroise*, 215 pairs of *pantalons à cheval*, 226 *gilet d'ecuries*, 395 pairs of stable trousers, 388 pairs of *caleçon* and 56 *bonnets de police*.[266] The February 1815 dress regulations gave them helmets, white-fringed epaulettes, aiguilettes and plumes. In theory they retained scarlet facings of the 1e *Chasseurs*.

The regiment took part in the Hundred Days' campaign, when an officer deserted to the allies at Waterloo. An idea of what it wore during the campaign can be gained from the inspection carried out when the regiment was disbanded on 1 October 1815. We note on that day the regiment was wearing 11 *schakos* and 233 helmets. Clearly it seems helmets had been worn during the Waterloo campaign. The *schakos*, we may suppose, were worn by trumpeters. Clothing and equipment in use on 1 October 1815 comprised:[267]

Item	Good Condition	Bad Condition	To be Replaced
Habits-vestes		258	
Gilet d'ecuries		208	
Pantalons à cheval		208	
Stable trousers		73	
Bonnets de police		262	
Capote Manteaux		193	
Porte-manteaux	5	225	
Helmets		233	
Schakos		11	
Schako covers	0	0	0
Culottes hongroise	0	0	
Gauntlets	0	0	0
Pairs of boots		179	
Gibernes	38	502	
Porte-gibernes	30	466	
Banderolles	88	445	
Waistbelts for sabre	22	338	
Sword knots		221	

Item	Good Condition	Bad Condition	To be Replaced
Pairs of gloves		31	
Waistbelts in buff		255	
Aiguillettes	31	25	
Sabres	315	80	41
Musketoons	275	64	40
Pistols	99	10	8

Insufficient aiguilettes existed to have equipped the entire regiment – one wonders what happened to the others. Where they destroyed at the start of the Hundred Days' campaign? Cloth in the regiment's magazine was as follows:[268]

5m 95 green broadcloth
0m white broadcloth
0m white broadcloth
0m *garance* broadcloth
33m 10 linen for *caleçon*
3m 50 green tricot
99m 90 scarlet serge
0m white serge
376m 80 white lace 10mm wide
269m 21 wool lace for corporal's stripes

General Excelmanns, the inspecting general in October 1814, notes that the regiment had 90 new entrants that had not been equipped due to the lack of materials. He told the officers to use the inherited cloth from the 26e *Chasseurs* in the production of new uniforms, including the *garance* cloth, so we are left to suppose that the regiment

We present a trooper of the *Chasseurs du Roi* as they appeared from November 1814 through to December 1815 based on the regiment's paper archive.

We also present speculative reconstructions of the trumpeter as they appeared from November 1814 through to December 1815 based on the regiment's paper archive. The regimental stores held eleven *schakos* that may have been used in the campaign by trumpeters, which we show, alongside the use of the helmet.

had dark red facings in 1815, and not scarlet. It is also clear from the clothing and equipment return that the regiment no longer wore *culottes hongroise*, but wore instead the more robust *pantalons à cheval*. The colour of these items is open to debate, they were likely green, although *garance* is a possibility. We also note that we have proof positive of helmets being worn in the Hundred Days, along with white epaulettes and aiguilettes. Indeed, the elite company had white plumes as forty-two white plumes and covers were brand new and waiting to be issued in *dépôt*. Another oddity we find is that regiment had 132 black stocks made from wool, and 89 pairs of wool ankle socks.[269]

Régiment des Chasseurs à Cheval Belge

This regiment was formed on 13 April 1815 and was to be recruited from Belgian soldiers who had been removed from the new Royalist Army in summer 1814 because they were not French. Colonel Hulimant was named the commanding officer and the staff comprised Chef d'Escadron Lazaneure, Adjutant-Major Grazier and Captain Chevalier, with 9 *sous-officiers* forming the *petit-etat major*. By 1 May 1815 Captain Louis Chevalier's squadron mustered in 1e Company 1 sergeant major, 4 sergeants, 1 fourrier, 3 corporals, 25 troopers and 35 horses, and in 5e Company 1 sergeant major, 4 sergeants, 1 fourrier, 3 corporals and 25 troops with 34 horses. In total the unit had 4 officers, 77 others ranks and 77 horses.[270] By 12 May the 1e squadron had 85 other ranks clothed, equipped and mounted.[271] How they looked we cannot say. The regiment was filled out with returned POWs and volunteers, and had been clothed with items taken from the central *dépôt* in Paris.[272] By 1 July 1815 the regiment fielded two squadrons, some 350 men and fought in a major cavalry action to defend the bridge at Sevres in Paris over 2 and 3 July. Following the capitulation of Paris, the regiment was disbanded in September 1815. The regiment likely looked incredibly ad hoc, with little uniformity, yet it existed and fought well in the defence of Paris.

Chapter 3

Chasseurs – Concluding Comments

What does all this data say? Well clearly some regiments, despite the 1806 edict, had clung tenaciously onto their *dolmans*, and even had non-regulation *pelisses*. Braided or facing colour *vestes* or *gilets* were clearly worn with cutaway old-style *habits*; both these factors show that the Bardin regulation was more theory than reality. The 1^{e}, 2^{e}, 3^{e}, 4^{e}, 5^{e}, 6^{e}, 9^{e}, 11^{e}, 12^{e}, 16^{e}, 19^{e} and 25^{e} were all in theory redressed in 1813 in Bardin-regulation clothing, twelve regiments out of thirty-one, with the regiments in Spain wearing whatever clothing they had. Yet this simplification of the facts ignores the whim of the colonel.

Dolmans, despite being abolished in 1805, were worn and had been adopted post-1808 and noted at the time of the 1814 inspections:

5e ***Chasseurs***: 67 *dolmans* in service in summer 1814
7e ***Chasseurs***: 275 *dolmans* and *pelisses* in use
8e ***Chasseurs***: 165 *dolmans* in use
21e ***Chasseurs***: 39 new *dolmans* and 20 needing repairs in *dépôt*
27e ***Chasseurs***: 39 *dolmans* and *pelisses* in use with elite company of 1e squadron

Furthermore, contrary to our expectations and what modern illustrators of the epoch show, the plates accompanying the Bardin regulation imply that pre-Bardin regulation *habit a revers* and or *kinski* were in use with every regiment of *chasseurs*: in 99 per cent of cases Bardin regulations were only introduced in summer 1814. Bardin regulation was never enforced with the cavalry during the 1st Empire. The peace following the abdication was the only time regiments had the chance to 'dump' worn out kit, and with the recent amalgamations regiments had to replace a lot of kit that did not fit in with the new regiments' facing colours. For the *chasseurs*, like the dragoons and *cuirassiers*, Bardin was only applied from early summer 1814 into 1815, when it was codified by the February 1815 regulations. Beyond reasonable doubt, Bardin regulation was an innovation of the First Restoration.

We remark that 21^{e} *Chasseurs* wore 116 infantry *habits-vestes* along with infantry *capotes* and equipment! These *chasseurs* would hardly have been recognisable as such, and this shows how acute the shortages of green cloth and appropriate equipment was at the end of the Empire.

It is undeniable that with the presence of *dolmans*, *habits a revers*, *kinski* and *habits-vestes* in use in 1814, the logical conclusion that we must draw is that in the 31

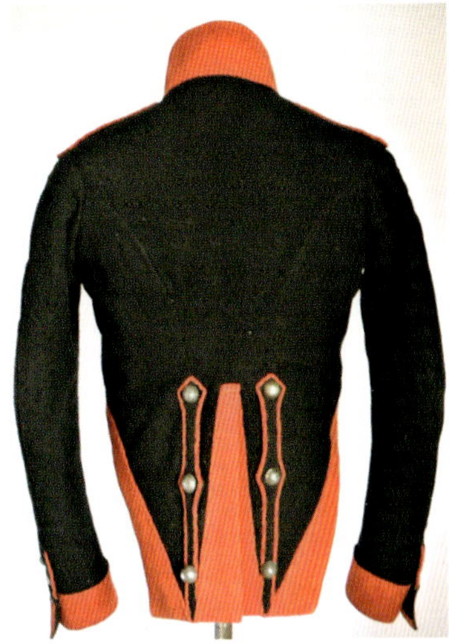

Incredibly well-preserved *habit-kinski*, adopted by most regiments of *chasseurs* at some time during their history. (*Private collection Switzerland*)

A trooper's *giberne* dating to the last months of the First Empire.

A trooper of an unknown *chasseur* regiment observed around Dresden in summer 1813. The non-regulation *giberne* is perfectly plausible given the shortages of the period. (*Collection KM*)

An officer of an unknown regiment of *chasseurs* in summer 1813. The grey broadcloth pantalons with leather inserts we know had been adopted by officers by 1808, if not earlier. (*Collection KM*)

regiments of *chasseurs*, official War Ministry decrees were ignored. The study shows overwhelmingly the importance of disregarding 'what we think we know' from books and other publications created over the last 200 years based on official decrees, as the creator of these works have made gross assumptions about the immediate implication of regulations that cannot be substantiated by archive sources. Regimental archives are the primary source for the understanding of how regiments were dressed and not official regulations, yet many dozens of books present 'pretty pictures' of the line *chasseurs* that are without a shadow of a doubt total fiction when compared to the primacy of regimental records and are in fact perpetuating total lies about how the army was dressed.

Elite Company

Formed under the decree of 10 October 1801, Article 13 of the Decree stipulates:

> The first company of the first squadron of each cavalry regiment, dragoons, *chasseurs* and *hussars* will take the name of Elite Company. This company will be formed of men chosen in all Corps, conforming to the instructions which will be given by the Minister of War.[273]

Thus, the fur-covered *schako* that later developed into the colpack was adopted by *chasseur* regiments. Yet how common were colpacks post-1812? What other distinctions did elite companies have? We find the following regiments with colpacks:

6[e] ***Chasseurs***: 71 colpacks in use August 1814.
10[e] ***Chasseurs***: 45 colpacks in use September 1814.
13[e] ***Chasseurs***: 27 new colpacks and 13 old colpacks in April 1813.
19[e] ***Chasseurs***: 49 colpacks in use September 1814.
26[e] ***Chasseurs***: 11 colpacks in use with 1[e] squadron June 1814.
27[e] ***Chasseurs***: 32 colpacks in use June 1814.
29[e] ***Chasseurs***: 87 colpacks in use, with 26 in store in June 1814.

Thus, we find seven regiments out of thirty-one still wearing colpacks. Arguably the 5e had these in 1813 and all had been lost by summer 1814. Under Bardin elite companies wore grenadier *schakos*, which we find worn in the following regiments:

3e ***Chasseurs***: 31 grenadier *schakos* listed in September 1815.
8e ***Chasseurs***: 4 grenadier *schakos* in *dépôt* in September 1815.
23e ***Chasseurs***: 30 grenadier *schakos* and 55 scarlet *aigrettes* purchased in 1813 for elite company.

Just three regiments out of thirty-one had the regulation Bardin *schako* and just one regiment had *aigrettes*! We find regiments clung tenaciously to plumes:

6e ***Chasseurs***: 400 plumes in use summer 1814.
12e ***Chasseurs***: 37 plumes with covers in *dépôt* September 1815.
13e ***Chasseurs***: 11 pairs of scarlet-fringed epaulettes, 10 plumes, 5 grenade plates in copper in *dépôt* in 1813.
21e ***Chasseurs***: 15 plumes in *dépôt* 1814.

In theory the elite company men wore scarlet-fringed epaulettes; yet these are not in universal use across all thirty-one regiments:

3e ***Chasseurs***: 38 pairs grenadier epaulettes in use September 1815.
6e ***Chasseurs***: 410 pairs of epaulettes in use August 1814 – every man was wearing a pair!
13e ***Chasseurs***: 11 pairs of grenadier epaulettes in *dépôt* August 1814.
23e ***Chasseurs***: 120 pairs of grenadier epaulettes in use August 1814.

The 10e used copper scale contre-epaulettes like those of the Marines of the *Garde Imperiale*! On balance of evidence, elite companies did not have *aigrettes*, grenadier *schakos* or colpack or wear epaulettes.

Sapeurs

No formal decree was published that authorised the light cavalry to adopt *sapeurs*, yet in July 1802 a circular advised the regiments of mounted troops that it was the intention of the government to provide the elite companies, as well as with their normal armament, the following tools: the sous-officiers with bill-hooks, one third of the men with axes, a third with spades and a third with pick-axes. The corps were authorised to pass contracts for their purchase and the tools were actually distributed in some companies.[274]

The only archive source to reference *sapeurs* is from 1811 and mentions that the 11e, 12e and 24e regiments had *sapeurs*.[275] Iconography adds the 26e. Therefore sapeurs were not present in every regiment and, moreover, seem to only have existed in the time frame of 1808 to 1813.

Trumpeters

In theory Bardin and the earlier 1811 simplified the dress of trumpeters and replaced the gaudily clad trumpeters in green and Imperial Livery. Yet we note the 3e *Chasseurs* had twelve trumpeters' *habits* made in 1813 from scarlet broadcloth with blue broadcloth facings, accompanied by scarlet pantalons with elaborate braiding; the 8e *Chasseurs* had 4 trumpeters' *dolmans* in use in 1815; the 12e *Chasseurs* had two trumpeters' *dolmans* in summer 1814 and had worn *bleu celeste kinski* with *czapka* in 1813 and 1814! Yet we note Bardin ascribes trumpeters with the same habit as used by drummers in the line infantry. However, in the plates accompanying the regulation, the trumpeters wear a standard *chasseur habit*, with Imperial Livery to the collar, cuffs, seven chevrons in each arm, on the tail facings, at the taille and around the revers![276] So what was the regulation? Both options of the Brandenburgs on the single-breasted *kinski* and the laced *habit* are both seemingly regulation, and we cannot tell from archive sources which was actually used. Indeed, we note that very few regiments are recorded with any trumpeters' lace. Regiments with specific trumpeters' lace were as follows:

1e ***Chasseurs***: 9m 78 Imperial Livery in *dépôt*, June 1814 and 3 new trumpeters' habits.
8e ***Chasseurs***: 100m 36 trumpeters' lace in *dépôt*, August 1814; the same amount remained in *dépôt* in September 1815.
23e ***Chasseurs***: 172m 90 Imperial Livery for trumpeters obtained in 1813 and 1814.
25e ***Chasseurs***: *dépôt* held June 1814 5 brand-new trumpeters' *habits* and 100m 36 of trumpeters' lace. Exactly the same amount of lace was in *dépôt* in 1815, which was 'burned' on the order of the inspecting officer. Therefore, the regiment had Bardin-regulation trumpeters' habits with Imperial Livery.
28e ***Chasseurs***: 60m Imperial Livery in *dépôt* in 1814.

Just four regiments out of thirty-one had adopted Imperial Livery, a very small number indeed.

We are therefore left to conclude that from 1800 to 1814 colonels of *chasseurs* regiments 'did their own thing' and dressed 'their regiment' the 'way they wanted' and that the War Ministry and official dress regulations 'could go to hell'.

Chapter 4

Hussars

The most flamboyant regiments of the French Army after the imposing *cuirassiers* must surely have been the gaudily dressed *hussars* with their flamboyant *pelisses* and *dolmans*. The *hussars* at the time of Napoléon coming to power comprised just fourteen regiments, of which six existed well before 1791. The famous 7e *Hussar* of Marbot were formed in 1792 along with the 8e; the 9e, 10e and 11e came along in 1793; the 12e in 1794; the 13e in 1795 in first incarnation, and the 14e in 1814. The 13e was disbanded in 1796 and re-raised on 28 January 1813 in Italy, before being re-formed as the *Jérôme Napoléon Hussars*. The regiment that was to become the 14e was raised in Turin on 28 January 1813 and was disbanded 13 December 1813, the men becoming the 14e *Hussar* with the men from the former 13e *Hussar* formed in Italy.

Uniform Regulations

The *dolman* and *pelisse* were the trademarks of the uniform of the *hussars*. Under the terms of the October 1801 regulations, the *hussars* adopted a new form of headgear to replace the mirliton – the *schako a flamme*. The *schako* was to measure 180mm tall and 217mm in diameter at the top, the body to be made from leather, with a leather top. Around the body of the *schako* was wrapped a *flamme*. This was a long triangular piece of serge, the colour of the regiment, 758mm long and 180mm tall at its origin, where it was sewn to the *schako*. The edge of the *flamme* was hemmed around its edges with worsted tape 23mm wide, the same colour as the regiment's lace. At the point of the *flamme* was a tassel, again in the same colour materials as the regiment's lace. At the front of the *schako* was a leather peak, which attached to the *schako* with three hooks and eyes. The *schako* was also issued a cord, 24m 74 long, with two raquettes at one end and a worsted tassel at the other. A black feather plume was authorised – worn since 1786 in any case – to be worn, some 325mm long with the shaft 81mm long. The shaft was made from whale bone.[277]

The decree of 22 February 1802 ordered that the undress *surtouts* were to be dismantled, and the materials used to make stable coats. Under the *dolman* a braided waistcoat was tolerated.[278] The order was repeated on 8 December 1802.[279] Clearly, colonels were unwilling to 'chop up' brand-new items. Indeed, brand-new *surtouts* made prior to February 1802 had an expected lifespan of three years, and it seems logical that these items would remain in use until they were worn out.

On 24 September 1803 yet another decree appeared. The 7e *Bis*, 11e and 12e *Hussar* were disbanded and became dragoon regiments. The decree also affected the facing colours of some regiments. The 5e *Hussar*, who since 1786 had had *garance* facings, suddenly found themselves with white. A new *dolman* made prior to September 1803 had at least a two-year lifespan, so the process in replacing the facing colours took time, at least two years if not more. The *schako a flamme* was officially supressed, with a *schako* made from felt 180mm tall and 217mm in diameter at the top with a fixed leather peak: no doubt the changeover would have taken time.[280]

Dolmans, *Habits* or *Kinski*?

The dress of the *hussars* underwent a major change in 1806. Away went the *dolman* and *pelisse*: in essence, *hussars* and *chasseurs à cheval* now formed a single cohesive formation of light cavalry all, in theory at least, dressed in the same uniform, the single-breasted *kinski* and the same headdress, the new pattern *schako*. The 1806 tariff for the *kinski* allowed for 1m 68 of body cloth and 1m 58 of linen to line it with; not a scrap of facing cloth was allowed. Yet at the same time, the tariff mentions a sleeveless *veste* made from 1m 9 of broadcloth, lined with 1m 56 of white serge and needing 0m 6 of linen for button stands, and also the *gilet d'ecurie*, which required 1m 25 of broadcloth, 0m 6 of facing cloth for piping the collar and cuffs, and not an inch of cloth was allowed to line the garment! The decree deleted from the use the braised waistcoat in favour of white, and confirms that the *gilet d'ecurie* was made from the *kinski* or *surtout* with the tails lopped off.[281]

The decree of 27 April 1807 introduced to the *hussars* the 1806 model infantry *schako*. In theory it was to replace the *schakos a flamme* and any other type in service, and confirmed the plate was to be stamped from copper, be diamond in shape and bear an imperial eagle over the regiment's number.[282]

Looking at regiments on service in summer 1807, we find the 1e had 685 *kinski* in use, the 5e were wearing *dolmans* and *pelisses*, and the 7e had 678 *kinski* in use: in both the 1e and 7e no *dolman* or *pelisse* were with the war squadrons, and clearly the colonel of the 5e refused to simplify his regiment's dress.[283] It also shows the leeway colonels had in ignoring officialdom! A more complete picture emerges of how regiments were dressed when we look at winter 1807 inspections. We find the 2e had 903 *habits-vestes* in use, of which 357 were in good condition, 133 needed repairs and 415 were life expired. The unit also used 833 *dolmans* and a mere 281 *pelisses*. It seems every man had a *dolman* and a *habit*, but only a select few had a *pelisse*. Indeed, a further 213 *pelisses* were in *dépôt* waiting repairs and a further 150 were awaiting disposal as life expired: just 78 in use were in good condition. Clearly these items had been 'worn to death', over winter 1806–07 with the *habit* used for summer? The inspector ordered the *habits-vestes* were to be replaced by *surtouts*.[284] We wonder how these non-regulation garments looked?

We know nothing more officially about the dress of *hussars* until 9 November 1810, when a new *schako* was introduced. Swept away at the same time were plumes and *schakos* cords.[285] Another major innovation of 1810 was the official sanction of *pantalons à cheval* – the leather-reinforced overalls, made at first from broadcloth.[286]

The War Ministry circular of 7 July 1809 had sanctioned the production of these overalls for replacement clothing for 1810, noting that regiments had unofficially made their stable trousers from broadcloth for campaign use, and now allowed a pair of stable trousers and *pantalons à cheval*.[287] The regulations were retrospectively confirming common practice.

Bardin

The 1812 regulations had very little impact on the *hussars*, they still had their flamboyant *pelisses* and *dolmans*:

> **Section 3eme Hussars**
> **Art 1 Clothing**
> 1326. The clothing of the *sous-officiers* and *hussars* will comprise a *pelisse*, a *dolman*, a waistbelt, a white *gilet sans manches*, a green tricot *gilet d'ecurie*, a pair of *culottes hongroise*, a pair of *caleçon*, a pair of *pantalons à cheval*, a *manteau* with sleeves.
>
> **Art.2 Headdress**
> 1349. The headdress of the *sous-officiers* and *hussars* will comprise a *schako* and *bonnet de police*. The Elite companies will wear a *schako*, the same as the grenadiers of the infantry.
> 1350. The *schakos* will be the same as the infantry; the plate and chinscales will be in the colour metal as the regiment's buttons.
> 1351. The *bonnets de police* will be made in the same colour broadcloth as the *pelisses* and take the form detailed in No. 45.
>
> **Art 3. Distinctive Marks**
> 1352. The distinctive marks of the sergeants and *fourriers* will be in gold or silver depending on the colour of the buttons and will be placed as for the light infantry (Viz. Nos 58 and 59). The corporals will have the same marks as the corporals of the light infantry (Viz. No. 63) and will be worn on the *pelisse* and *dolman*.
> 1353. The veterinarians and farriers will be distinguished as detailed in the general dispositions, Viz. No. 328 to 336.
> 1354. Trumpeters of *Hussars* will wear a *dolman* and *pelisse* in green broadcloth with lace and a pair of *culottes hongroise* in green broadcloth with the same lace and braiding as for the *hussars*; they will wear the same headdress as their regiment, except the *bonnet de police* is made from green broadcloth, and they will be armed like their regiment.
> 1355. The distinctions of the *dolman* and *pelisse* will be different to that of the *hussar* as it will be adorned with lace of the arms of the Emperor, and will be placed where the *tresse platte* [flat square braid] is worn. The back of the

dolman will be adorned with the braid placed exactly as for a *hussar*. The sleeves will be decorated with seven chevrons, not comprising the cuff. The *pelisse* will be not different to that of the *hussar*, except that for those of the trumpeters the *tresse platte* will bear the arms of the Emperor, the edge of the collar will be embellished with this lace; the sleeves will be decorated with seven chevrons, not including the cuffs.

Art 4. Weapons and Equipment

1356. The armament of the corporals and *hussars* will comprise a *mousqueton*, a short sabre and a pistol; they will conform to the models adopted. The sergeants and *fourriers*, trumpeters and farriers will not have the *mousqueton*.

1357. The equipment will comprise a sabretache, a waistbelt from which the sabre and sabretache are suspended, a *giberne* with belt, a *banderolle-porte-mousqueton*, a sabre knot, a pair of boots and a *porte-manteau*.

Art 5. Petit Equipement, Linen and footwear

1378. The Petit Equipement will comprise a *trousse*, a pair of black gaiters, three shirts, two stocks, three *rabats*, a handkerchief, two serviettes, and a pair of boots, a pair of shoes, all to conform to the general model Viz. No. 372.

Art 7. The dress of the Officers

1382. The clothing of the officers of *hussars* will comprise a *pelisse*, a *dolman*, a braided waistcoat, a waistbelt, a pair of *culottes hongroise*, a pair of *pantalons à cheval*, a *frac*, a *manteau* and a pair of gloves. The clothing will be the same as the *hussar*, made from the same colour but from super-fine broadcloth. The buttons will be silvered or gilded. The braid and lace will be in silver or gold depending on the colour of the buttons. The *pelisse* will be bordered in fur from the throat of the fox. The *manteau* will be made from green broadcloth and conform to those of the troops. The frac and the redingote will be cut from green broadcloth and conform to the details No. 431 and 435, except the retroussis will be decorated with a patch in the distinctive colour and will conform to engraving No. 1382.[288]

The 'waistbelt' that we know more commonly as a barrel sash was made from crimson wool with white knots and tassels. It was made in the manner of a Kamer band and measured 60mm wide. The body of the barrel sash was to be made from five lengths of crimson cord, secured by three white knots on each portion. The *pantalons à cheval* were officially to be made from green tricot for all regiments, reinforced with black basane leather, each leg being closed by a row of eighteen bone buttons. The button stand was piped in the regiment's facing colour. *Culottes hongroise* were again to become green for all regiments. Under Bardin the decorative festoon around the *schabraque*, which had been made from tricot in the regiment's distinctive colour, now became green, as did the *porte-manteau*, which became a lot smaller than the previous type.[289]

Chapter 5

Hussars – Regulations in Practice

As with all historical research, we are limited by the paper archives that exist in 2022 – which is a very small proportion of the paperwork that was generated in the epoch. What follows is a discussion of the fourteen regiments of *hussars* from the paperwork that the author has been able to track down in various French archives.

1e *Hussar*

Created as the *Hussard de Bercheney*, the 1e Hussar of the Republic and Empire retained the basic colours of the regiment. This cloth sample for the regiment from *c*.1794 shows top to bottom *bleu celeste, garance* – madder red for cuff facings – and *vert dragon* for the manteau. (*A S K Brown Collection. Photograph R A Cooper*)

An officer of elite company by Aaron Martinet. In our second image we present an elite company trooper by Martinet in a print published in 1810.

Under the terms of the Bardin regulation, all *hussar* regiments were to adopt green *culottes hongroise*. The regimental archive and Martinet agree that the 1e *Hussar* did indeed wear these garments.

Contemporary, eyewitness painting of an elite company trooper. He wears his scarlet *culottes hongroise* and his *giberne* belt is decorated with a copper flaming grenade device. The centre company troopers sport light blue *schako rouleau*, which must date the image to the last years of the Empire.

Incredibly rare sabretache of the 1e *Hussar*. This model was adopted as early as 1804 and remained in use with the elite company until after Waterloo. On physical examination we see that a device was sewn over the number 1 during the Hundred Days – no doubt the arms of France – which were hastily removed in the Hundred Days. (*Private Collection*)

The dress of the trumpeters of the 1e *Hussar* is not recorded by any archive sources or contemporary depictions. Later writers such as Ernest Fort, Boucquoy and Rene Louis all rely on the Petit soldat de Strasbourg, created sometime in the 1830s or 1840s. The use of reverse colours is within the known practice of the epoch. The centre companies wore *schakos* as we show. The uniform shown is a best guess and should be considered that rather than definitive.

The regiment was created in 1720 by the count Ladislas-Ignance de Bercheny in Turkey and renamed the 1e *Hussar* in 1791. The regiment was with the Grande Armée in 1805 and marched to Spain following Friedland. It was inspected on 20 July 1805. Clothing in use comprised:[290]

Item	In Good Repair	In Need of Repair	To be Written Off	Total	Total Made Since 23 May 1802	To be Replaced
Habits	Nil					
Dolmans	165	59	150	674	402	
Pelisses	516	48	110	647	221	
Surtouts	318	216	140	674	309	
Manteaux	312	80	120	512	91	
Gilets	584	40	50	674	584	
Gilet d'ecuries	124	322	163	609	124	
Culottes hongroise	636	38		674	636	
Stable trousers	78		536	614	49	
Colpacks	101			101	1	
Barrel sashes	414	97	163	674	141	
Schakos	318	26	330	674	283	
Bonnets de police	95	426	157	678	48	
Waistbelts	614	60		674	129	
Gibernes	534	66	74	674	106	
Porte-gibernes	514	58	102	626	106	
Porte-carabines	536		90	626	89	
Porte-manteaux	604		70	674	240	
Boots	654			654	115	
Sabretaches	464		210	674	437	

Cloth and other materials in the *dépôt* included *bleu celeste* broadcloth, green broadcloth for the *manteaux*, and madder red broadcloth for facings. Clothing in the *dépôt* comprised:[291]

Item	In *Dépôt* 1802	Purchased since 1802	Total	Amount Used	Remaining in *Dépôt*	Issued new
Dolmans	402		402			402
Pelisses	21	200	221			221
Surtouts	1	308	309			91
Manteaux		91	91			91
Gilets	476	124	600		6	584
Gilet d'ecuries	15	100	115		115	

Item	In *Dépôt* 1802	Purchased since 1802	Total	Amount Used	Remaining in *Dépôt*	Issued new
Culottes hongroise	600	61	661		24	636
Stable trousers	43	300	343		294	49
Barrel sashes	42	169	211		70	141
Colpacks		1	1			1
Schakos	198	133	331		48	283
Bonnets de police	3	36	39			39
Sabretache	458		458		21	437

The inspecting general authorised the production of 202 new *dolmans*, 202 new *pelisses*, 57 new *manteaux*, 404 new *surtouts*, 202 new *gilets*, but no new *gilet d'ecuries*. Furthermore, 808 new pairs of stable trousers and *culottes hongroise* were authorised for production and 16 new colpacks for the elite company, 177 new *schakos* and 134 new sabretaches. In theory, *surtouts* had been discontinued in 1802, yet here the inspector was ordering more to be made: this shows neatly the need to look beyond the written word of the official decree and explore what happened at regimental level. Theory and practice are often two totally different things. We wonder if we are missing a written order authorising the production of more *surtouts*, contiguous to the lost order for the *chasseurs* to abandon *dolmans* in October 1804? I would say we are.

We know nothing more until the regiment was reviewed 1 June 1807. We record:[292]

Item	In Good Repair	In Need of Repair	To be Replaced	Total	Observations
Surtouts	585	100		685	
Gilets en drap	150	535		685	
Gilet d'ecuries	150	535		685	
Culottes hongroise	150	535		685	
Pantalons à cheval	240	445		685	
Stable trousers	The regiment has none				
Caleçon					
Manteaux	150	535		685	
Bonnets de police					
Schakos		582		582	
Colpacks	103			103	
Schako covers	The regiment has none				
Pompoms					
Plumes					

The men were clearing wearing *kinski* and non-regulation *pantalons à cheval* as well as their parade *culottes hongroise*. The elite company had colpacks. The regiment was inspected six months later at Liege on 16 December 1807. Clothing and equipment in use then was as follows:[293]

Item	In Good Repair	In Need of Repair	To be written off	Total	Total made since 23 May 1805	Comment
Habits				Nil		
Dolmans	400	100		500	200	Since the last review, a portion of the new items of clothing and equipment has been sent out to the War squadrons as replacement items for those lost during the campaign of Austria ... We are ignorant of the losses of clothing and equipment sustained during the last campaign [i.e. 1807]
Pelisses	600	46	226	872	717	
Surtouts	600	322	78	1,000	1,152	
Manteaux	600	72	82	869	690	
Gilets en drap blanc	600	69	200	869	690	
Gilet d'ecuries					80	
Culottes hongroise	443	69	498	1,012	1,910	
Stable trousers	450	64	498	1,012	1,850	
Colpacks	28		40	68		
Schakos	600	78	130	808	684	
Bonnets de police	600	218	194	1,012	941	
Waistbelts	600	182	104	886	633	
Gibernes	690	172	30	894	553	
Porte-gibernes	820	44	30	894	553	
Porte-carabines	820		20	840	536	
Porte-manteaux	600	60	140	800	926	
Boots	650	242	120	1,012	1,219	
Plumes	620		160	780	620	
Sabretaches			251	251	458	
Barrel sashes	70		260	330	70	

The men were still wearing their *kinski*, but *hussar* rig was slowly being taken back into service. Of note, elite company had colpacks and all ranks it seems had plumes, the first recorded instance of them in use with the regiment. Cloth used since 1805 and 16 December 1807 is worth commenting upon. Unlike up to 1805, when only a tiny amount of red cloth was used, after 1805 230m of scarlet cloth was used. This amount far exceeds the quantities needed for the collar and cuff of the dolman. Therefore, we postulate that the elite company adopted scarlet *culottes hongroise* at some stage in 1806. It also worth noting that the *pantalons à cheval* have disappeared from use.[294] No doubt the scarlet *culottes hongroise* reflected the regiment's prestigious appointment to be the service squadron to the Emperor during the 1806 in the absence of the Guard cavalry. Scarlet legwear was a hallmark of the staff.

From 1809, the 1e squadron was detached and served in Germany with the Grande Armée, while three squadrons remained in Spain. Sadly, the regiment's archive says nothing about its appearance. At the end of the 1814 campaign the regiment had 1,110 other ranks under arms when inspected on 21 July. The inspecting general reported that every single bit of clothing in use that day was to be urgently replaced as nothing was in serviceable condition:[295]

Item	Good Condition	In Need of Repair	Need Replacing	To be Replaced	Items Need
Pelisses				809	301
Dolmans				809	301
Veste d'ecuries				728	382
Gilets			367	442	301
Culottes hongroise			809		301
Pantalons à cheval				913	197
Pantalons d'ecurie			1,110		
Caleçon			1,110		
Manteaux			22	124	964
Bonnets de police			813	297	
Pairs of boots			410	399	301
Pairs of gloves			809		301
Barrel sashes			128	681	301
Sabretaches				809	301
Waistbelts	189	300		312	309
Gibernes	160	400		259	299
Porte-gibernes	203	313		295	299
Porte-carabines	540	79		200	291
Sabre knots				809	301
Trumpets	5			15	
Trumpet cords	5			15	
Schakos				809	301
Schako cords					1,110
Schako covers					1,110
Pompoms				809	301
Plumes					1,110

The men were also issued 1,120 shirts and 203 black stocks. Some of the equipment was useable, 189 waistbelts, 160 *gibernes*, 203 *porte-gibernes*, 540 *porte-carabines* and 5 trumpets. The regiment had 420 carbines in good condition, 262 needing repairs and 39 to be written off. Likewise, 503 sabres were in good condition, 202 need repairs and 45 were 'knackered'. Of the pistols, 309 were in good condition, 58 needed repairs and 25 were to be cannibalised for spares. The *dépôt* held little in terms of cloth: 521m 18 *bleu celeste* broadcloth, 95m 70 scarlet broadcloth, 159m 47 green broadcloth, 16m of flannel to line *pelisses*, 455m 32 of linen for lining and 244m 30 linen to make caleçon with. *Dépôt* also held 15 shirts and 3 pairs of boots, 6 *gilets*, 39 pairs of green *culottes hongroise* and 35 pairs of *caleçon*. Vernet shows the 1e *Hussar* with green *culotte* in his series of plates; here is proof positive that these did indeed exist![296] The regiment was disbanded on 1 August.

2e *Hussar*

Martinet presents four differing images of a centre company trooper. They are consistent in showing a light blue plumes with a green base, and the use of *schako* cords. Three models of sabretache are shown: one brown with white lace and an embroidered eagle; red with white lace and a white metal numeral 2; and lastly black leather with a white metal eagle. The embroidered item matches a known example for the regiment, so we can be sure that Martinet's observations are reliable.

Officer, elite company of the 2e Hussar.

A trooper of the 2e Hussar in winter 1807 from the Otto manuscript. We can date this image fairly precisely. When reviewed in June 1807, the regiment was wearing habits-vestes rather than the pelisses shown here: just 101 pelisses were in use. Clearly the Otto artist captured a trooper wearing one of the elusive pelisses worn in winter 1807. The grey overalls are also recorded in use as far back as June 1805, 380 pairs being in use in 1808. (*Collection KM*)

Eyewitness drawing of a trooper of the 2e Hussar dated to 1815 by Lieutenant Bregeot of the 16e Chasseurs à Cheval. (*Collection KM*)

Created in Strasbourg on 25 January 1735 from Hungarian Volunteers, the regiment was named the *Chamborant Hussard*, becoming the 2e *Hussar* in 1791. The regiment was at Austerlitz and Friedland, and saw service in Spain in 1808–13 before fighting at Leipzig and in the campaign of France. When inspected on 9 August 1805, the clothing in use comprised:[297]

Item	In Good Repair	In Need of Repair	To be written off	Total	Total made since 23 September 1803	Observation
Habits				Nil		
Dolmans	617		2	619	183	
Pelisses	482	130	60	672	198	
Surtouts	377	291	47	715	273	
Manteaux	393	197	124	623	204	
Gilets	504	47	9	560	148	
Gilet d'ecuries				Nil		
Culottes hongroise	388	13	266	607	346	
Stable trousers	51	80	581	682	19	
caleçon	388	4	277	667	576	
Barrel sashes	465	6	3	474	7	
Schakos a poil	73		2	75	13	
Schakos	508	36	47	301	2	
Bonnets de police	291	94	378	703	18	
Adjutants *redingote*	2			2	1	

In the eighteen months prior to the inspection, some 748m 69 of blue – presumably *bleu celeste*? – broadcloth had been used, 1,065m 17 green broadcloth to make *manteaux*, 877m 48 brown broadcloth, 362m *treillis*, 650m flannel, 20m 80 brown tricot, 486m 91 white serge and 2,162m 58 linen. Rather than *gilet d'ecuries*, the regiment used smocks made from linen, 42 being made and 17 issued. In terms of armament, the regiment had 726 carbines, 518 pairs of pistols and 818 sabres.

We present reconstructions of elite company troopers based on notes by Rousselot. We do not know the source of Rousselot's information.

Among Rousselot's papers are images of centre company trumpeters. Up first is this image of a trumpeter made by the regiment's colonel in the 1803–05 period, therefore we can be certain of its reliability. Our first reconstruction is based on this image. The second reconstruction is based on Rousselot's notes, for which he does not give a source, but dates to 1810. Lastly, Rousselot, based on Marckolsheim's manuscript, argues that trumpeters wore a trooper's *dolman* and *pelisse* and a *schako* with sky-blue body with white lace top and bottom bands. Such a *schako* can be found in the former Brunon Collection, now part of the *Musée de l'Armée* and a second example in a private collection in France.

When reviewed on 5 January 1808, 833 *dolmans*, 281 *pelisses,* of which 101 had been issued since 1805, and 903 *habits* were in use, some 1,032 being made since 1805. Every man on parade was wearing a *habit* and white *veste*. Just 50 sabretaches were in use and not a single colpack existed for the elite company. The inspecting general ordered that 1,000 *culottes hongroise* were to be made and the same number of pairs of stable trousers, which were made from green tricot, reinforced with black leather and closed down the outside legs with bone buttons. No *gilet d'ecuries* existed, and instead the *habit-veste dit surtout* i.e., a *kinski,* was worn in its place. Only 250 *pelisses* were to be made, so clearly these were restricted to the elite company, *sous-officiers* and trumpeters. Just 166 sabretaches were authorised for production, again suggesting these were for *sous-officiers* only or the elite company. The regiment was not allowed to buy any more colpacks.[298]

Incredibly well-preserved trooper's *schako* with its black plume dating to the 1808–12 period. (*Photograph and Collection of Bertrand Malvaux*)

We know nothing more until summer 1814:[299]

Item	Good Condition	In Need of Repair	Need Replacing	To be Replaced	Items Need
Pelisses	418	52	2	16	166
Dolmans	376	17	7	16	238
Gilets	301	4	96	10	243
Gilet d'ecuries	279	47	101	43	121
Culottes hongroise	27	1	18	8	600
Pantalons à cheval	267	32	86	49	220
Bonnets de police	490		59	17	88
Manteaux-capote	335	7	10	13	289
Schakos	473	3		1	173
Stable trousers	143	4	2	121	421
Caleçon			15	9	630
Gibernes	421	7			226
Porte-gibernes	421	7			226

Item	Good Condition	In Need of Repair	Need Replacing	To be Replaced	Items Need
Porte-carabines	374	7			196
Sword knots	413				241
Sabretaches	395	4			255
Waistbelts	406	18		17	213
Barrel sashes	Nil				
Gloves					654
Pompoms	314			8	332
Pairs of boots	283	91	31	18	231
Schako covers	473	3		1	177

The *dépôt* held just 1m 84 of *bleu celeste* broadcloth and 452m 90 of flannel to make new uniforms. Brand-new clothing and equipment in the *dépôt* included 57 *dolmans*, 30 *bonnets de police*, 14 pairs of *surculottes* made from tricot, 61 pairs of *caleçon*, 7 *gibernes* with belts, and 60 sword knots. Clothing and equipment needing repairs included 54 *pelisses*, 3 pairs of *pantalons à cheval,* 187 *gibernes* and belts, 168 *porte-carabines*, 79 waistbelts, 19 sword knots and 64 sabretaches. Clothing to be disposed included 37 *pelisses*, 2 *dolmans*, 40 *capotes-manteaux*, 10 pairs of *pantalons à cheval* and

Incredibly well-made example of a trooper's *dolman*, preserved in a private collection. In the years before 1812, it was worn over a sky-blue waistcoat with white braid, ten rows of frogging with three vertical rows of buttons.

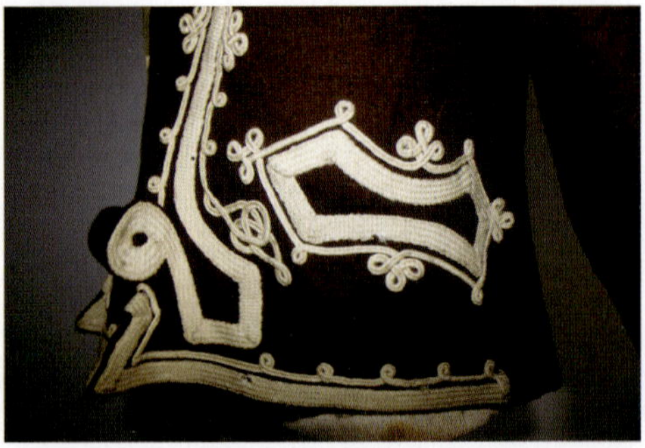

25 sabretaches. Various grades of leather were held in the *dépôt:* cow hide for *pantalons à cheval,* black sheepskin for *pelisses*, and red Moroccan leather to line *dolmans.*[300]

The regiment was disbanded at the end of 1815. Not an inch of broadcloth was in the *dépôt,* but it did hold 459m 83 green *tricot*, 12,984m 98 square worsted braid and 12,081m 10mm wide worsted braid. In addition, there was 308m of red and white worsted lace 22mm wide and 34m of silver lace 22mm wide. Clothing in the *dépôt* included 36 *dolmans* needing repairs and 29 that were life expired, 307 new *pelisses*, 42 needing repairs and 42 that were life expired. Other items included 2 white *gilets*, 5 *schako* covers, 204 *manteaux*, 34 *porte-manteaux*, 410 brand-new barrel sashes and 24 needing repairs, 174 *schakos*, 157 pairs of boots, 247 sabre belts, 653 *gibernes*, 413 *porte-gibernes*, and 310 sabretaches.

The *dépôt* admits to the loss of 98 *pelisses* in the Hundred Days' campaign, 472 *dolmans*, 383 *schakos*, 351 pairs of *culottes hongroise*, 121 white *gilets*, 275 *gilet d'ecuries*, 371 pairs of *caleçon*, 184 *bonnets de police*, 580 pairs of boots and 288 *porte-manteaux*. Not a single barrel sash was lost, from which we surmise that they simply were not worn on the campaign. Again, not a single *manteau* is recorded lost – were these worn we ask?[301] We know nothing else of the regiment made famous by the memoirs of Hussar Rocca.

3e *Hussar*

For a short period, the 3e *Hussar*, otherwise known as the *Esterhazy Hussars*, were numbered 5. This incredibly rare cloth sample is the only known example of the famous *gris argentin* used by this regiment. The samples are, top to bottom, *vert dragon*, *rouge-garance* i.e. madder red, and lastly *gris argentin*. (*A S K Brown Collection. Photograph R A Cooper*)

Martinet presents four troopers of the regiment, all with slight differences of sabretache design, plume and *porte-manteaux* colour.

An officer of the elite company, 3ᵉ *Hussar*. The regiment adopted colpacks for the elite company in 1803.

An exceptional sabretache for a 3ᵉ *Hussar* trooper dating from 1804 to 1808, give or take. We see that the regiment's uniform colour was not a light pale grey. (*Private collection*)

When reviewed on 1 June 1807, the men were all wearing *surtouts*: clearly the *surtout* was worn in lieu of the *dolman* on campaign. The elite company wore colpacks. The regiment's leather was noted as being blackened cow hide. At the time of the February 1808 review, the 3ᵉ *Hussar* was decked out in 875 *pelisses* and *pantalons à cheval* and the stores held 37 *pelisses* and 394 *dolmans*. All bar the trumpet major wore a *schako*, with 59 colpacks being in store and a single example in use. Clearly, the *surtout* was summer wear and the *pelisse* was worn in the winter. Quite how the trumpeters were dressed we know not. Our image is based on a contemporary sketch in the Bibliotheque Nationales, Paris.

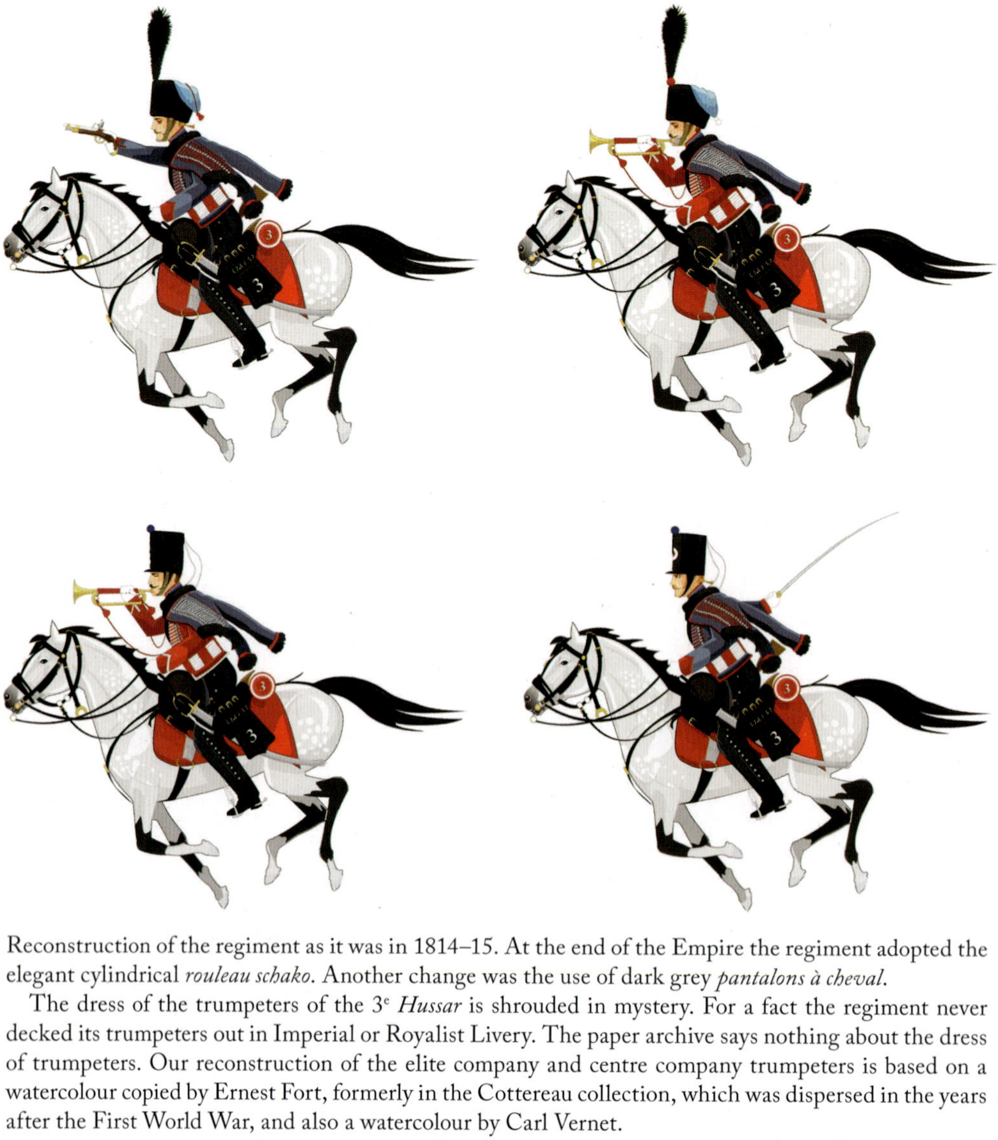

Reconstruction of the regiment as it was in 1814–15. At the end of the Empire the regiment adopted the elegant cylindrical *rouleau schako*. Another change was the use of dark grey *pantalons à cheval*.

The dress of the trumpeters of the 3e *Hussar* is shrouded in mystery. For a fact the regiment never decked its trumpeters out in Imperial or Royalist Livery. The paper archive says nothing about the dress of trumpeters. Our reconstruction of the elite company and centre company trumpeters is based on a watercolour copied by Ernest Fort, formerly in the Cottereau collection, which was dispersed in the years after the First World War, and also a watercolour by Carl Vernet.

Raised as the *Esterhazy Hussards* on 15 January 1742, the regiment became the 3^e *Hussar* in June 1793. When inspected on 8 August 1805, it was wearing:[302]

Item	In Good Repair	In Need of Repair	To be Written Off	Total	Total Made Since 23 May 1802
Dolmans	470	141	193	504	198
Pelisses	314	154	193	661	55
Surtouts	559		386	936	550
Manteaux	266	367	85	718	40
Gilets	371	269	193	833	227

Item	In Good Repair	In Need of Repair	To be Written Off	Total	Total Made Since 23 May 1802
Gilet d'ecuries	The regiment has none. *Surtouts* are used				
Culottes hongroise	561		772	1,333	561
Stable trousers	868		772	1,640	208
Caleçon	796		772	1,568	
Kolpacks	83		17	100	
Barrel sashes	401	150	122	673	
Schakos		504	168	672	
Bonnets de police	471		386	857	85
Waistbelts	560		127	687	14
Gibernes	485	150	38	673	
Porte-gibernes	485	150	38	673	
Porte-manteaux	171	515	86	772	171
Boots	418		386	804	804
Sabretaches	401	150	172	673	

The inspecting officer recorded that all the regiment's equipment was 'incomplete and totally defective' and was to be immediately replaced. He commented that the regiment used *surtouts* with the tails cropped short as *gilet d'ecuries*. Of interest, the elite company had 100 colpacks, 17 being life expired. The *dépôt* held 14 brand-new *dolmans*, 101 needing repairs and 193 awaiting disposal, 15 brand-new *pelisses* and 150 awaiting disposal. Also held were 208 new *surtouts*, 40 new *manteaux* and 180 that were little more than rags, 50 new *gilet*s made from *gris argentin* broadcloth with a further 114 examples that were awaiting disposal, 18 pairs of brand-new *caleçon*, 252 pairs of *culottes hongroise* and a single colpack.

Worthy of comment, the regiment's *manteaux* since the 1760s had been green – clearly not the case for the 3e *Hussar* as not an inch of green broadcloth existed on 23 May 1802 or later! Stores also reported 156m 10 of madder red tricot being used, perhaps for the *porte-manteaux* and perhaps *culottes hongroise* of trumpeters?[303]

The dress of the trumpeters before 1814 is not known. Rousselot, based on Marckolsheim's manuscript, argues that trumpeters wore a madder red *dolman* and *culottes hongroise*, and *gris argentin pelisse* and *schako*. This is perfectly plausible as Vernet in 1814 shows the same *dolman* and *pelisse* arrangement as Marckolsheim but with red cuffs. He also shows the use of the dark grey *pantalons à cheval*, which we know the regiment used. Conversely, he also depicts a red-garance *schabraque* with crimson lace, and a black sheepskin over the saddle. Vernet also shows black oilskin covers over the *schako*. (*Collection KM*)

On 1 June 1807 every man under arms was wearing a *surtout*, 99 colpacks were in use and 829 *schakos* with cords and plumes.[304] We know nothing else about the dress of the regiment until it was inspected on 4 January 1808. The regiment's inspection return offers us new details about the dress of this famous unit. Rank and file were wearing '*schakos garnis*' i.e. *schakos* with a garnish that we suppose to be cords and plumes. Some 604 *schakos* were in good condition, 225 were '*hors de service*' and the regiment had 829 in total, 660 being issued since 1805. The elite company wore colpacks, 60 being in good condition, 22 needing repairs, 17 *hors de service* making 99 examples, 60 being issued since 1805. Upper body wear included 929 *pelisses*, 929 *dolmans* and 929 *surtout* – clearly the regiment had campaign dress for the campaign of 1806–07. Of the *surtouts*, 500 were considered *hors de service*, whereas only 250 *pelisses* and *dolmans* were considered such. Every single pair of *culottes hongroise*, pantalons and *caleçon*, 929 pairs of each, were life expired and needed total replacement. Also in use were 929 pairs of *Keoppy* – we suppose to be *pantalons à cheval.* The *dépôt* held a large selection of cloth and materials. The *dolmans* and *pelisses* were *gris argentin* with red facings and crimson lace – indeed *dépôt* had used 7,071m 60 *gris argentin* broadcloth, 24m 76 red broadcloth, 2,886m 40 green broadcloth and 731m 98 of tricot since 1805. Since 1808, 25,642m 25 of flat worsted braid had been bought, 23,232m 32 square worsted braid, 10,436m 98 of worsted soutache and 2,785m 93 of crimson and blue worsted lace! Was this for rank stripes? Perhaps.[305]

In 1811 the regiment purchased seventy new colpacks for the elite company at 40 francs each and ten sets of trumpet cords costing 7 francs 50 apiece. Some 19,687 francs was spent buying 1,061 pairs of boots in 1813. In addition, 519 francs 20 was spent buying twenty trumpets, eight more than was allowed for by the War Ministry. Some 100 bridles were purchased at the same time, along with 100 saddle blankets and *schabraques*. Some 687m 70 of linen to make pantalons was obtained at the same time, for the sum of 801 francs 90. Five pairs of boots costing 139 francs 50 were purchased, costing 27 francs 9 a pair rather than the 19 francs for other ranks, and a further five pairs costing 128 francs, costing 25 francs 60 rather than 19 francs for the adjutant-*sous-officiers* and trumpet major and corporals.[306]

The regiment was inspected on 1 August 1814, when it mustered 364 other ranks and 5 *enfant de troupe*, as well as 45 officers. The clothing was in tatters:[307]

Item	Good Condition	In Need of Repair	Need Replacing	To be Replaced	Items Need
Pelisses	23	32	95	44	74
Dolmans	7	4	10	3	204
Gilets en drap blanc	32	4	25	2	205
Culottes hongroise	16		5	1	251
Caleçon	21	4			248
Pantalons de Peau		4		36	264
Stable trousers	113				115

Item	Good Condition	In Need of Repair	Need Replacing	To be Replaced	Items Need
Veste d'ecuries	29	9	9	8	118
Bonnets de police	85	83	66	13	26
Schakos	101	32	25		114
Manteaux	55	42	20	19	130
Barrel sashes	9		4		255
Sabretaches	120	3	2		143
Waistbelts	141	3	2		122
Sword knots	140				128
Gibernes	134	3	2		129
Porte-gibernes	136	3			129
Banderole-porte-carabines	86	1	2		96
Porte-manteaux	20	76	45	27	90
Pairs of boots	6	31	139		92
Fusils	74	3			
Sabres	140	4			
Pistols	31	15			
Trumpets	10	2			

The men had 638 shirts issued, just 9 pairs of shoes, and instead of the regulation stock wore black silk cravats, 208 being in use. We note 264 men had '*pantalons de peau*', which we assume are *pantalons* with the inner leg reinforced with leather. Clearly the regiment wore a mix of legwear – not enough of any type existed to give man a pair of each – the regiment must have presented a very mixed appearance, given some men had *pelisses*, some had *dolmans*, but no man had both, and very few had a *gilet*. The regiment's *dépôt* was captured by the allies on 5 January 1814, so we can say nothing else about the dress of the regiment.[308]

The regiment was disbanded at the end of the Hundred Days' campaign. The contents of the *dépôt* are recorded, as well as the loss of clothing and equipment during the campaign.

The *dépôt* of the 1e and 2e squadrons contained:[309]

129 *pelisses*
127 *gilet d'ecuries*
128 pairs of *pantalon*s in broadcloth
128 pairs of *pantalons* in linen
128 *manteaux*
128 *bonnets de police*
128 *schakos*

128 *porte-manteaux*
51 sabretaches in good condition, 39 new sabretaches, 70 needing repairs
134 sword knots
157 waistbelts
67 *gibernes* and belts
156 *banderole-porte-carabines*
129 pairs of boots
147 carbines
6 pistols
160 sabres
6 trumpets

The *pantalons* in broadcloth are shown in a print by Vernet as being dark grey, with leather reinforcement to the inner leg. *Dépôt* did indeed hold such a fabric! Vernet also shows the use of *schako rouleaux* and black leather work. Certainly, blackened cow hide had been purchased for the regiment's equipment during the First Restoration, so we can be sure that the unit had both these distinctions. The regiment had spent vast sums on clothing the men:[310]

102 saddles, bridles, *schabraques* and blankets. Total 13,566fr
Production of 67 sabretaches, *schakos*, *gibernes*, *porte-gibernes* waistbelts. Total 2,803fr 95
Production of new clothing. Total 5,022fr 90
Blackened cow hides and red Moroccan leather. Total 2,429fr 76
Lace and *passamenteries*. Total 1,579fr 50
Boot repairs. Total 4,446fr
Purchase of broadcloth, serge and linen. Total 5,985fr 10

The *dépôt* held the following materials:[311]

16m 33 *gris argentin* broadcloth
4m 20 grey-black broadcloth
0m 7 scarlet broadcloth
21m 80 green broadcloth for *manteaux*
0m 78 green tricot
24m 99 *treillis*
31m 22 linen
74 leather hides
222 dozen bone buttons
23m 20 white lace

Clearly by the end of the Empire the *manteaux* were once more green. Furthermore, we are left to wonder as to the use of the white lace. Was this for corporal's stripes? Not an inch of braid or lace to make *dolmans* and *pelisses* existed, nor any white broadcloth for *gilets*. Also standing out in the return is the presence of scarlet broadcloth: we assume a change in the regiment's facing colour occurred during the First Restoration, no doubt to create a contrast with the madder red lace on the cuffs of the *dolman*. Clearly by 1815 the regiment had taken on a very exotic look to previous years. At no stage does the regiment ever seem to have adopted Imperial Livery for the trumpeters. Indeed, we are left with no clues at all to their appearance from the archive sources.

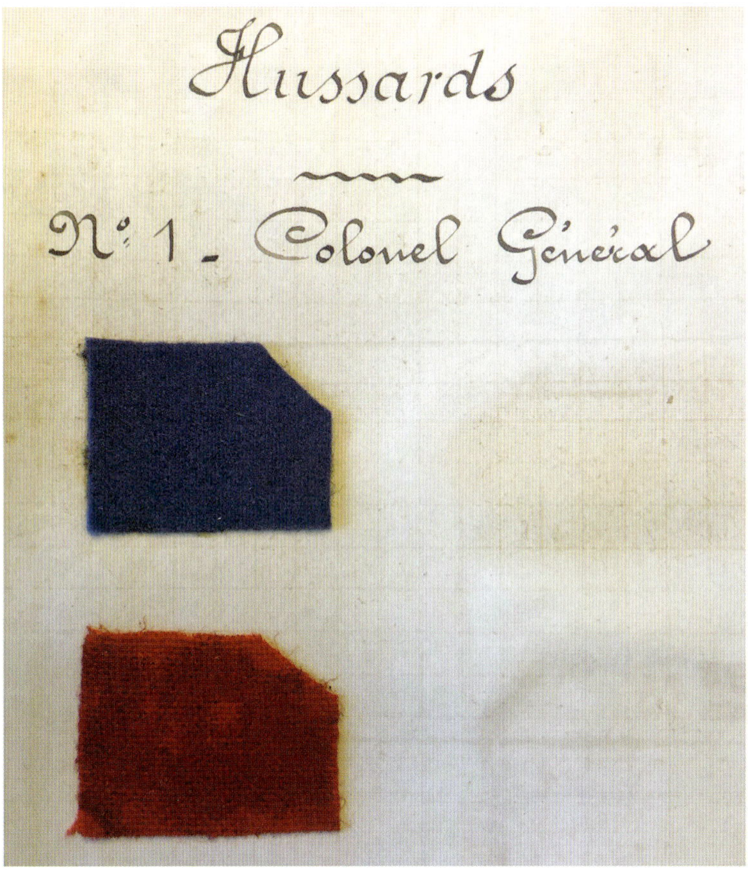

This cloth sample is dated 1791 has a surprise for students of the period: it shows that the *Hussar Colonel General* and the successor 4ᵉ *Hussar* had *bleu* celeste for the *dolman*, and *garance* for the *pelisse* and facings. The regiment only changed facings it seems as part of the Bardin regulation. (*A S K Brown Collection. Photograph R A Cooper*)

4^{e} *Hussar*

Created with the Royal Ordinance of 31 July 1783, the regiment became the 5^{e} *Hussar* in 1791, thence the 4^{e} *Hussar* with the decree of 4 June 1793 when the original 4^{e} *Hussar* of the *Hussards de Saxe* emigrated as a man. The regiment's archive is sporadic for inspection returns during the course of the Empire that can be located by the author. The 1805 and 1808 inspection returns are missing alas. One of the few documents that exists dates from 1814 and contains details of the regiment's clothing. Inspected in July 1814, the unit had the following items of clothing and equipment.[312]

Item	In Good Repair	In Need of Repair	Need Replacing	Total Needed	Items Needed
Pelisses	341	206	7		
Dolmans	147	100		7	
Gilets en drap blanc			Nil		
Gilet d'ecuries	349	55	62	75	13
Bonnets de police	494	40		20	
Pantalons à cheval en drap vert	345	69	41	68	31
Stable trousers	305	35	15	38	161
Schakos	488	27	39		
Manteaux	454	15			
Pompoms	488	27	39		
Waistbelts	554				
Gibernes	554				
Porte-gibernes	554				
Sabretaches	554				
Sword knots	213		331		
Barrel sashes	375				179
Pair of boots	473	79			2
Porte-carabines	549				
Sabres	554				
Pairs of pistols	469				
Carbines	549				
Bayonets			Nil		
Shirts	1,662				
Black stocks	552				
Pair of socks	445				
Pairs of shoes	522				

No man had the regulation white *gilet*, no man had *culottes hongroise*, and the regiment seemingly still had the old *manteaux* rather than the new *manteaux-capote*! Cloth in the *dépôt* was minimal and included 57m 79 blue broadcloth, 20m 77 scarlet broadcloth, 335m 88 tricot and 83m 30 of white flannel. Brand-new clothing in the *dépôt* included 2 *pelisses*, 97 *dolmans*, 3 *gilet d'ecuries*, 12 *bonnets de police*, 1 *manteau*, 33 pairs of *culottes hongroise* – all the examples the regiment possessed! – 19 pairs of *caleçon*, 16 white *gilet*s – again all that the regiment had – 3 barrel sashes and 16 pairs of boots. Clothing in good condition that could be issued to make up shortages comprised 50 *manteaux* and 50 *schakos* with 100 further examples needing repairs. *Dépôt* also held 152 waistbelts, 99 *gibernes*, 87 *porte-gibernes*, 80 *banderole-porte-carabines* and 99 sabretaches with

Elite company trooper painted by an eyewitness from the 2e *Hussar* in 1805. Of interest is the black sheepskin *schabraque*, but also the bright blue of the *pantalons à cheval*: proof that the 4e retained the *bleu celeste* of the *Hussar Colonel General.*

Found among Lucien Rousselot's papers is this evocative image of the 4e *Hussar* in Germany in 1809. Of interest the men are wearing *bleu celeste dolman* and *pantalons à cheval.* Rousselot states the image was painted in 1811.

Martinet gives us two troopers of the regiment. Firstly, Martinet shows a very dark blue in use with the regiment. Secondly, Martinet adds yellow cords to the *schako.* He suggests a black plume was commonly worn, which is shown by other period illustrations.

Rousselot's coloured copy of the Zimmerman manuscript: Rousselot states the image is dated to 1808. The yellow cords to the *schako* and no plate can be matched with Martinet, so too the dark blue hue of the uniform, but the colour shown is Rousselot's choice and not Zimmerman, so is likely not reliable. (*Collection KM*)

Officer of the elite company of the 4[e] *Hussar* in a print by Martinet.

Reconstruction of the 4e *Hussar* as they appeared in 1814–15. Both the elite and centre companies wore the same *schako*, which the regiment's archive tells us were distinguished solely by the colour of the pompom, and furthermore it reports that the *pantalons à cheval* were green. The records show *pelisses* were not worn on campaign it seems, nor the barrel sash, and not a single pair of stable trousers existed.

The regimental standing orders helps us to reconstruct the dress of the regiment. Up first is a *sapeur* of the 4e *Hussar* in 1811. The reconstruction is based on notes from the regiment's colonel found in the Bibliotheque Nationales in Paris. Secondly, is an elite company trooper reconstructed from the regimental colonel's orders. In a letter dated 15 September 1811, Colonel Christopher wrote:

> All my elite company are mounted on the most handsome black horses, with black schabraques … The men have for their headgear the Kolbaks [*sic*] with the red bag, copper grenades as well as eagles. When I pass them in Review, it is said that they have come out of a toy box of model soldiers.

He noted that the leather work was made from blackened cow hide that had been polished and waxed. We are at a loss as to where the eagles were worn. He makes no mention of sabretaches, so we have omitted them, although this may be an error on my part.

slings, all in good condition. A mix of whitened buff and blackened cow hide leather work was in use: black presumably with the elite company? We can say alas nothing about the dress of the trumpeters.[313]

When we delve into the regiment's accounts, we find that in the second quarter of 1813 224 pairs of *culottes hongroise* had been made, the tailoring costing 110 francs 63. The inspecting officer reported that they had been made from blue broadcloth and not green tricot, and had been fully lined in linen. The regiment was ordered to take them out of service and replace them with regulation green. Perhaps this explains the absence of *culottes*![314]

The regiment was disbanded at the end of 1815. The disbandment records add more details to the clothing of the regiment during the First Restoration and Hundred Days. Cloth purchased and used was as follows:[315]

	Broadcloth				Flannel	Treillis	Linen
	Blue	Green	Madder Red	Green Tricot			
In *dépôt* 16 July 1814	62m 43	2m 45	97m 77	426m 11	83m 30		129m 47
Purchased	1,290m 84	3,022m 20	425m 15	3,695m 68	1,825m	2,668m 99	3,592m 88
Total	1,353m 27	3,024m 65	522m 92	4,121m 79	1,908m 30	2,668m 99	3,723m 35
Amount used	1,348m 36	3,023m 32	522m 92	4,121m 42	918m 82	2,629m 92	3,723m 35
Total remaining	4m 91	1m 33	0m	0m 37	989m 48	39m 27	0m

The records for clothing production reveal that in January 1815 every single one of the regiment's barrel sashes, some 790 examples, were written off when the regiment was inspected, along with 16 *pelisses*, 308 *dolmans*, 123 *gilet d'ecuries*, 92 pairs of *pantalons à cheval*, 11 *gilets*, 343 *manteaux*, 391 *porte-manteaux*, 404 *schakos* and 82 *bonnets de police*! The inspector authorised the production of 222 *pelisses*, 225 *dolmans*, 255 *gilet d'ecuries*, 229 pairs of *pantalons à cheval,* 23 *gilets*, a mere 46 *manteaux*, just 18 *porte-manteaux*, 105 *schakos*, 87 *bonnets de police* and 67 barrel sashes.

With regard to clothing production and use, the regiment's archive reports that in total 649 *pelisses* were made, 1,221 *dolmans*, 1,119 pairs of *gilet d'ecuries*, 1,359 pairs of

Found among Rousselot's papers is this painting of an elite company trooper. The black *schabraque* we know to have been in use from 1805 – if not earlier – and the colpack from 1802. Interestingly, the trumpeter has whitened buff leather work, suggesting that the adoption of blackened cow hide took place after the image was painted. We present our reconstruction of the uniform before black leather work was adopted: we assume the same uniform was retained but with changes to the equipment. We furthermore assume the centre companies to be dressed the same, but with *schakos* that we show as tentative reconstruction.

pantalons à cheval, 34 white *gilets*, 1,030 *manteaux*, 997 *porte-manteaux*, 1,105 *schakos* and 1,205 *bonnets de police*. Not a single *pelisse* was used during the Hundred Days' campaign, but 50 were repaired. Huge quantities of kit were lost during the campaign: 172 *dolmans*, 54 *gilet d'ecuries*, 227 pairs of *pantalons à cheval*, 131 *manteaux*, 42 *porte-manteaux*, 109 *schakos* and 87 *bonnets de police* through men deserting the regiment or lost in action. At disbandment the *dépôt* held:[316]

Item	New	Good Condition	Need Repair	To be Replaced	Total
Pelisses	275	147			422
Dolmans	79	24		1	104
Gilet d'ecuries	92		9		101
Pantalons à cheval	16				16
Manteaux	106	95	43	41	285
Porte-Manteaux	145	35			180
Schakos	176	5	23		204
Bonnets de police	31				31
Barrel sashes		261	138		399
Sabretaches		260	130		390
Waistbelts		403	42		253
Gibernes		240	253		493
Porte-gibernes		444	104		548
Banderole-porte-carabines		368	113		481
Pair of boots	45				45

Not a single pair of stable trousers were in use, so we must imagine the *pantalons à cheval* were worn in every order of dress, and would have been incredibly dirty and smelly! The accounts list the use of 646m 80 of red and white worsted lace between July 1814 and 30 June 1815, as well as 461 *pelisse* cords, 13,303m 50 of yellow square worsted braid and 11,033m 28 of yellow worsted braid 13mm wide. As in 1814, a mix of whitened buff and blackened cow hide leather work was in use.[317]

5e *Hussar*

The regiment was raised in 1783 with the Ordonnance of 14 September from the cavalry of the *Legion de Lauzun*, which had been formed in 1778. The *Legion* had served in America and had recently returned when it was re-christened the *Hussards de Lauzun*. In 1791 it became the 6e *Hussar* and then in 1793 the 5e *Hussar* with the decree of 4 June. Dressed in white and *bleu de ciel* with yellow lace and trim, the uniform of the 5e *Hussar* was one of the most elegant of the epoch. General de Beaumont, notable for his act of treason during the Waterloo campaign that overshadowed his entire military

Martinet presents us with four different versions of the 5e *Hussar*. Up first is a plate that shows an embroidered sabretache, bearing a yellow eagle and a black No. 5. The *schako* has no plate but carries white, or perhaps even very light blue cords, that match the plume colour. Secondly, we have the same sabretache shown, but we know it has a brass binding to the *schako* peak, which now has an eagle on a plinth plate. Thirdly, we have an all-red sabretache with no device, but the *schako* now has no cords but a diamond plate: presumably 1808 or thereabouts. Lastly, is a trooper of the *Hussard d'Angoulême*. We can make out copper *fleur des lys schako* plate bellow the white cockade. The sabretache carries a No. 5.

Trooper of the 5e *Hussar*, winter to spring 1808, from the Otto Manuscript. (*Collection KM*)

An officer of the 5e *Hussar* in a print by Weiland issued in 1812. Of note, is the very dark shade of the *bleu de ciel*, which matches with known garments for the regiment. Contrary to Martinet, Weiland shows a black plume. (*Collection KM*)

Officer's undress *habit*, a sensible and practical replacement for the *dolman*. Of interest is the dark hue of the 'sky blue' used by the regiment. (*Musée de l'Empéri, Collections du Musée de l'armée, Anciennes collections Jean et Raoul Brunon*)

career, reviewed the regiment in summer 1803. The regiment's manoeuvres were good, the men overall rode well and cared well for their horses. Discipline in the regiment was good – in fact everything about the regiment met his satisfaction. The clothing in use was as follows:[318]

Item	In Good Repair	In Need of Repair	To be written off	Total	Total made since 1802	Observation
Barrel sashes	409	77	166	652	363	
Dolmans	131	80	298	509	114	
Pelisses	187	120	282	589	263	
Surtouts	57		1	58	57	
Manteaux	200	98	289	587	9	
Gilets	18			18	14	
Gilet d'ecuries	101	70	256	427	149	
Culottes hongroise	24	34	297	355	33	
Stable trousers	378	50	270	698	571	
Schakos	160	105	323	588	296	
Bonnets de police	222	32	390	644	233	
Caleçon			772	772		
Gloves			386	571		

Portrait of an unknown officer of the 5e *Hussar*. The black leatherwork suggests a late Empire date. (*Musée de l'Empéri, Collections du Musée de l'armée, Anciennes collections Jean et Raoul Brunon*)

We assume the *surtouts* were issued to trumpeters and *sous-officiers*, and may in reality be *habits* based on extant garments. From the returns of the *dépôt*, 860 black plumes existed in 1802, 386 were issued after this, making 1246 plumes delivered to the regiment, of which 860 were in use. *Dépôt* held 867m 17 blue broadcloth and 1m 75 white broadcloth. *Dépôt* also held 1,069m 36 serge, 26m 35 white tricot, 636m 27 white flannel and 1,960m 31 linen. The regiment was armed with 816 musketoons, of which 103 had been lost, 602 pairs of pistols and 878 sabres.[319] General Ney had inspected the regiment a year earlier, when he commented that the *surtouts* and *schakos* were 'all detestable' and the government was being slow in issuing new uniforms. The *manteaux* were clearly green as Ney notes 1,168m 66 of green broadcloth had been used to make 377 *manteaux*. Ney also records that 1,798m 48 of blue tricot had been employed to make 1,022 pairs of *culottes hongroise*.[320]

An officer of 5e *Hussar* wearing undress made from nankeen, set off with a *bleu de ciel confederakta* headdress. (*Musée de l'Empéri, Collections du Musée de l'armée, Anciennes collections Jean et Raoul Brunon*)

History has not been kind to the regimental archive of the 5e *Hussar*. There is a regrettable gap in the paper archive between 18 August 1803 and 7 June 1807, when the regiment was wearing:[321]

Item	In Good Repair	In Need of Repair	To be Replaced	Total	Observations
Dolmans	400	100	60	560	
Pelisses	200	201	190	591	
Gilet d'ecuries	500		159	659	
Culottes hongroise	The regiment has none				
Pantalons à cheval	500		159	659	
Stable trousers	The regiment has none				
Caleçon	659			659	
Manteaux	570	59	30	659	
Bonnets de police	500		159	659	
Schakos	114		440	554	
Colpacks	105			105	
Schako covers	The regiment has none				659 of each needed
Pompoms					
Plumes					

Clearly, the regiment had just one set of legwear for all duties. We know nothing more until 1814. Inspected on 11 August 1814, the regiment had the following clothing and equipment in use:[322]

Item	In Service, but Due to Expire in the Next Year	In need of Repair	To be Replaced in the Next Year	To be Replaced	Items Short	Observations
Dolmans	171	16	2			The effectives are 316 men.
Pelisses	108	5	47			
Gilets en drap blanc	151					
Gilet d'ecuries	59	5	40			
Culottes hongroise	15	2	3			
Caleçon	5	12				
Pantalons à cheval	60	35	12			
Stable trousers	71		4			
Manteaux	149	14	5			
Porte-manteaux	105	4	43			
Bonnets de police	54	10	32			
Schakos	160	18	32			
Sabretaches	194	35		10		

The bulk of the regiment's clothing was either in good condition or entirely missing. The regiment was primarily decked out in *pantalons à cheval,* with a mix of *culottes hongroise* and stable trousers having to be used to give every man some form of legwear. Not every man had a *dolman* or *pelisse*, we suspect, and these were mixed in with *gilet d'ecuries* to give every man an upper body garment. The regiment must have looked shocking! Of interest, the regiment had old-pattern *manteaux*. No barrel sashes were in use, ditto *schako* pompoms. The men were also issued 575 shirts – with another 234 in store, 116 black silk cravats, 35 pairs of linen ankle socks – with another 51 pairs in store, 95 pairs of woollen stockings and 68 pairs of linen pantalons.

The regiment had virtually nothing in the *dépôt* to make new clothing from, merely 1m 19 of white broadcloth, 72m 50 green broadcloth, 20m 18 white milled serge, 200 flat worsted braid, and 12m 6 red leather. Clothing in the *dépôt* included 1 *habit-veste*, 1 *surtout*, as well as 301 brand-new *dolmans*, accompanied by 381 *gilet d'ecuries*, 108 pairs of stable trousers, 320 sabre belts and 47 sabretaches.[323]

Disbanded in 1815, the regiment mustered 6 adjutants, 2 vets, 4 master workmen, 9 sergeant majors, 55 sergeants, 12 *fourriers*, 45 corporals, 14 trumpeters, 228 troopers and 2 children. They were wearing:[324]

195 *pelisses*
166 *dolmans*
337 white *gilets*
292 *gilet d'ecuries*
194 *pantalons à cheval*

Reconstruction of the sapeurs of the 5e *Hussar*.

The dress of the *sapeurs* is problematical. Our only reference comes from summer 1811. Our first image is tentative: Kolbe provides us with the dress of the trumpeters and also kettledrummers in 1810. Presumably if the regiment went to the expense of a kettledrummer and costly trumpeters' clothing, it would make sense that the *sapeurs* – assuming that they existed before summer 1811, and we cannot see why they would not despite the lack of any archive evidence to support our contention – would be dressed like the rest of the head of column.

Certainly by 1811, the *sapeurs*, like the trumpeters, were wearing totally different uniforms. We know from archive documents that the *sapeurs* wore a *dolman* and *pelisse*, but were missing their axe case and belts: we have assumed that they were dressed in the manner of trumpeters and wore a colpack. They may have been dressed as rank and file. We added a lance in both cases as period iconography shows *sapeurs* so armed in regiments of light cavalry. These reconstructions are 'best guesses' and should not be taken as hard fact.

171 stable trousers
44 *manteaux*
373 *bonnets de police*
320 *schakos*
19 *surtouts*

The *surtouts* were presumably for the master workmen, adjutants and perhaps senior *sous-officiers*, and a further 7 were in store, making 26 examples in total. In the *dépôt* we find 2 *habits* for the condemned, 206m 17 white broadcloth, 472m 82 *bleu celeste* broadcloth, 1m 28 green broadcloth, 4m 50 *rouge-garance* broadcloth, 139m 90 green tricot, 68m 19 linen, 201m 38 red Moroccan leather to line *dolmans*, 3,161m 28 square yellow worsted braid, and 6,853m 36 flat yellow worsted braid. Clothing in the *dépôt* included 8 *pelisses*, 8 *dolmans*, 30 *manteaux*, 120 sabre belts, 506 barrel sashes and 94 sabretaches.[325]

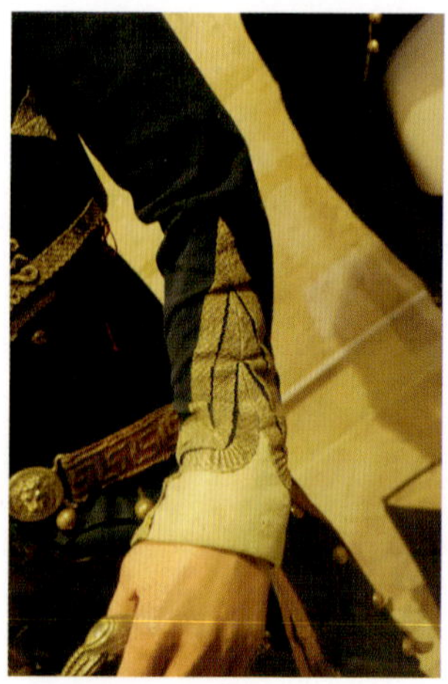

A gorgeous ensemble of an officer's uniform of the 5e *Hussar*, created by the Brunon brothers in the years before the Second World War. The legwear on the mannequin is not original, but was made to the Brunon's exacting standards to complement the original items. (*Musée de l'Empéri, Collections du Musée de l'armée, Anciennes collections Jean et Raoul Brunon*)

We present four tentative reconstructions of trumpeters.

Up first, a trumpeter wearing campaign dress taken from Rousselot's papers based on the Marckolsheim manuscript. Secondly, a trumpet major based on a naïve period portrait. It is possible that all trumpeters wore a *czapka* and also blue epaulettes. No other source presents this uniform. In both cases, an identical habit to that shown can be found in a private collection in France, so we can be sure that this representation has some degree of reliability to it.

Dressed in red, this striking uniform for the trumpeters of the 5e *Hussar* is reconstructed from a colour plate published by Wilhelm Kobel. Kobel also gives us the kettledrummer we show here. We have no archive sources to confirm or deny this uniform. However, interestingly for us, clothing in the depot in 1814 included a *habit-veste* and a *surtout* – these may well be trumpeters' items. The depot also held a single pair of crimson pantalons: were these for trumpeters or the elite company? We shall never know.

Lastly, a reconstruction of a centre company trumpeter of the 5e *Hussar* from the Elberfeld manuscript illustration of 1814.

We present four figures of the regiment from the last year of its existence.

Up first a reconstruction of a trooper of the 5ᵉ *Hussar* in late summer 1814. A crucial change to the appearance of the regiment came during the First Restoration. The inspector general who reviewed the regiment in summer 1814 informed the War Ministry in a letter dated 9 August:

> the white pelisse has proved very difficult to keep and get clean, and that according to many opinions 'sous tous les rapports' the pelisse are better made out of the same colour as the dolman.

At the same time, the inspector noted due to the high number of madder red *culottes hongroise* and *pantalons à cheval* inherited from the 8ᵉ *Hussar*, that rather than jettison these items into the trash, the 5ᵉ *Hussar* legwear should be changed to madder red. The War Ministry agreed in a reply dated 12 August. So clearly, legwear changed almost immediately.

Despite official sanction being granted in 1814 to remove the white *pelisse* from use, in May 1815 Colonel Liegeard complained to the War Ministry that this had not been done. He reported to the ministry that the *pelisses* were impossible to keep clean and added that the soldiers were constantly obliged to whiten and clean them. Furthermore, he informed the ministry that the regiment's clothing was far from uniform and the changes that had been demanded by the inspector in the previous year had not yet been fully carried out due to shortages of funds and cloth, and funds to buy materials so that the blue *pelisse* could be taken into universal use. Liegeard noted some blue *pelisses* were in use and made from *bleu de ciel*, a mid-blue broadcloth. However, we note the regiment's paperwork argues they were made from *bleu celeste* – is the difference in recording the eye of the beholder? Certainly, under Bardin the regiment had *bleu celeste* facings and not *bleu de ciel*. Had the 5ᵉ only changed its facing colour during the Hundred Days? Certainly, the regiment had been dressed in *bleu de ciel* up to the First Restoration. How far the changes were made to the regiment's *pelisse* and *dolman* colour is almost impossible to comment further without additional archive sources. We show a trooper with his garance *pantalons à cheval* and *bleu de ciel dolman* and *pelisse*, as Liegard envisioned.

Thirdly, is a reconstruction of a trumpeter based on the regiment's paper archive, assuming the orders of the Inspector General of Cavalry ordering the trumpeters into Royalist Livery was carried out. Lastly, a tentative reconstruction of a trumpeter during the Hundred Days. At disbandment, stores held trumpeters' lace, but we do know which pattern was held: it could be Royalist or Imperial pattern, and therefore these reconstructions are hypothetical and not hard fact.

6ᵉ *Hussar*

A fabulous officer's *dolman* for the 6ᵉ *Hussar*. (*Photograph and Collection of Bertrand Malvaux*)

The regiment was formed in 1792 from the *Hussards Defenseurs de la Liberté et de l'Egalite* as the 7ᵉ *Hussar* and renumbered 6ᵉ *Hussar* in June 1793. The regiment was clad in scarlet with imperial blue facings. The regiment's paperwork is fragmented and has very little about clothing and equipment. When reviewed in 1808 by General Pully, he tells us in his almost unintelligible scribble that the regiment had no colpacks for the elite company, the men were wearing *surtouts* [some 991 being in use with 811 white *gilets*] and needed 204 *schakos*,

An officer of the 6[e] *Hussar* in a period portrait. (*Photograph and Collection of Bertrand Malvaux*)

Officer of the elite company of the 6e in a print by Aaron Martinet.

57 pairs of boots, 161 sabretaches, 18 *gibernes*, 54 waistbelts, 208 *porte-carabines* and 197 *manteaux*. The *dépôt* held 445 pairs of *culottes hongroise*, 167 *vestes* in broadcloth, 20 *bonnets de police* and 50 *manteaux*.[326] It's interesting to note that on campaign the regiment had dispensed with traditional *hussar* clothing of *dolman* and *pelisse*.

We know nothing else until summer 1814, when the regiment had the following items:[327]

Item	New	In Good Repair	In Need of Repair	Need Replacing	Total Items
Pelisses	151	44	1	20	141
Dolmans	240	12		20	85
Gilets en drap blanc	183	4		4	166
Gilet d'ecuries	76	16		42	223
Stable trousers	6		4	10	337
Caleçon	54	11	2	40	250
Bonnets de police	227	5	12	12	101
Schakos	264	4		5	79
Pompoms	269			4	84
Manteaux	126	14		2	215

Martinet presents four different troopers of the regiment. The plumes are variously black-tipped red, or black with a red base, and *schako* cords are shown as yellow.

Item	New	In Good Repair	In Need of Repair	Need Replacing	Total Items
Pantalons à cheval	113	30	62	45	107
Pair of gloves	6				351
Braces	70	12	9	44	222
Schako covers					357
Sabretaches	143	41			173
Barrel sashes	259			5	93

Schako of Colonel Louis Vallin, 6[e] *Hussar*. Louis Vallin (16 August 1770 in Dormans–25 December 1854 in Paris) was named colonel of the 6[e] in 1807 and was promoted to general in 1812. He was involved on the Royalist side in the French intervention in Spain. His name is inscribed on the twelfth column on the Arc de Triomphe in Paris. He was a commander of the Order of Saint Louis and a grand officier of the Legion of Honour, as well as being made a baron under the First French Empire. (*Private collection Switzerland*)

Trooper of the 6e *Hussar* in an eyewitness drawing completed in 1815 by Lieutenant Bregeot of the 16e *Chasseurs à Cheval*. (*Collection KM*)

The regiment had no stocks of cloth in the *dépôt*, merely 2m 38 of *treillis* to make stable trousers. *Dépôt* held 62 white *gilets*, 93 pairs of *caleçon*, 195 pompoms, 439 pairs of gloves, 375 sets of braces, 133 *gibernes*, 152 *porte-gibernes*, 100 waistbelts, 203 sabretache, 245 sword knots and 123 pairs of boots. Overall, we learn very little about the dress of the regiment. The regiment was armed with 141 carbines, of which 11 needed repairs, 177 sabres, of which 21 needed repairs, and 107 pistols, 11 of which needed repairs. Remarkably, 194 *banderole-porte-carabines* were in used, all listed as good condition, with a further 5 needing repairs or to be replaced: were men on parade with the shoulder belt and no firearm? Clearly! We also note that 95 men had no *giberne* and belt, 174 had no sabretache, 93 men had no barrel sash and 127 no boots! Not a single pair of shoes was issued, so we must imagine the men without boots were wearing clogs or similar footwear like *espadrilles*. Despite this, 769 shirts were in use and 169 black stocks, and the bulk of the men had linen neckcloths.

The regiment was disbanded in 1815, when the *dépôt* held no stocks of materials. Clothing in the *dépôt* comprised 7 *pelisses* that were to be disposed of, 69 *dolmans*, 29 brand-new *gilets*, 19 brand-new *bonnets de police*, 72 *manteaux*, 31 *porte-manteaux*, 7 pairs of *culottes hongroise*, 135 pairs of under wear, 42 s*chakos* needing repairs, 20 brand-new sets of braces, 279 waistbelts, 247 sword knots, 442 *gibernes* with 434 belts, 371 *banderole-porte-carabines*, 351 sabretaches, 145 barrel sashes and 6 trumpets.[328] The paper archive says nothing about the elite company or trumpeters.

We present two uniform reconstructions. Firstly, a trooper of the 6ᵉ *Hussar* from the regiment's paper archive from 1814 and 1815. Secondly, an elite company trooper from notes by Lucien Rousselot from a naïve drawing dated August 1814. The cloth schabraque is unexpected.

We present an elite company trumpeter of the 6ᵉ *Hussar* in a naïve drawing dated August 1814. The *culotte de peau* and white colpack are most surprising! We know of no other depiction of a trumpeter that shows *culotte de peau* for any regiment of *hussars*. Rousselot, in his notes, presents a second trumpeter, wearing campaign dress in 1813 to 1814. Ostensibly similar to a dated naïve sketch of a trumpeter from 1814, it does seem to be the case that the trumpeters had white colpacks.

7[e] *Hussar*

Established as the 8[e] *Hussar* on 23 November 1792, the regiment became the 7[e] on 4 June 1793. The regiment's archive is sparse of records of clothing. Marbot's famed 7[e] *Hussar* was inspected by General Oudinot on 23 May 1803, when the clothing in use comprised:[329]

Item	In Good Repair	In Need of Repair	To be Written Off	Total	Total Made Since 24 May 1802	To be Replaced
Habits				6		
Dolmans	503	79	109	691	300	
Pelisses	492	110	44	646	89	
Surtouts	107	25	20	152	104	
Manteaux	210	97	119	426	1	
Gilets	649			649	592	
Gilet d'ecuries	379	74	247	700	379	
Culottes hongroise	430	101	140	671	246	
Stable trousers	201	83		269	201	
Chapeaux	16			16	16	
Schakos	384	78	124	586	129	
Bonnets de police	748			748	748	
Barrel sashes	261		142	403	Nil	
Porte-manteaux	464	109	83	660	174	

Clothing in the *dépôt* comprised:[330]

Item	In *Dépôt* 1802	Purchased Since 1802	Total	Amount Used	Remaining in *Dépôt*	Issued New
Dolmans		300	300			300
Pelisses		89	89			89
Surtouts		104	104			104
Manteaux		1	1			1
Red *gilets*		592	592			592
Gilet d'ecuries		379	379			379
Culottes hongroise		246	246			246
Stable trousers		201	201			201
Chapeaux		17	17			17
Schakos	1					1
Bonnets de police		766	766			766
Porte-manteaux	1	173	174			174
Sabretaches	1	160	161			161

Martinet presents four troopers of the 7e *Hussar*. It is hard to place them in chronological sequence: presumably the lack of *schako* cords marks out later Empire illustrations?

Schako of the 7[e] *Hussar* complete with original cords. (*Private collection Switzerland*)

General Oudinot authorised the production of 182 new *dolmans* and *pelisses*, 81 *manteaux*, 365 *surtouts*, 162 white *gilets*, 731 pairs of *culottes hongroise*, 731 pairs of stable trousers, 122 *schakos*, 365 *bonnets de police*, 122 sabretaches and 122 barrel sashes. The *chapeaux* were presumably worn by adjutants when wearing the undress *surtout*.

When inspected on 27 July 1805 the clothing in use comprised:[331]

Item	In Good Repair	In Need of Repair	To be Written Off	Total	Total Made Since 23 May 1803	To be Replaced
Habits	Nil					
Dolmans	513	156	139	808	17	
Pelisses	515	56	229	808	4	
Surtouts	702		106	808	585	
Manteaux	263	94	441	808	51	
Gilets	543	150	107	808	4	
Smocks	367	140		507	207	
Gilet d'ecuries			386	386		
Culottes hongroise	525	42	240	868	525	
Stable trousers	449		359	808	277	
Barrel sashes	423		385	808	72	
Schakos a poil	64			64		
Schakos	761		56	817	70	
Bonnets de police	472	340		812	518	
Waistbelts	762		46	808	14	
Gibernes	690		118	808		

Item	In Good Repair	In Need of Repair	To be Written Off	Total	Total Made Since 23 May 1803	To be Replaced
Porte-gibernes	632		176	808		
Musket slings	88		88	88		
Porte-manteaux	401		407	808	1	
Boots	300		508	808	27	
Sabretaches	481		300	781	8	

We present four reconstructions drawn from differing sources. Firstly, a reconstruction of a trooper of the 7e *Hussar* in summer 1814 from the regiment's paper archive. Secondly, a reconstruction of the 7e *Hussar* based on the regiment's paper archive for 1815. Thirdly, is a tentative reconstruction of a trumpeter based on an original *dolman* housed in the Musée de l'Armée. Lastly, is an elite company trumpeter from Rousselot's notes citing the Marckolsheim manuscript.

Clothing in the *dépôt* comprised:[332]

Item	In *Dépôt* 1803	Purchased Since 1803	Total	Amount Used	Remaining in *Dépôt*	Issued New
Dolmans		300	300			300
Pelisses		89	89			89
Surtouts		104	104			104
Manteaux		1	1			1
Red *gilets*		592	592			592
Gilet d'ecuries		379	379			379
Culottes hongroise		246	246			246
Stable trousers		201	201			201
Chapeaux		17	17			17
Schakos	1					1
Bonnets de police		766	766			766
Porte-manteaux	1	173	174			174
Sabretaches	1	160	161			161

The *chapeaux* were for the adjutants, we assume, and perhaps also senior *sous-officiers*: the trumpet-major and such like. Given the amount of clothing to be written off as life expired, it is odd to find not a single scrap of clothing in the *dépôt*. What the men were wearing was literally everything the regiment possessed as it marched to war.

Reviewed on 7 June 1807, the regiment was wearing:[333]

Item	In Good Repair	In Need of Repair	To be Replaced	Total	Observations
Dolmans	The regiment has none				
Surtouts	678				
Gilets en drap blanc	678				
Gilet d'ecuries	678				
Culottes hongroise	649				
Pantalons à cheval	678				
Stable trousers					
Caleçon	The regiment has none				
Manteaux	608				
Bonnets de police	678				
Schakos	578				
Colpacks	100				
Schako covers					
Pompoms	The regiment has none				
Plumes					

Clearly, the men were all in *kinski* and traditional *hussar* rig had been lost during the 1805 campaign and not replaced. The 7e *Hussar* were inspected again on 13 January 1808. The inspection showed most of the clothing was missing or had to be replaced:[334]

Item	In Good Repair	In Need of Repair	To be Written Off	Total	Total Made Since 1805	Comment
Habit	Nil					
Dolmans	141		69	210	843	Since the last review, a portion of the new items of clothing and equipment has been sent out to the War squadrons as replacement items for those lost during the campaign of Austria … We are ignorant of the losses of clothing and equipment sustained during the last campaign [i.e. 1807]
Pelisses	664	87	60	811	1,063	
Surtouts	700		200	900	740	
Manteaux	636		50	686	558	
Gilets	617		150	767	576	
Gilet d'ecuries	The regiment has none					
Smocks						
Culottes hongroise	722		192	914	1,416	
Stable trousers in broadcloth	344			344	216	
Barrel sashes	379		100	479	293	
Kolpacks	91			91	29	
Schakos	573		200	773	292	
Bonnets de police	887			887	649	
Sabretaches	571			571	415	
Pairs of boots	1569			1569	294	

The *dépôt* held 492 new *dolmans* and 50 *gilet*s. Between 1804 and 1808 1,323 *dolmans* had been made, of which 843 had been issued, but due no doubt to the regiment being away from France since 1805, the replacements had languished in *dépôt* as the *dolmans* wore out. Likewise, 571 braided *gilets* had been made in the same period, all bar one being issued and this remained in *dépôt* with 49 old *gilets.* A similar story exists concerning barrel sashes. Some 148 were in *dépôt* in 1805, a further 149 had been made, some 297 items, all bar two being issued. It is clear therefore that, as with the *gilet*s, not every man was entitled to these for whatever reason. Two types of stable trousers existed: 772 pairs of regulation stable trousers had been made in durable treillis and 216 pairs in broadcloth, reinforced in the inner leg in black leather. We also note 18 smocks in linen and 517 made from twill linen mix. Given the huge shortfall of *dolmans*, the *pelisse* was the only garment the men had overall. Not a single *gilet* existed to be worn under the *dolman* or *pelisse.* Indeed, the reviewing inspector noted that the regiment needed as matter of urgency some 950 *dolmans*, 950 *pelisses*, 111 *manteaux*, 500 *surtouts*, 250 *gilets*, 800 *gilet d'ecuries*, 21 colpacks, 219 *schakos* with cords and plumes and 500 *bonnets de police.* The inspection return also lists surprises for us. Among the list of cloth, which includes the expected green, white and scarlet broadcloth, green tricot, green serge, we find 8m 50 of rose, i.e., pink, broadcloth. The amount of cloth used strongly indicates that the rose broadcloth was the facing cloth for, we assume, trumpeters' clothing. Green – or even scarlet – and pink would have been a challenging combination of colours. We have insufficient information to recreate this uniform. The white broadcloth was clearly destined for the regulation *gilet.*[335]

We know nothing else until the regiment was inspected 2 September 1814, when it was reduced to 210 others ranks, 14 officers and 9 *enfant de troupe*. The clothing was as follows:[336]

Item	In Good Repair	In Need of Repair	Need Replacing in 1 Year	To be Replaced	Items Needed
Pelisses	127	31	6	5	33
Dolmans	136	63	1		7
Gilets en drap banc					187
Gilet d'ecuries	125	17	5		23
Bonnets de police	150	20	5	2	30
Manteaux-capote	150	32		7	9
Culottes hongroise	133	32	11	4	7
Pantalons à cheval	120	56	8	4	9
Stable trousers					187
Caleçon	141	5		2	37
Schakos and pompoms	170	8		1	8
Gibernes	170	8		1	8
Porte-gibernes	170	8		1	8
Banderole-porte-carabines	131	1			7
Sabre belts	172	5		1	9
Sword knots	170	4		1	12
Pair of gloves	33			26	128
Barrel sashes	169	7		1	50
Sabretaches	169	8		1	9

Armament wise, the regiment had 137 carbines, 169 sabres and 106 pistols – not enough to give every man a sabre, pistol and carbine that needed them. The *dépôt* held some brand-new clothing, which included 113 *pelisses*, 177 *dolmans*, 62 *gilets*, 127 pairs of *culottes hongroise* and 10 *capotes-manteaux*. Equipment included 70 *schakos* with covers, 125 *gibernes* with belts, 105 sabre belts and 125 *banderole-porte-carabines*. No cloth was held at all in the *dépôt.*[337] We have been unable to locate any disbandment paperwork for the regiment.

8e *Hussar*

Martinet presents four troopers of the 8e *Hussar*, all with subtle differences, the most notable being the presence of *schako* cords, and the change to a scarlet *schako*, presumably at the end of the Empire.

Three period images show the 8e *Hussar* at the end of the Empire. Up first is a data sketch from 1814, which shows a scarlet *schako*, as does Martinet. Secondly, we have an elite company trooper with his colpack and scarlet *pantalons à cheval*, which we know from archive sources the regiment did indeed possess. Our third image dates from *c.*1817 in gouache painting by an officer of the 10e *Dragons* from the mid-1820s. The officer was a veteran of the First Empire, so his paintings are based on what he remembers, and therefore may not be totally accurate. (*Collection KM*)

Created as the *régiment des éclaireurs de Fabrefonds* by Colonel Joseph Fabrefonds on 23 November 1792, it became the 9e *Hussar* on 26 February 1793, and the 8e only a matter of weeks later on 4 June. The regiment's paper archive concerning the dress of the regiment is sparse. One document that does exist gives a list of the clothing and equipment lost when the *dépôt* at Vilna was captured, as well as losses made during the retreat from Leipzig:[338]

> 249 *pelisses*, 417 *dolmans*, 250 *gilets*, 430 pairs *culottes hongroise*, 457 *gilet d'ecuries*, 140 barrel sashes, 390 pairs of *caleçon*, 560 pairs of stable trousers, 314 pairs *pantalons à cheval*, 132 *gibernes* with belts and *banderole-porte-carabines*, 217 waistbelts and sword knots, 191 *porte-manteaux*, 130 pairs of boots, 217 sabretaches.

Trooper's sabretache of the 8e *Hussar.* The dark green edging is shown by Martinet as adorning both the *culottes hongroise* and sabretache. This extant item confirms Martinet's observations. (*Musée de l'Empéri, Collections du Musée de l'armée, Anciennes collections Jean et Raoul Brunon*)

Oddly no headgear is listed, no saddles, no weapons! We assume the men still had these.

Nothing else is known until the regiment was inspected on 1 August 1814. By this date, the regiment was reduced to a mere 258 other ranks and

26 officers. The regiment was broken up between the 3^{e}, 5^{e} and 6^{e} *Hussar*. Clothing in use with 1^{e} and 2^{e} squadron was as follows:[339]

Item	In Service, but Due to Expire in the Next Year	In Need of Repair	To be Replaced in the Next Year	To be Replaced	Items Short	Observations
Pelisses	187	13				
Dolmans	181					
Red broadcloth *pantalons*	204	17				
Linen *pantalons*	68	17				
Gilet d'ecuries	207	17				
Bonnets de police	175					
Schakos	192					
Manteaux	224					
Gilets	200	20				
Caleçon			None			
Barrel sashes	186					
Sabretaches	175					
Waistbelts	186	1				
Sword knot	186					
Gibernes and belts	186					
Porte-manteaux	207					
Banderole-Porte Carabine	149					
Pairs of boots	182	25				

In addition, 199 pairs of linen overalls, 119 shirts, and 199 black stocks were in use, along with 174 black cravats! Remarkably the regiment's *culottes hongroise* were made from red broadcloth, as were the *pantalons à cheval* – in theory they were to be made from green tricot according to the Bardin regulations! Based on an original sabretache for the regiment, as well as a coloured print by Aaron Martinet, it seems the regiment adopted green lace rather than white for the *culottes hongroise* and red and green braid and lace for *dolmans* and *pelisses*.

Furthermore, the *dépôt* of the 1e and 2e squadron was sent to the 3e *Hussar* and included a lot of brand-new clothing, including 50 *pelisses*, 1,109 *dolmans*, 30 pairs of *culottes hongroise*, 47 *schakos*, 191 *gilets*, 170 pairs of *pantalons à cheval* and 216 *manteaux* – clearly described as such rather than *manteaux-capote*! Also, transferred from the *dépôt* were brand-new and unissued 432 barrel sashes, 377 *gibernes*, 365 *porte-gibernes*, 439 *banderole-porte-carabines*, 301 waistbelts and 25 *porte-manteaux*. Cloth in the *dépôt* included 28m scarlet broadcloth, 1,709m 54 green broadcloth and 174m 40 tricot.[340]

We present four uniform reconstructions. Up first is a trooper as they appeared in summer 1814, according to the regiment's paper archive. Secondly, an elite company trooper at the end of the Empire. The sabretache is based on a known example housed in the collections of the *Musée de l'Armée*. Lastly, we present reconstructions of trumpeters based on notes by Ernest Fort. On the left we have an elite company trumpeter and the right a centre company trumpeter in 1814 from a now lost eyewitness sketch held in the long-dispersed Cottereau collection.

The 5e *Hussar* inherited from the *dépôt* 62 *pelisses*, 62 *dolmans*, 64 sc*hakos*, 63 pairs of *pantalons à cheval*, 54 *bonnets de police*, 61 *gilet d'ecuries*, 60 *manteaux-capote* and 67 barrel sashes – all in good condition but they could not be used by the 5e *Hussar*.[341] Alas, we learn nothing about the elite company or trumpeters from the regiment's paper archive.

9ᵉ *Hussar*

Martinet presents four different plates for the 9ᵉ *Hussar*. Each has subtle differences, primarily concerning the sabretache, *schako* plate and cords.

Reconstruction of the elite company of the 9ᵉ *Hussar* from the regiment's archive. We have shown a darker shade of sky blue than many would expect: the regiment's archive is clear that between 1805 and 1808 4,199m of dark celestial blue broadcloth was used: therefore, the regiment's facings were much darker than have been heretofore understood. In the centre is a corporal and on the right is an NCO. We remark that the regiment's archive reports that the *pelisses* of different ranks carried differing trim: when reviewed on 19 March 1802 the regiment listed *pelisse* trim in white sheepskin, black sheepskin and fox fur. When inspected on 20 October 1804 we find 154 black sheepskin boarders for troopers, 15 grey fox fur trim for NCO *pelisses*, and white sheepskin trim for corporals and trumpeters *pelisses* had been used since March 1802. On 19 January 1808 we again find 503 black sheepskins for troopers' pelisses had been used since 1804, 500 white sheepskins for trumpeters and corporals – we also assume for the *schabraques*! – and 40 grey fox fur trims for NCOs' *pelisses*. We assume this custom continued to the end of the Empire.

Incredibly well-preserved *dolman* for a trooper of the 9ᵉ *Hussar*. (*Private Collection Australia*)

Formed on 2 September 1792 as the *Hussards de la Liberté*, the 2e squadron became the cadre of the 10e *Hussar* on 25 March 1793. On 1 May 1794 the first squadron of the *Hussards de la Liberté* became the 7e *régiment bis de hussars*. The 10e was renumbered as 9e on 4 June 1794. Dressed in scarlet *dolmans* with yellow lace and braid, and *bleu celeste pelisses* and *culottes hongroise*, the 9e was one of the most picturesque regiments of *hussars*. One of the earliest documents we have for the dress of the regiment is dated 9 June 1803. We note the regiment had 624 *dolmans*, 620 *pelisses*, 581 *surtouts*, just 102 barrel sashes, as well as 559 *schakos* with cords. *Dépôt* held yellow basane leather for lining trumpeters' *dolmans* and also red basane leather for lining troopers' *dolmans*. The elite company had 64 colpacks and one was left in *dépôt*.[342]

Inspected on 5 September 1805, the elite company had 100 colpacks, and 629 *schakos* with cords were in use. In addition, 691 *dolmans* were in use, 685 *pelisses*, 343 *surtouts* and 348 barrel sashes – not enough for every man to have one – of which 178 were newly issued, and 680 sabretaches.[343]

Reviewed on 19 February 1808, the regiment had 1,423 *schakos* with cords and plumes, 1,247 *dolmans*, 1,213 *pelisses*, 534 *surtouts*, 1,099 green *manteaux,* 124 colpacks, 1,095 sabre

Three almost contemporary illustrations show the dress of the trumpeters.

Up first, an eyewitness sketch made in 1814 from the Elberfeld manuscript. The regimental archive at no stage presents the use of yellow broadcloth for trumpeters clothing: however, every single representation of a trumpeter from the epoch shows the trumpeters wore yellow *pelisses*, one of which can be found in the *Musée de l'Armée*. Quite why the yellow broadcloth does not appear in regimental accounts, or for that matter colpacks, we cannot adequately answer. Despite the lack of archive corroboration, we cannot dismiss period iconography.

Secondly, a trumpeter of the elite company of the 9e *Hussar* by Major Jolly. The black fur trim to the *pelisse* is matched by the Elberfeld and Marckolsheim manuscripts. Lastly, a trumpeter of the elite company of the 9e *Hussar* observed in summer 1813 by Sauerweid. Nothing in the regiment's archive supports a cloth *schabraque*, but the white fur trim to the pelisse is recorded in the 1803 and 1808 inspections. The use of a trooper's *dolman* is unexpected, or maybe due to shortages of 1813–14 they were used out of necessity or maybe on campaign only, keeping the yellow *dolman* for parade? We assume the white colpacks were in fact sheepskin rather than bear pelt. Exactly the same uniform is shown in notes made by Rousselot from items in the Vanson collection, but with a black sheepskin *schabraque*. (*Collection KM*)

We present four more images of trumpeters.

Up first a centre company trumpeter *c.*1806 based on a lost coloured sketch in the Cottereau collection, copied by the early nineteenth-century artist JOB. Secondly, a reconstruction of a trumpeter of the elite company of the 9e *Hussar* from an original watercolour dated to 1812. Formerly held in the Cottereau collection, it passed to the historian Gembrazewksi.A copy can be found in the collections of the *Musée de l'Armée*. Of note is the high degree of synchronicity with the Sauerweid illustration. The *schabraque* is the same, as are many other details. The *dolman* cuffs and collar are shown as red: we suppose they should be blue, which supports the contention that the trumpeters wore troopers' *dolmans* in 1812 and 1813.

Thirdly, a trumpeter of the 9e *Hussar* from the notes of Rousselot concerning the Marckolsheim manuscript. The similarity in dress between this image and the Elberfeld manuscript is striking, dated to 1813.

knots and 140 barrel sashes, which were clearly reserved it seems for the elite company and trumpeters, or maybe just the *sous-officiers*. In addition, 880 sabretaches were in use, almost one for each man, and importantly, we find that the clothing of the regiment was made from dark celestial blue broadcloth and not the light shade of blue re-enactors and artists show. Rather than the regulation stock, black linen cravats were used.[344]

We present three more images of the regiment created in the period or shortly after. Firstly, the Dresden manuscript image of an elite company trooper of the 9e *Hussar* in summer 1813 by Alexandre Saurweid, Secondly, a centre company trooper from a dated eyewitness sketch by Lieutenant Bregeot of the 16e *Chasseurs à Cheval*. Lastly, an elite company trooper at the end of the Empire, rendered by an officer of the 10e *Dragons* just after the Second Restoration. If the image is reliable, it shows that the elite company took back the sheepskin schabraque. (*Collection KM*)

One of the few documents we have concerns the 4e and 5e squadrons, from when some 13 officers and 481 men with just 44 horses were reviewed on 29 May 1813. The inspecting officer noted that virtually everything was missing – no man had been clothed or equipped, and the regiment's Administrative Council had issued contracts to have the clothing and equipment made. No man had a sabre, let alone carbine or pistol. The men did have a pair of shoes, underpants, linen overalls, a shirt, stock, night cap, but were wearing whatever clothing they had arrived with from 'civvy street'.[345]

Clothing in use with the 9e *Hussar* at the end of the 1814 campaign comprised:[346]

Item	In Service, but Due to Expire in the Next Year	In Need of Repair	To be Replaced in the Next Year	To be Replaced	Items Short	Observations
Pelisse	36	35	17	51	233	The effectives are 572 men.
Dolmans	78	43	20	62	369	
Gilest en drap blanc	37	21	6	58	450	
Culottes hongroise	69	28	2	3	440	
Stable trousers	16	2	9	34	511	
Caleçon					572	
Bonnets de police	73	23	3	101	372	
Schakos	175	22	21	6	348	
Pompom					572	
Manteaux	80	12	7	20	453	
Pairs of gauntlets					572	
Braces					572	
Schako covers					572	

The vast majority of the clothing was either missing or needed to be replaced. The regiment was in deplorable condition by the time it was disbanded. We can say distressingly little from the return. The following items of equipment were in use at the date of disbandment:[347]

Item	In Service, but Due to Expire in the Next Year	In Need of Repair	To be Replaced in the Next Year	To be Replaced	Items Short	Observations
Gibernes	281	9		13	269	The effective is 572 men.
Porte-gibernes	281	9		13	269	
Banderole-porte-carabines	236	10		13	313	
Sabre belts	202	2			468	
Sabretaches	98	1			473	
Sword knots	20				552	
Barrel sashes	44	28	13	127	360	
Pairs of boots	44	28	13	127	360	

The men were issued 802 shirts and just 36 regulation black stocks. The *dépôt* held no clothing or equipment of any kind whatsoever, and stocks of material was minimal: 6m 87 of *bleu celeste* broadcloth, 1m 3 green broadcloth, 54m 10 white serge, 359m 85 worsted lace 30mm and 228m worsted lace 22mm wide.[348] The 9e were in shambolic condition at the end of the 1814 campaign. Thankfully, several *dolmans* for the regiment exist, as well as undoubted contemporary images by Aaron Martinet and Major Jolly of the 6e *Lanciers*, which allow us to reconstruct the dress of the regiment.

10e *Hussar*

The 10e *Hussar* had been formed in 1793 from the '*Hussard Noirs*', otherwise known as the '*Hussards de la Mort*', organised in the *Département du Nord* as a free corp.

The regiment was dressed in light blue and scarlet with white lace. Many writers state that the *pelisse* and *dolman* were '*bleu celeste*', whereas it seems in reality they were '*gris*

These six images by Martinet show subtle differences concerning the colours of the barrel sash, the type of *schako* plate and presence of cords, as well as the plume colour.

A trooper of the 10e *Hussar* as rendered by Weiland sometime between 1808 and 1812. Secondly, an elite company trooper of the 10e in the middle years of the Empire by Martinet. The red *schabraque* is not shown by other period images, but their use can be demonstrated in other regiments. Lastly, an elite company trooper depicted in gouache painting by an officer of the 10e *Dragons* from the mid-1820s. The officer was a veteran of the First Empire, so his paintings are based on what he remembers, and therefore may not be totally accurate. (*Collection KM*)

argentin', which was a melange cloth very much a light blue in hue. On 13 March 1802 the regiment's *dépôt* had used 352m 68 of blue broadcloth but held none, and held 86m 78 scarlet broadcloth, 366m 83 green broadcloth for *manteaux*, some 37m 34 *gris argentin* broadcloth, 16m 44 red tricot, 8m 14 milled serge, 275m 19 wool flannel, 1,419m 10 blue tricot, 368m 86 red leather, 2,295m flat white worsted braid, 5,880m white worsted square braid, and remarkably 324 plumes! Clearly the regiment used blue – presumably *blue de celeste*? – and *gris argentin* side by side. The small amount of *gris argentin*, 13m used in eighteen months, imply this was for facings only – trumpeters? Or all ranks? The use of just 2m 70 of red tricot suggests this was used for trumpeters or elite company pantalons, which in theory were to be *bleu celeste*, of which 169m 90 had been used, yet only 4 pairs of *culottes hongroise* had been made and 13 *porte-manteaux*, which were also made from tricot. It is arguable that the four pairs of *culottes hongroise* were made from the red tricot and were destined for trumpeters. If so, what colour were the trumpeter's *dolman* and *pelisse*? Scarlet-faced *gris argentin* or the opposite? Arguably, *gris argentin* with scarlet facings, worn with scarlet *culottes hongroise*. A remarkable ensemble.[349] When we look at the inspection return of 4 August 1803, not an inch of *gris argentin* or scarlet cloth is in *dépôt*! The report reveals the regiment had 401 *dolmans* in use and had been issued 535 since 1802, not a single *pelisse* existed, and 54 *surtouts* had been issued. Some 168 brand-new *pelisses* were in *dépôt*, and 3,369 had been issued, so we wonder where they were that day in 1803![350] Rolling forward two years on 8 August 1805, we once again find scarlet broadcloth in use and in the *dépôt*: 1,177m 55 of *bleu celeste* broadcloth being used, 420m 74 green broadcloth for *manteaux* and 191m 57 scarlet broadcloth being used in the 1803 to 1805 period. The regiment had 566 *dolmans*, 529 *pelisses* and 59 *surtouts* in use, accompanied by 509 green *manteaux*, 557 *gilet*s, 647 *gilet d'ecuries*, 629 pairs of *culottes hongroise* and 528 pairs of stable trousers. The elite company had 96 colpacks and the remainder of the regiment wore *schakos*. The colpacks were clearly an innovation after 1803. The *dépôt* held 68 new *dolmans*, 178 having been repaired, while 93 *pelisses* were in *dépôt* and 168 had been repaired. Brand-new and ready to be issued clothing included 1 *surtout*, 39 *gilets*, 206 *manteaux*, 31 *gilet d'ecuries*, 68 pairs of *culottes hongroise*, 107 pairs of stable trousers and 155 *bonnets de police*.[351]

The regiment was next inspected in January 1808:[352]

Item	In Good Repair	In Need of Repair	To be Written Off	Total	Total Made Since 8 August 1805	Comment
Habits				Nil		
Dolmans	790			790	731	Since the last review, a portion of the new items of clothing and equipment has been sent out to the War squadrons as replacement items for those lost during the campaign of Austria ... We are ignorant of the losses of clothing and equipment sustained during the last campaign [i.e. 1807]
Pelisses	820			820	927	
Surtouts	20		20	40	76	
Manteaux	564			564	633	
Gilets	781			781	569	
Gilet d'ecuries	567		200	767	1,026	
Culottes hongroise	798			798	1,463	
Stable trousers	541		200	741	1,112	
Colpacks	56			56		
Schakos	858			858	652	
Bonnets de police	720			720	860	
Waistbelts	895			895	659	
Gibernes	781		200	981	504	
Porte-gibernes	781		200	981	504	
Porte-carabines			Nil			
Porte-manteaux	743			743	860	
Boots	779			775	886	
Plumes			Nil			
Sabretaches	759			759	669	
Barrel sashes						

In the preceding two years 6,072m 11 of *bleu celeste* broadcloth had been used, 2,222m 87 green broadcloth, 938m 74 scarlet broadcloth, used to make 814 *dolmans*, 1,458 *pelisses*, 78 *surtouts*, 657 *manteaux*, 800 *gilets*, 1,120 *gilet d'ecuries*, 1,618 pairs of *culottes hongroise* – clearly the trumpeters no longer had scarlet *culottes* and the *gris argentin* clothing had disappeared by 1803. *Dépôt* held 141 new *pelisses* and *dolmans*, 58 *manteaux*, 457 *gilets*, 119 *gilet d'ecuries*, 213 pairs of *culottes hongroise*, 169 pairs of stable trousers and 116 *bonnets de police*. No colpacks were in *dépôt* and none had been obtained, so those in use clearly dated from 1803, and must have been rather shabby by 1808! Despite having not a single *banderole-porte-mousqueton*, the regiment had 984 *mousquetons* and 910 bayonets! We are baffled as to how the firearms were carried![353]

Regimental accounts furthermore report that during the course of 1808, 848m 30 blue broadcloth was purchased, 306m 80 red broadcloth, 3,000m squared worsted braid and 1,500m flat worsted braid was purchased for the total sum of 12,646 francs. The cloth was used to make 264 *gilet*s and 892 pairs of pantalons – clearly the *gilet*s had braid on them, and the *culottes hongroise* were made from broadcloth and not the regulation tricot! Each pair of *culottes* required 4m 50 of flat worsted braid. The report also states the stable trousers were made from broadcloth, lined in linen, with buttons on the outside leg and the inner leg reinforced with leather, which was 'highly irregular' and not according to the regulation – clearly the regiment adopted *pantalons à cheval* strictly against regulation as early as 1808, four years before they were officially sanctioned.[354]

Nothing else is known until the regiment was disbanded in summer 1814. The remaining men under arms were sent to the 2e and 3e *Hussar*. The clothing of the regiment in summer 1814 was as follows:[355]

Item	Good Condition	In Need of Repair	Need Replacing	To be Replaced	Items Need
Pelisses	184	88	53	42	
Dolmans	291	13	8	4	
Gilets en drap blanc	123	22	18	19	88
Gilet d'ecuries	180	59	6	7	22
Culottes hongroise	139	16	13	8	99
Pantalons à cheval	139	46	16	36	38
Bonnets de police	205		14		56
Manteaux-capote	240	65	17	39	
Schakos	269	15	4	2	
Pantalons du Treillis	8	27	41		204
Caleçon	109		37		139
Gibernes	207	82		2	
Porte-gibernes	292				
Banderole-porte-carabines	202	8			10
Waistbelts	291	13		2	
Sword knots	218				57
Sabretaches	225	65	2		
Barrel sashes	217				58
Gloves	38				207
Pompoms	104				171
Pairs of boots	108	76	23	4	64

We present three uniform reconstructions for the 10^{e} *Hussar*. Up first is a trooper based on the regiment's archive from the time of disbandment in 1814.

Secondly, we present a reconstruction of a trumpeter as they appeared in 1814. The regimental archive of the 10^{e} informs us that in summer 1814 it held 187m green broadcloth, 120m of trumpeters' livery, 0m 20 of green leather ready to be cut out and 0m 55 of cut-out green leather: presumably this was destined to line trumpeters' *dolmans*. The 10^{e} *Hussar* are the only regiment to have used beyond reasonable doubt Imperial Livery. Lastly, a reconstruction of an elite company trooper based on the 1808 inspection return. We assume such a uniform remained in use until 1813.

In addition, the inspector noted, the regiment had 11 instruments – are these trumpets or are they band instruments? If the latter, this is the only evidence of a *hussar* regiment actually having a band beyond some iconographic sources. Clothing sent to the 2e *Hussar* comprised kit ready to be 'dumped in the trash', notably 155 *pelisses*, 3 *dolmans*, 8 white *vestes*, 22 pairs *pantalons à cheval* and 78 *capotes-manteaux*.[356]

Cloth in the *dépôt* included 589m 70 *bleu celeste* broadcloth – for making *pelisse* and *dolmans* – 244m scarlet broadcloth – for collar and cuffs of *dolmans* and what else we ask as this is a large amount of cloth for a purpose that required minimal quantities. Martinet suggests that the elite company had scarlet broadcloth *schabraques*, which this archive record seems to confirm. Also in *dépôt* was 1,358m 90 white serge, 448m 60 green tricot for *porte-manteaux*, 56m linen for lining, 50m linen for *caleçon*, 62m 6 white flannel for lining *pelisses*, and 44m red worsted lace for chevrons. Clothing held in the *dépôt* comprised 21 brand-new *pelisses* accompanied by 10 brand-new *dolmans*, 3 pairs of *culottes hongroise*, 1 white *veste*, 20 *gilet d'ecuries* and 58 pairs of *pantalons à cheval*. The inspector also recorded that the *dépôt* held 19 sabretaches with eagles and 182 'without eagles', which were presumably made from black varnished leather, and simply bore '10' in white metal numerals. We assume the other type were either black leather with an eagle, or were they the much older embroidered type, perhaps retained by the elite company as they were also listed as brand new?[357]

11^{e} *Hussar*

Raised in 1793, the regiment became the 29^{e} *Dragons* in 1803. It was recreated in 1810 from the *regiment de Hussards Hollandaise*, and was disbanded in 1814. Hardly any paperwork exists for its dress and equipment in French service. When inspected

Martinet presents for us three troopers of the 11e *Hussar*, all of which are broadly similar except for the colour of the fur to the *pelisse*.

on 3 June 1813, General Legrange reported that the men were wearing *pelisses*, and *pantalons à cheval* made from green broadcloth with red piping to the button stands. Men were armed with sabres, pistols and carbines. No *dolmans* were issued and the *pelisse* was worn over a white *veste*. We know nothing else until August 1814, when the *dépôt* held 4m 50 *rouge-garance* broadcloth, 378m 85 red wool flannel, 254m 13 green

Two further contemporary images show the dress of the 11e *Hussar*. Up first, an eyewitness drawing of a trooper of the 11e *Hussar* by Lieutenant Bregeot of the 16e *Chasseurs à Cheval*. Secondly, a centre company trooper depicted in gouache painting by an officer of the 10e *Dragons* from the mid-1820s. (*Collection KM*)

Up first we have a trumpeter of the 11e *Hussar* from Rousselot's notes. Secondly, a reconstruction of an elite company trumpeter based on notes created by Ernest Fort in the years prior to the First World War. We have found no archive evidence to support or deny this uniform. (*Collection KM*)

tricot, 30m 40 white sheepskin, 1,400m square worsted braid, 4,100m soutache, 80 leather hides and 300m of cording with olives for *pelisse*. White fur is listed for *pelisses*, but not was in store. Also in *dépôt* were 450 shirts, 22 pairs of *caleçon* and 82 black stocks. The regiment also possessed 177 *pelisses*, 163 *dolmans*, 142 white *gilets*, 5 *gilet d'ecuries*, 121 pairs of *culottes hongroise*, 46 pairs of *pantalons à cheval*, 32 *manteaux a manche*, 189 *bonnets de police*, 394 *schakos* with 227 covers, 205 waistbelts, 214 *gibernes*, 214 *porte-gibernes*, 196 *porte-carabines*, 153 sabretache, 112 pairs of gloves, 484 barrel sashes and 6 trumpets, as well as 281 saddles with 227 *schabraques*.[358]

12e *Hussar*

The regiment was formed on 9 January 1812 from three squadrons of the 9e *Hussar* serving in Spain, the 2e, 3e and 4e squadrons, which had been renamed the 9e *Bis Hussar*. Based at Saragossa in January 1813, the regiment had three squadrons 175 men per squadron and totalled 622 men. By Imperial Decree dated the Tuileries, 17 February 1813, the 9e *Bis Hussar* became the 12e *Hussar*.[359] A report of 10 February 1813 sent to the Minister of War reported that the 13e *and* 14e *regiment des Hussars* and also the 12e regiment, formerly the 9e (*bis*), were to have silver and white lace, the buttons to be tin or silvered.[360] This was not confirmed until 3 March 1813 when the regiment's colonel was ordered to replace yellow and gold lace with silver and white.[361]

Trooper and elite company officer of the 12^{e} *Hussar* by Martinet.

A reconstruction of a trumpeter of the 12e *Hussar* as they appeared in 1813, based on notes made by Rousselot from a naïve contemporary image housed in the library of the *Musée de l'Armée*. The image seems to be that created by 'Captain Baty' presented by Boisselier and Ernest Fort and may well be a phantom source rather than being authentic, as no trace of the original can be found.

In the spring of 1813 the 1e, 2e, 3e squadron were in Spain, and the newly raised 4e, 5^{e} and 6^{e} squadrons based at Niort were sent to the army in Germany. On 31 January 1814 the regiment had a total of 523 men in six squadrons, the strength of which varied from 63 to 125 men. The regiment was in action at Chateau-Thierry on 12 February 1814.

The regiment was disbanded in summer 1814 when it had 92 officers' horses and 218 troop horses, of which 40 were passed to the 5^{e} regiment of Dragoons as they were unsuitable for light cavalry mounts. On 11 August 1814 the men of the 12^{e} *Hussar* were wearing the following items:[362]

Reconstruction of the centre and elite companies of the 12e *Hussar* as they appeared in 1813. Formed on 9 January 1812 from three squadrons of the 9e *Hussar*, by Imperial Decree dated the Tuileries, 17 February 1813, the 9e Bis Hussar became the 12e *Hussar*. A report of 10 February 1813 sent to the Minister of War reported that the 13e and 14e *regiment des Hussars* and also the 12e regiment, formerly the 9e (*bis*) were to have silver and white lace, the buttons to be tin or silvered. However, a letter of 10 November 1813 sent from the minister of war reminded the colonel of the regiment to adopt white lace and braid. Clearly, the changeover took almost a year to enact.

Item	In Service, but Due to Expire in the Next Year	In Need of Repair	To be Replaced in the Next Year	To be Replaced	Items Short	Observations
Pelisse	112	27	97	4	110	The effectives are 350 men.
Dolmans	95	26	101	4	124	
Gilets en drap blanc	92	17	61		180	
Gilet d'ecuries	68	35	110	39	98	
Bonnets de police	100	23	137	13	77	
Culottes hongroise	20	10	51	10	259	
Pantalons à cheval	83	50	93	56	68	
Caleçon	21				329	
Stable trousers	28				322	
Manteaux	170	42	74	17	47	
Schakos	249		71	50	2	
Barrel sashes	184		67	25	124	
Colpacks	38					

Thus, we see that in 1814 the regiment wore *pelisses* and *dolmans*, but it seems sous-officiers and elite company alone had *culottes hongroise*, the centre companies having *pantalons à cheval*. The elite company had also managed to hang on to colpacks despite these items being officially discontinued from February 1813.

Firstly, we present a reconstruction of centre company troopers of the 12e *Hussar* in 1814, by which time the regiment had changed to white trim from yellow. We know this as at disbandment the stores held over 3,000m of white braid to frog *dolmans* and *pelisse* and a similar amount of flat white braid to edge the *dolmans* and *pelisses* and to decorate the *culottes hongroise*. The sabretache is based on an extant item held in a private collection.

Secondly, a reconstruction of a trooper of the elite company in summer 1814. At disbandment, the regiment's elite company is recorded as wearing thirty-eight colpacks. These were clearly inherited from the 9e *Hussar* and would have been very 'scruffy' in appearance, being issued as far back as 1811 if not earlier. Regimental stores held at disbandment two grades of scarlet broadcloth: presumably the superfine was destined for the *sous-officiers* and the 'common' broadcloth was used by other ranks. For campaign dress, the *pantalons à cheval* were made from gris-beige broadcloth.

Lastly, we present a reconstruction of a trumpeter as they appeared in 1814. At the time of changeover from yellow to white trim, it seems that the regiment took up Imperial Livery. The regimental stores in summer 1814 held 4m 63 of first-quality green broadcloth, 105m green broadcloth of second quality for *manteaux-capotes*, and 135m 95 of green tricot destined for trumpeters' *culottes hongroise*. No lace remained in stores: the inspector noted that the colonel had not enacted the recent decree to dress the trumpeters in blue with Royalist Lace and remove Imperial iconography from use. Presumably this meant that the trumpeters wore Imperial Livery.

The following items of equipment were in use at the date of disbandment:[363]

Item	In Service, but due to Expire in the Next Year	In Need of Repair	To be Replaced in the Next Year	To be Replaced	Items Short	Observations
Porte-Manteaux	174	35	39	41	61	The effective is 350 men.
Waistbelts	198	40	27	20	65	
Sword knots	253				67	
Gibernes	180	51	31	21	67	
Giberne belts	201	30	31	21	67	
Carbine slings and clips	207	30		14	51	
Sabretaches	206	41			65	
Gloves					350	
Trumpets	2	4	4	1		
Carbines	212	25	4			
Sabres	268	13	4			
Pistols	241	24				

Stocks of material in the regiment's *dépôt* comprised:[364]

Item	Amount	Observation
Bleu de Celeste broadcloth	0	
Bleu de Roi broadcloth	326m 55	Passed to 64ᵉ de Ligne
Scarlet broadcloth 1st quality	0m 34	
Scarlet broadcloth 2nd quality	46m 99	Passed to 64ᵉ de Ligne
Green broadcloth	4m 63	
Green broadcloth 2nd quality	105m	
White flannel	360m 38	
White serge	193m	Passed to 64ᵉ de Ligne
Green tricot	135m 95	
Green tricot 2nd quality	187m	
Linen for linings	449m 66	
Large buttons	625 dozen and 6	
Small buttons	75 dozen and 10	
Medium buttons	1,996 dozen 10	
Item	**Amount**	**Observation**
White square braid	3,962m 76	
White flat worsted lace	3,811m 56	
Cording to fastening barrel sashes	147m	
Lambskins	757	
Cow hide	37	
Red Moroccan leather	252 hides	

The green broadcloth was used to make the regiment's *manteaux-capote* and the tricot was used to make the *pantalons à cheval* and *porte-manteaux* as outlined under the Bardin regulation. The two grades of scarlet broadcloth hints that the *sous-officiers* had a finer grade of cloth for their *dolmans* than the other ranks. The two qualities of green broadcloth hint that the superior grade was perhaps used for the trumpeters' clothing, yet not an inch of Imperial Livery was in *dépôt*. The white broadcloth was for the sleeveless *veste* worn under the *dolman*. Of interest, the facing colour is not the specified *bleu celeste*, but the darker and richer *Bleu de Roi*, which we assume was later used by the drummers of the 64ᵉ de Ligne.

In the regiment's magazine were the following items:[365]

Item	**New**	**In Good Condition**	**To be Repaired**	**To be Replaced**	**Items Short**	**Observations**
Vestes en drap blanc	26					
Culottes hongroise	50					
Caleçon	8					
Manteaux	18		6			
Schakos	62					
Barrel sashes	64					
Gibernes	131		410			
Carbine slings and clips	200		17			
Waistbelts	108		50			
Sabre slings	66					
Sword knots	199					
Pelisses	3					
Sabretaches	55		16			

Of interest, the *dépôt* held 184 pairs of grey linen gaiters for stable duties, 600 pairs of woollen ankle socks, as well as 175 pairs of shoes, again for stable duties, but none were in use.

13e *Hussar*

Martinet presents two troopers of this short-lived regiment for us.

We present three uniform reconstructions for the 13[e] *Hussar*.

Firstly, a centre company trooper based on the regiment's paper archive. Secondly, an elite company trumpeter of the 13[e] *Hussar* based on notes by Ernest Fort. We have been unable to locate Fort's source material for the image. The image presents several issues, most notably that the regiment possessed not an inch of red broadcloth. However, Fort may have had access to now lost sources, and therefore we include the image as a possible representation.

Lastly, a centre company trumpeter of the 13[e] *Hussar* based on the regiment's paper archive.

The regiment was raised on 28 January 1813 from recruits in Turin and Verona with Prince Baciocchi, husband of Elisa Bonaparte, at its head. The regiment existed for little less than a year, being merged with the 14[e] *Hussar* on 11 December. The unit was dressed in the same colours as the 2e *Hussar*, i.e., chestnut brown and sky blue. The 13e possessed the following items at disbandment:[366]

	Pelisse		*Dolman*		*Gilet*		*Gilet d'ecurie*	
	New	Good condition	New	Good condition	New	Good condition	New	Good condition
In *Dépôt*	618		89	1,219	99		7	
In Service						154		95
Total	618		89	129	99	154	7	95

	Pantalons à cheval		*Culotte Hongroise*		*Bonnet de police*	
	New	Good condition	New	Good condition	New	Good condition
In *Dépôt*	19		86		7	
In Service		123		129		95
Total	19	123	86	129	7	95

In addition, 119 *schakos* were in *dépôt* and 127 were in use, 96 *manteaux* were in *dépôt* and 96 in use, 118 barrel sashes were in *dépôt* and 114 in use. The regiment had a large stockpile of *dolmans* and *pelisse* but very little else. Thus is the sum total of our knowledge on this enigmatic regiment's uniform and equipment.

13e *Hussar dit Hussar Jérôme Napoléon*

By Imperial Decree of 6 August 1813, Napoléon 'presented' his brother Jérôme – King of Westphalia – with a regiment of *hussars*. The regiment was formed at Kassel under the orders of Colonel Brincard. The *sous-officiers*, corporals and other key personnel were to come from French and Westphalian regiments, as well as new recruits from Lorraine. This regiment became the *hussar* regiment 'Jérôme Napoléon' of the Westphalian Guard and was initially supplied with horses from the *dépôt* of the Westphalian Guard *Chevaux-leger*, because the majority of the complement arrived in Kassel without horses.

Trooper of the *Hussard Jérôme Napoléon* in a print by Aaron Martinet.

The regiment was established on 5 August 1813 by converting the 'Westphalian Hussar'. The Westphalian Hussar regiment was formed at the end of June from men in the report *dépôt* at Hanau, being drawn from *chasseur*, dragoon, *hussar*, lancer and *cuirassier* regiments! Four men came from the Red Lancers of the Imperial Guard.[367] It was a collection of raw conscripts who had never seen action, nor ever would! A report dated 3 July lists that 230 men were drawn from the 6 French lancer regiments, 540 men from the line *chasseurs* and 350 from the *hussars*, making 1,120.[368] The clothing and equipment on 3 August 1813 was as follows:[369]

Regiment	Number of men	*Gilet d'ecurie*	Stable trousers	*Pantalons à cheval*	*Bonnets de police*
5e *Hussar*	29	29	29		29
6e *Hussar*	79	79	75		77
7e *Hussar*	70	69	69	2	69
8e *Hussar*	88	88	88	88	88
10e *Hussar*	33	33	33	33	33
3e *Chasseurs*	10	10	10	9	10
7e *Chasseurs*	38	36	33		35
8e *Chasseurs*	59	60	60	59	60
25e *Chasseurs*	68	70	70		70
6e Lancers	39	53	55		55
Total	533	529	502	211	526

The dragoons and *cuirassiers* had been transferred to new regiments by August. The regiment must have presented an incredibly mixed appearance. The new regiment had 88 *porte-manteaux*, 465 sabre-belts, 381 sword knots, 1,093 shirts, 489 stocks, 408 pairs of shoes, 33 pairs of gaiters and 398 pairs of boots, as well as 465 sabres.[370] Not an inch of *hussar* dress yet existed. Clearly *hussar* kit was made and issued, as on 11 December 1813 the *Hussard Jérôme Napoléon* had the following clothing and equipment:

> 54 *pelisse*, 78 *dolmans*, 2 pairs of *culottes hongroise*, 267 *gilet* d'ecuries, 253 pairs of stable trousers, 233 *bonnets de police*, 64 *manteaux*, 54 *schakos*, 84 pairs of boots, 251 *gibernes*, 120 *porte-carabines*, 195 sabre belts, 83 barrel sashes, 83 sabretaches.[371]

The regiment to be fully equipped needed 685 *pelisses*, 661 *dolmans*, 737 pairs of *culottes hongroise*, 472 *gilet d'ecuries*, 486 pairs of stable trousers, 506 *bonnets de police*, 605 *manteaux* and 685 *schakos*, among other items. In essence the cadre of the regiment was badly and incompletely dressed and the regiment needed clothing and equipping from scratch.

In October 1813, the regiment accompanied the king during his flight to France, becoming on 1 January the 13e *Hussar*. Baron Grundler, in a letter to Marshal MacDonald, reported on 22 December 1813 that the regiment mustered 1,064 men and 717 had been forced to evacuate Kassel and had abandoned the regiment's *dépôt* there, as well as many old soldiers and horses who remained in the *dépôt*.[372] He further reported that 400 men had been clothed at Kassel, and that clothing and equipment had been ordered for 110 further men. The cloth in use was mediocre, and the men were wearing *pantalons à cheval* and *gilet d'ecuries*. By 23 December, 280 *dolmans* were in use, 201 *pelisses*, 453 *gilet d'ecuries*, 450 pairs of *pantalons à cheval*, 118 pairs of stable trousers, 230 capotes-*manteaux*, 420 *bonnets de police* and 329 *schakos*. A further 781 *pelisses* and 863 *dolmans* were needed, 606 *gilet d'ecuries*, 614 pairs of *pantalons à cheval,* 946 pairs of stable trousers, 644 *bonnets de police* and 644 *schakos*.[373]

A report of 31 December 1813 notes that when the regiment arrived in France, to be brought up to full strength it needed 1,000 men – having only 200 men under arms in various forms of dress – and needed 700 horses. The regiment had 300 and had provisionally purchased 400 others.[374] A letter of 9 February informs us that the newly organised 13e *Hussar* had:

1. clothing and equipment. Westphalian blue *Culottes hongroise*
2. dolman dark blue with five rows of buttons; pelisse is white with white fur, grey astrakhan for officers
3. barrel sash is scarlet with blue and white knots. *Schabraque*, sabretache scarlet, eagle in yellow metal on the sabretache
4. sheepskin *schabraque*
5. scarlet Schakos
6. *gilet*, and stable trousers in blue, stripes on the outside leg in scarlet
7. sleeved cloak in grey
8. buff work in yellow
9. white plumes[375]

It was proposed that items that that were not 'in harmony' with the other *hussar* regiments in the army were to be changed to the French model.[376] A letter of 12 February 1814 implies that Jérôme Napoléon himself authorised the regiment to wear scarlet *dolmans*,[377] and a few days later General Clarke, the minister for war, reported in a letter of 16 February 1814 that 'The King of Westphalia, has authorised that the regiment Jérôme Napoléon 13e regiment de Hussar is to substitute the blue dolman for scarlet.' Clarke noted also that the *pelisse* became blue rather than white.[378] The regiment was re-formed at Maastricht, which become a temporary *dépôt*.

The new 13e *Hussar* existed for a matter of months: with the restoration of the Bourbons, it was disbanded. On 11 August, the regiment had 44 officers, namely 1 colonel, 2 first majors, 2 squadron commanders, 3 adjutants, 1 quarter-master, 3 surgeons, 14 captains, 9 lieutenants and 9 sub-lieutenants. For the other ranks, 159 men were present with 118 horses. On 11 August 1814 their uniform comprised:[379]

Item	In Service, but Due to Expire in the Next Year	In Need of Repair	To be Replaced in the Next Year	To be Replaced	Items Short	Observations
Pelisses	61	16			15	The effectives are 130 men, including 8 men who had been given their discharge, two have been passed to the Gendarmerie.
Dolmans	3	1			126	
Schakos	81	15		3	31	
Manteaux	71	3			56	
Gilet d'ecuries	65	24		5	36	
Pantalons à cheval	58	22			50	
Bonnets de police	14	8		9	99	
Trompettes	4					
Waistbelts	104	18		4	4	
Gibernes	118	12				
Porte-gibernes	130					
Sword knots					130	
Porte-manteaux	94	4		2	30	
Gloves					130	
Pairs of boots	17	21	1	2	89	
Banderole-porte-carabines	91				39	
Sabretaches	58	1		1	70	
Sword knots	11	1			118	
Musketoons	57	11				
Sabres	128	1				
Pistols	10					

Thus, we see that in 1814 the regiment wore *pelisses* and *pantalons à cheval*, and not a single pair of stable trousers existed: the *pantalons à cheval* must have been worn in all orders of dress, and must have been incredibly smelly and dirty.

Stocks of material in the regiment's *dépôt* comprised:[380]

Item	Amount	Observation
Bleu de Roi broadcloth	223m 64	
White broadcloth	58m 60	
Iron grey broadcloth	1m 3	
Iron grey tricot	5m 98	
Bleu de Roi tricot	317m 43	
Large buttons	92 dozen and 3	
Lambskins	5	
Yellow worsted square braid	1,107m 70	
Yellow worsted flat lace	909m 56	For 18 cordons and tresses

What is noticeable, is the total absence of any scarlet cloth from which to make *dolmans*. Therefore, were they ever made? Or, was it all used in making new clothing and none remained? In 1813, as we noted earlier, the *dolman* was dark blue and the *culotte hongroise* Westphalian Blue, which we assume is the same as *Bleu de Roi*, the *dolman* and *pelisse* being laced and braided presumably in yellow. We can say that the *manteau-capote* was indeed made from iron grey broadcloth, and the *pantalons à cheval* were likewise iron grey, a change from 1813 when they had been listed simply as blue. The lambskins are noted as being white, again according to the 1813 uniform.[381] The archives of the regiment at disbandment in 1814 show us that only three *dolmans* were issued, to the regiment's adjutant-sub-officiers. Every man was wearing a *pelisse*. We are totally ignorant of the appearance of the trumpeters as nothing from the period gives us details of their clothing.

14e *Hussar*

The regiment was raised in Turin on 28 January 1813 from recruits in Turin and Verona and organised by Prince Camille Borghese, estranged husband of Pauline Bonaparte.

By 3 March 1813, 20 men had been mounted and equipped from the department of Marengo and had originally been destined for the 4e *Artillerie à cheval*. The department of Taro provided 19 men, clothed, equipped and mounted, and they had arrived at Verona on 23 February 1813; 46 men had arrived at Turin by 16 February from the department of the Po; 145 men, fully equipped, clothed and mounted, had come from the *dépôt* of the 19e *Chasseurs à Cheval*; 67 men had been drawn from the department of Florence – in total 900 men had been raised in north Italy for the regiment, of which 414 had arrived fully clothed and equipped with 354 horses – clearly each department had to provide a number of clothed and equipped conscripts in the same manner as the Guards of Honour would be raised in France. The men were described as intelligent and standing 5ft 1 pouce, [around 5ft 3in!]. Despite the optimism that the men or departments would provide clothing, the reality was that of the 414 men, 350 were wearing *gilet d'ecuries*, and that it was proposed to make another 50. Some 300 pairs of linen *pantalons* were in use, and leather had been bought for *pantalons à cheval* – clearly things were not going to plan and the state had had to step in to clothe the regiment. On 1 March contracts had been passed to make *dolmans*, *pelisses*, *culottes hongroise* and

Trooper of the Italian 14e *Hussar* by Martinet.

Reconstruction of a trooper of the 14ᵉ *Hussar* from the regiment's archive for 1813. We also present a trumpeter of the elite company from a now lost contemporary illustration in the Cottereau collection. We assume the centre company trumpeters wore the same uniform but with a *schako* as headdress.

Re-formed in late 1813, we present a reconstruction of centre company troopers of the 14ᵉ *Hussar* from the regiment's archive for 1814.

white *gilets*, as well as *bonnets de police*, which were in theory to arrive by 15 March. Some 100 *schakos* were to be delivered on 15 March, with further batches after this date. Leather work was ordered on 10 March 1813 – the men had supplied none, and 200 pairs of boots were expected by 1 April 1813.[382]

The 13ᵉ and 14ᵉ *Hussars* were merged on 11 December as the 14ᵉ *Hussar*, the *Jérôme Napoléon Hussars* becoming the new 13ᵉ *Hussar*. The paperwork for the two regiments is confused as we have four regiments with two numbers! At amalgam, *dépôt* held:[383]

	Pelisses		*Dolmans*		*Gilets*		*Gilet d'ecuries*	
	New	Good condition	New	Good condition	New	Good condition	New	Good condition
In *Dépôt*	93		67		62		62	
In Service		205		109		109		109
Total	93	205	67	109	62	109	62	109

	Pantalons à cheval		*Culottes Hongroise*		*Bonnet de police*	
	New	Good condition	New	Good condition	New	Good condition
In *Dépôt*	62		62		62	
In Service		109		109		109
Total	62	109	62	109	62	109

The *dépôt* held 216 brand-new *schakos*, 86 *manteaux* and 162 barrel sashes.

At the time of the amalgam cloth and materials in the *dépôt* was:[384]

Regiment	Brown Broadcloth	*Bleu de Ciel* Broadcloth	Green Broadcloth	Grey Tricot	Flannel	Linen
14e	285m	225m	700m	685m	240m	966m 27
13e	0m 45	4m 96	2m 50		0m 13	
Total	285m 45	229m 96	700m 50	685m	240m 13	966m 27

Both regiments were dressed exactly the same, chestnut brown *dolmans* faced in *bleu de ciel*, a rich mid-blue colour, making them distinct from the 2e *Hussar*, which had the lighter shade of *bleu celeste* as the facing colour. We assume the grey tricot was destined for *pantalons à cheval*.

The new 14e *Hussar* was again organised by Prince Camille Borghese and mobilised on 1 January 1814: the regiment lasted little over seven months and was disbanded on 16 July. The rump of the regiment was taken into the 4e *Hussar*; a mere 38 officers, 100 other ranks and 2 *enfant de troupe*. The clothing in use was:[385]

Item	Good Condition	In Need of Repair	Need Replacing	To be Replaced	Items Need
Pelisse	55	4	1		4
Dolmans	The regiment has none				
Gilet d'ecuries	34	7	4	7	12
Bonnets de police	22			22	42
Pantalons à cheval	30	14			20
Stable trousers	21	14	2	8	19
Schakos	52	6			6
Manteaux	31	6			27

Item	Good Condition	In Need of Repair	Need Replacing	To be Replaced	Items Need
Culottes hongroise	25	10	1		28
Caleçon	15	6	3	14	26
Gilets en drap blanc	37				27
Pompoms	28				36

The bulk of the regiment's clothing was missing in most cases, a mix of legwear was used, no *dolmans* existed, and the *pelisse* were presumably worn in most orders of dress, except stable duties. Not every man had a *gilet* to wear under the pelisse, and not every man had a *gilet d'ecurie* – their *pelisse* was, we guess, their only item of upper body wear. Just forty-two sabretaches were in use and not a single barrel sash. The *dépôt* had almost nothing, holding 87m of scarlet broadcloth – was this for facings? – and fifty dozen small white metal buttons.

The lack of materials, we suppose, was due to the high numbers of brand-new, ready to be issued clothing in the *dépôt*, which included 334 *pelisses*, 280 *dolmans* and 130 *gilet d'ecuries*, as well as 452 brand-new sabre belts, 43 sword knots, 437 barrel sashes. Clothing and equipment in good condition included 120 *dolmans*, 4 pairs of *pantalons à cheval,* 15 pairs of linen *pantalons*, 69 *schakos*, 4 *manteaux,* 147 pairs of *culottes hongroise*, 48 pairs of *caleçon*, 475 *gibernes*, 675 *porte-gibernes*, 569 *banderole-porte-carabines* and 329 sabretaches with slings.[386]

Hussars du Roi

Raised on 23 April 1814 from Royalist volunteers, the *Hussars du Roi* were given a shake-down inspection in July 1814. The men were wearing:[387]

Item	Good Condition	In Need of Repair	Need Replacing	To be Replaced	Items Needed
Pelisses	180				51
Dolmans	176				55
Veste d'ecuries					231
Gilets					231
Culottes hongroise					231
Pantalons à cheval	180			40	21
Pantalons d'ecuries			210		21
Caleçon					231
Manteaux					231
Bonnets de police			89	142	
Pairs of boots	181				50
Pairs of gloves					231

Item	Good Condition	In Need of Repair	Need Replacing	To be Replaced	Items Needed
Barrel sashes	166				55
Sabretaches					231
Waistbelts				188	43
Gibernes	45	130		117	39
Porte-gibernes	42	150			39
Porte-carabines	60	112			59
Sabre knots					231
Trumpets	8				
Trumpet cords	8				
Schakos	157				74
Schako cords	157				74
Schako covers					231
Pompoms	185				
Plumes	231				

The men were clearly wearing 1812 or similar *schakos* with both a white plume and pompom. Most of the clothing was missing or worn out, and we assume it had been badly treated by the men, or was second-hand when it was issued. The 231 men were

Colonel Clary at the head of the 1e *Hussar* in 1815. The elite company trooper is wearing a colpack, which is not verified by archive sources, but the use of these is perfectly plausible as this is a posed portrait. We see centre company troopers have *schako rouleau*. The officer in the background firing his pistol has a white plume and scarlet *pantalons*.

A portrait of a senior officer of the *Hussard du Roi* said to be Colonel Merlin. Note the silver embroidery to the *schako*. (*Private collection France*)

armed with 283 sabres, 56 carbines – which were either in need of repair or were life expired – and 37 pistols in similar condition. The *dépôt* held no stocks of cloth and materials, but held 4 brand-new *dolmans*, 12 barrel sashes, 86 *schakos*, 103 *porte-manteaux*, 200 *schako* covers and 215 pompoms.

During the Hundred Days the *Hussars du Roi* became the 1e *Hussar*. Disbanded in September 1815, the men present were wearing 240 *pelisses*, 41 *dolmans*, 222 *veste d'ecuries*, 109 white *gilets*, 259 pairs of *pantalons à cheval*, 236 pairs of *culottes hongroise*, 254 pairs of *caleçon*, 261 *bonnets de police*, 29 *manteaux*, 236 pairs of boots, 239 *schakos* and 227 *porte-manteaux*. Clearly, *dolmans* were restricted perhaps to either *sous-officiers* and/or the elite company. The idea the regiment wore *dolmans* with *pelisses* at the shoulder for all ranks is wrong. The regiment used two types of sabretaches, 257 black leather and 180 red. No colpacks, let alone grenadier *schakos*, existed for the elite company by the end of the Empire. The *dépôt* held a substantial amount of clothing and equipment:[388]

Item	Good condition	In Need of Repair	Need Replacing	Total
Pelisses	Nil			
Dolmans	464			464
Veste d'ecuries	Nil			
Gilets en drap blanc	6			6
Culottes hongroise	4			4
Capote Manteaux	105			105
Schakos			4	4
Barrel sashes	549	84		633
Red sabretaches		180		180
Black sabretaches		11		11
Trumpets			12	12
Waistbelts	193	40		233
Gibernes	386	50		436
Porte-gibernes	407	32		439
Porte-carabines	250	100		350
Sabre knots	101			101

Two contemporary images give us the dress of the trumpeters of the *Hussard du Roi*: first a detail by Vernet and second a portrait by Gericault. Both artists show the same uniform.

We present three uniform reconstructions of the *Hussard du Roi*. Firstly, a reconstruction of a trooper based on the regiment's archive, as they appeared in 1815. The same uniform shown in the Vernet portrait of Colonel Clary, and a naïve period drawing by Charles Brun dated 1815 housed in the library of the *Musée de l'Armée*. The regiment became the 1e *Hussar* during the Hundred Days, which was achieved by replacing Royalist symbols. The regiment had two types of sabretache: red embroidered examples and a simpler plain black model. Both, it seems, were used side by side. Perhaps the embroidered examples were used by the elite company. All ranks wore the *schako rouleau* during the Hundred Days. Secondly, a trumpeter based on a sketch by Theodore Geriacult housed in the library of the *Musée de l'Armée* that largely corroborates an image by Vernet in showing a white pelisse and red *schako rouleau*. Nothing Gericault shows can be disputed by the regiment's paper archive. Lastly, a *sapeur* of the regiment in 1815 based on a now lost – presumably contemporary – watercolour in the Cottereau collection.

We also find in *dépôt* 2 *pelisse*s and 2 *dolmans* '*de modèle*', as well as 220 *mousquetons*, 348 sabres, 21 pistols and 20 bayonets with scabbard. Cloth comprised 21m of *bleu celeste* broadcloth, 80m 56 scarlet broadcloth, 237 dozen medium buttons and 623 dozen small buttons. The men were clearly not issued *dolmans*; regimental archives show just 78 were issued in the First Restoration compared to 556 *pelisses*. Just 88 manteaux-capote were issued, 581 pairs of *pantalons à cheval*, 488 pairs of *culottes hongroise* and 554 *schakos*. No plumes or cords were made or issued in the First Restoration, unless they were counted with the schako.[389]

An image by Brun dated to 1814 shows the regiment with *schako rouleaux*, with no *schakos* plate but a central white cockade held in place by a white lace *ganse*. A scarlet-tipped white plume is worn. The *pantalons à cheval* are shown as *bleu celeste*, with a broad scarlet side stripe and black leather inner leg reinforcement. The figure is a sergeant of elite company and he has a slung *pelisse* and copper grenade to his *giberne* belt. The sergeant also wears a moustache and goatee beard coupled with a *queue* and *cadenettes*. Nothing in the paper archive discounts this. In a portrait by Horace Vernet of Colonel Clary, trumpeters are show with a white *pelisse*.

Two primary sources created at the end of the Empire show the *Hussards du Roi*. Up first a trooper drawn sometime before August 1814, and second a *sapeur*. Of note is the cloth schabraque, under the black sheepskin. This is presumably the image formerly in the Cotterau collection incorrectly copied by Ernest Fort. The schabraque is identical to those used by the 3e: seemingly this was a semi-official standard issue item.

Chapter 6

Hussars – Concluding Comments

So what does our data say? *Hussars* wore, at least in the first regiment, green *culottes hongroise* just like Vernet shows, and likely the 4^{e}. Given virtually no difference existed between pre- and post-Bardin *dolmans*, *pelisses* etc., we cannot state explicably what parts of Bardin regulation were or were not adopted.

Elite Company

Formed under the decree of 10 October 1801, the men were allowed bear fur headdress in imitation of the grenadiers of the infantry.[390] These items were not in universal use after 1808, and the only regiment with colpacks post 1812 was the 12^{e}. Not a single grenadier-style *schako* was issued to elite companies, unless recorded with the centre company *schakos*, likewise not a single *aigrette* either. We can be sure, therefore, that elite companies had no distinctions what soever.

Sapeurs

No formal decree was published that authorised the light cavalry to adopt *sapeurs*, yet in July 1802 a circular advised the regiments of mounted troops that it was the intention of the government to provide the elite companies with tools.[391] Many artists show *sapeurs* in a number of regiments, yet we can only prove their existence in the 4^{e} and 5^{e}.[392] Beyond reasonable doubt, most depictions of *sapeurs* are 'fake news'.

Trumpeters

Well, the headline news is that in most cases we can say nothing about the dress of trumpeters. We have to rely on contemporary iconography. Just two regiments out of sixteen studied had trumpeters' lace, the 8^{e} in 1814 and the 5^{e} in 1815, and this was very likely Royalist Livery: therefore, the notion of trumpeters of *Hussar* regiments decked out in Imperial Livery is wrong. Therefore, we have to assume that the *Hussar* regiments never fully adopted this provision under the Bardin regulations, and clung on to reversed colours or other distinctions.

Bibliography

Printed sources

Etienne Alexandre Bardin (1808) Manuel *d'infanterie, ou Résumé de tous les règlements, décrets, usages, renseignements concernant l'infanterie, dans lequel se trouve renfermé tout ce que doivent savoir les sergents et caporaux.* Paris: Chez Magimel.

Les Gupil (1812) *Administration du masses.* Chez Magimel, Paris.

Archives Nationales de France

C2, AF/IV/1179.

Bibliotheque Musée de l'Armée

Fonds Rousselot.

Manuscripts and printed books, Volume 1 du projet de règlement sur l'habillement du major Bardin.

Service Historique Armée de Terre

Xc 23, Xc 186 1e *Chasseurs*, Xc188 2e *Chasseurs*, Xc 189 3e *Chasseurs*, Xc 190 3e *Chasseurs*, Xc 191 4e *Chasseurs*, Xc 192 4e *Chasseurs*, Xc 193 5e *Chasseurs*, Xc 194 5e *Chasseurs*, Xc 196 6e *Chasseurs*, Xc 198 7e *Chasseurs*, Xc 200 8e *Chasseurs*, Xc 202 9e *Chasseurs*, Xc 203 10e *Chasseurs*, Xc 204 10e *Chasseurs*, Xc 206 11e *Chasseurs*, Xc 207 12e *Chasseurs*, Xc 208 12e *Chasseurs*, Xc 211 13e *Chasseurs*, Xc 213 14e *Chasseurs*, Xc 214 15e *Chasseurs*, Xc 217 16e *Chasseurs*, Xc 218 17e *Chasseurs*, Xc 220 19e *Chasseurs*, Xc 222 20e *Chasseurs*, Xc 223 21e *Chasseurs*, Xc 224 21e *Chasseurs*, Xc 226 22e *Chasseurs*, Xc 228 23e *Chasseurs*, Xc 230 24e *Chasseurs*, Xc232 25e *Chasseurs*, Xc 233 26e *Chasseurs*, Xc 234 27e *Chasseurs*, Xc 235 28e et 29e *Chasseurs*, Xc 236 30e et 31e *Chasseurs*, Xc 237 1e *Hussar*, Xc 238 1e *Hussar*, Xc 240 2e *Hussar*, Xc242 3e *Hussar*, Xc 243 4e *Hussar*, Xc 244 4e *Hussar*, Xc 245 5e *Hussar*, Xc 246 5e *Hussar*, Xc 248 6e *Hussar*, Xc 249 7e *Hussar*, Xc 250 7e *Hussar*, Xc 251 7e *Hussar*, Xc 252 8e *Hussar*, Xc 253 8e *Hussar*, Xc 254 9e *Hussar*, Xc 255 9e *Hussar*, Xc 256 10e *Hussar*, Xc 258 11e *Hussar*, Xc 259 12e *Hussar*, Xc 260 12e *Hussar*, Xc 261 13e et 14e *Hussar*, Xc 263 *Régiments Provisoire.*

Xs 525, Xs 526, Xs 528.

Notes

1. 1 Service Historique du Défense Armée de Terre (hereafter SHDDT), E31 fol.6.
2. 2 Bibliotheque Musée de l'Armée, Manuscripts and printed books, Volume 1 du projet de règlement sur l'habillement du major Bardin, pp.27–31.
3. Etienne Alexandre Bardin (1808) Manuel *d'infanterie, ou Résumé de tous les règlements, décrets, usages, renseignements concernant l'infanterie, dans lequel se trouve renfermé tout ce que doivent savoir les sergents et caporaux*. Paris: Chez Magimel, p.335.
4. Archives Nationales [hereafter AN] C2 471, Situation report, 25 February 1807.
5. Napoleon to Kellerman, 6 March 1807, Nos. 11949.
6. Service Historique Armée de Terre [hereafter SHDDT] Xc 263 régiments provisoire.
7. Fonds Rousselot, Journal Militaire 2e semester 1814, p.28.
8. Ibid.
9. SHDDT Xs 525 PROJET D'ARRÊTÉ Relatif à l'Habillement des troupes pour l'an X.
10. Fonds Rousselot Journal Militaire, 6 Juillet 1806.
11. SHDDT Xs 525 No. 34 Devis de Chasseurs.
12. SHDDT GR 2C 247 bis Habillement.
13. SHDDT Xc 186 1e Chasseurs. Rapport 11 Décembre 1807.
14. SHDDT Xc 188 2e Chasseurs. Rapport 23 Novembre 1807.
15. SHDDT Xc 190 3e Chasseurs. Rapport 21 Janvier 1808.
16. SHDDT Xc 192 4e Chasseurs à Cheval AnXI a 1815. Dossier 1808. Rapport 23 Juin 1808.
17. SHDDT Xc 196 6e Chasseurs. Rapport 9 Juillet 1808.
18. SHDDT Xc 202 9e Chasseurs. Rapport 16 Juin 1808.
19. SHDDT Xc 208 12e Chasseurs. Rapport 1 Janvier 1808.
20. SHDDT Xc 217 16e Chasseurs à Cheval An XI a 1811. Dossier 1808. Rapport 25 Janvier 1808.
21. SHDDT Xc 217 16e Chasseurs à Cheval An XI a 1811. Dossier 1808. Rapport 25 Janvier 1808.
22. SHDDT GR 2C 247 bis Habillement. Rapport 1 Juin 1807.
23. AN, AF/IV/1179. RAPPORTS ET PROJET DE DÉCRET Relatifs à une nouvelle Fixation de la Masse générale d'habillement, 11 Mars 1811.
24. Les Gupil (1812) *Administration du masses*. Chez Magimel, Paris, p.131.
25. Bibliotheque Musée de l'Armée, Manuscripts and printed books, Volume 1 du projet de règlement sur l'habillement du major Bardin, pp.310–313.
26. Bibliotheque Musée de l'Armée, Manuscripts and printed books, Volume 1 du projet de règlement sur l'habillement du major Bardin, p.14.
27. Bibliotheque Musée de l'Armée, Manuscripts and printed books, Volume 1 du projet de règlement sur l'habillement du major Bardin, pp.313–316.
28. Journal Militaire, 3e tremestre 1812. Décret 17 Septembre 1812.
29. Archives Nationales (here after AN) AN AF/IV/1179. Lettre a Napoleon 14 8bre 1812.
30. AN AF/IN/1179. Lettre a Napoleon 14 8bre 1812.
31. AN AF/IV/1179 rapport 18 Fevrier 1813.
32. SHDDT Xs 525. Décret 22 Juin 1813.
33. SHDDT Xs 525 Décret 25 Janvier 1814.
34. SHDDT Xs 528 Décret 22 Avril 1814.
35. Ibid.
36. SHDDT Xc 23 pièce 10 Rapport 10 Janvier 1815.
37. AN AF/IV/1941, Rapport fait l'Empereur par le ministre de la Guerre, le 26 mars 1815.
38. SHDDT Xc 186 1e Chasseurs. Rapport 5 Prairial An XI.
39. SHDDT Xc 186 1e Chasseurs. Rapport 5 Prairial An XI.
40. SHDDT Xc 186 1e Chasseurs. Rapport 10 Vendémiaire An XIII.
41. SHDDT Xc 186 1e Chasseurs. Rapport 10 Vendémiaire An XIII.
42. SHDDT Xc 186 1e Chasseurs. Rapport 3 Thermidor An XIII.
43. SHDDT Xc 186 1e Chasseurs. Rapport 3 Thermidor An XIII.

44. SHDDT Xc 186 1e Chasseurs. Rapport 11 Décembre 1807.
45. SHDDT Xc 186 1e Chasseurs. Rapport 11 Décembre 1807.
46. SHDDT Xc 186 1e Chasseurs. Dossier 1812. Rapport 5 Juillet 1812.
47. SHDDT Xc 186 1e Chasseurs. Dossier 1814. Rapport 14 Juin 1813.
48. SHDDT Xc 186 1e Chasseurs. Dossier 1814. Rapport 11 8bre 1814.
49. SHDDT Xc 186 1e Chasseurs. Dossier 1814. Rapport 11 Octobre 1814.
50. SHDDT Xc 186 1e Chasseurs. Dossier 1814. Rapport 11 8bre 1814.
51. SHDDT Xc 186 1e Chasseurs. Dossier 1814. Rapport 11 8bre 1814.
52. SHDDT Xc 188 2e Chasseurs. Rapport 9 Thermidor An XIII.
53. SHDDT Xc 188 2e Chasseurs. Rapport 9 Thermidor An XIII.
54. SHDDT Xc 188 2e Chasseurs. Rapport 4 Vendémiaire An XIII.
55. SHDDT Xc 188 2e Chasseurs. Rapport 23 Novembre 1807.
56. SHDDT Xc 188 2e Chasseurs. Rapport 23 Novembre 1807.
57. SHDDT Xc 188 2e Chasseurs à Cheval 1812–1815. Dossier 1812. Rapport 27 Avril 1812.
58. SHDDT Xc 188 2e Chasseurs à Cheval 1812–1815. Dossier 1814. Rapport 1 Aout 1814.
59. SHDDT Xc 188 2e Chasseurs à Cheval 1812–1815. Dossier 1815. Rapport 8 Octobre 1821.
60. SHDDT Xc 188 2e Chasseurs à Cheval 1812–1815. Dossier 1814. Rapport 1 Aout 1814.
61. SHDDT Xc 188 2e Chasseurs à Cheval 1812–1815. Dossier 1815. Rapport 19 8bre 1815.
62. SHDDT Xc 188 2e Chasseurs à Cheval 1812–1815. Dossier 1815. Rapport 25 9bre 1815.
63. SHDDT Xc 190 3e Chasseurs. Rapport 29 Vendémiaire An XII.
64. SHDDT Xc 190 3e Chasseurs. Rapport 29 Vendémiaire An XII
65. SHDDT Xc 190 3e Chasseurs. Rapport 21 Brumaire An XIV.
66. SHDDT Xc 190 3e Chasseurs. Rapport 21 Brumaire An XIV.
67. SHDDT Xc 190 3e Chasseurs. Rapport 21 Janvier 1808.
68. SHDDT Xc 190 3e Chasseurs. Rapport 21 Janvier 1808.
69. SHDDT Xc 190 3e Chasseurs. Rapport 21 Janvier 1808.
70. SHDDT Xc 190 3e Chasseurs Cheval. Dossier 1812. Rapport 30 Juin 1812.
71. SHDDT Xc 190 3e Chasseurs Cheval. Dossier 1813. Rapport 30 Mars 1813.
72. SHDDT Xc 190 3e Chasseurs Cheval. Dossier 1814. Rapport 14 Aout 1814.
73. SHDDT Xc 190 3e Chasseurs Cheval. Dossier 1814. Rapport 14 Aout 1814.
74. SHDDT Xc 190 3e Chasseurs Cheval. Dossier 1814. Rapport 14 Aout 1814.
75. SHDDT Xc 190 3e Chasseurs Cheval. Dossier 1814. Rapport 14 Aout 1814.
76. Musée de l'Armée Gb1907.2.
77. SHDDT Xc 190 3e Chasseurs Cheval. Dossier 1814. Rapport 14 Aout 1814.
78. SHDDT Xc 190 3e Chasseurs Cheval 1812–1815. Dossier 1815. Rapport 30 Aout 1815.
79. SHDDT Xc 190 3e Chasseurs Cheval. Dossier 1815. Rapport 5 Septembre 1815.
80. SHDDT Xc 190 3e Chasseurs Cheval. Dossier 1815. Rapport 1 8bre 1815.
81. SHDDT Xc 192 4e Chasseurs. Rapport 19 Frimaire An XIV.
82. SHDDT Xc 192 4e Chasseurs. Rapport 19 Frimaire An XIV.
83. SHDDT Xc 192 4e Chasseurs à Cheval AnXI a 1815. Dossier 1808. Rapport 17 Juin 1808.
84. SHDDT Xc 192 4e Chasseurs à Cheval AnXI a 1815. Dossier 1814. Dossier 1813. Proces Verbal 13 Décembre 1813.
85. SHDDT Xc 192 4e Chasseurs à Cheval AnXI a 1815. Dossier 1814. Rapport 6 Juillet 1814.
86. SHDDT Xc 192 4e Chasseurs à Cheval AnXI a 1815. Dossier 1814. Rapport 6 Juillet 1814.
87. SHDDT Xc 192 4e Chasseurs à Cheval AnXI a 1815. Dossier 1814. Rapport 6 Juillet 1814.
88. SHDDT Xc 192 4e Chasseurs à Cheval AnXI a 1815. Dossier 1815. Rapport 30 Mars 1820
89. SHDDT Xc 192 4e Chasseurs à Cheval AnXI a 1815. Dossier 1815. Rapport 30 Aout 1815.
90. SHDDT Xc 194 5e Chasseurs à Cheval 1811 a 1815. Dossier 1813. Rapport 2 Novembre 1813
91. SHDDT Xc 194 5e Chasseurs à Cheval 1811–1815. Dossier 1813. Rapport 13 Aout 1816.
92. SHDDT Xc 194 5e Chasseurs à Cheval 1811–1815. Dossier An13. Rapport 15 Thermidor An13.
93. SHDDT Xc 194 5e Chasseurs à Cheval 1811–1815. Dossier 1808. Rapport 19 Janvier 1808.
94. SHDDT Xc 196 5e Chasseurs à Cheval 1811–1815. Dossier 1814. Rapport 1 Aout 1814.
95. Bibliotheque Musée de l'Armée. Fonds Rousselot. Fiche Chasseurs à Cheval 1e Empire.
96. SHDDT Xc 194 5e Chasseurs à Cheval 1811–1815. Dossier 1814. Lettre au Ministre de Guerre 2 Septembre 1814.
97. SHDDT Xc 194 5e Chasseurs à Cheval 1811–1815. Dossier 1814. Rapport 1 Aout 1814.
98. SHDDT Xc 196 6e Chasseurs. Dossier An XIII Rapport 12 Brumaire An13.
99. SHDDT Xc 196 6e Chasseurs. Dossier An XIII Rapport 26 Thermidor An13.
100. SHDDT Xc 196 6e Chasseurs. Dossier 1808. Rapport 9 July 1808.
101. SHDDT Xc 196 6e Chasseurs. Dossier 1814. Rapport 15 Juillet 1814.
102. SHDDT Xc 196 6e Chasseurs. Dossier 1814.

103. Henckens (Lieutenant), Mémoires se rapportant à son service militaire au 6e régiment de chasseurs à cheval français de février 1803 à août 1816. La Haye, 1910.
104. SHDDT Xc 198 7e Chasseur à cheval An13 a 1815. Dossier An13.
105. SHDDT GR C2 247 Bis Habillement.
106. SHDDT Xc 198 7e Chasseurs. Dossier 1814. Rapport 21 Aout 1814.
107. SHDDT Xc 198 7e Chasseurs. Dossier 1815. Rapport 1 Janvier 1820.
108. SHDDT Xc 198 7e Chasseurs. Dossier 1815. Rapport 30 Novembre 1815.
109. SHDDT Xc 200 8e Chasseurs à Cheval. Dossier 1814. Rapport 21 Juillet 1814.
110. SHDDT Xc 200 8e Chasseurs à Cheval. Dossier 1814. Rapport 21 Juin 1814.
111. SHDDT Xc 200 8e Chasseurs à Cheval. Dossier 1815. Rapport 3 Décembre 1815.
112. SHDDT Xc 200 8e Chasseurs à Cheval. Dossier 1815. Rapport 3 Décembre 1815.
113. SHDDT Xc 202 9e Chasseurs. Rapport 24 Nivose An XIII.
114. SHDDT Xc 202 9e Chasseurs. Rapport 24 Nivose An XIII.
115. SHDDT Xc 202 9e Chasseurs. Rapport 24 Nivose An XIII.
116. SHDDT Xc 202 9e Chasseurs. Rapport 25 Fructidor An XIII
117. SHDDT Xc 202 9e Chasseurs. Rapport 16 Juin 1808.
118. SHDDT Xc 202 9e Chasseurs. Rapport 16 Juin 1808.
119. SHDDT Xc 202 9e Chasseurs. Rapport 16 Juin 1808.
120. SHDDT Xc 202 9e Chasseurs à Cheval. Dossier 183. Rapport 13 Janvier 1813.
121. SHDDT Xc 202 9e Chasseurs à Cheval. Dossier 1814. Rapport 9 Juin 1814.
122. SHDDT Xc 202 9e Chasseurs à Cheval. Dossier 1814.
123. SHDDT Xc 202 9e Chasseurs à Cheval. Dossier 1814.
124. SHDDT Xc 202 9e Chasseurs à Cheval. Dossier 1814.
125. SHDDT Xc 203 10e Chasseurs à Cheval. Dossier AN 13. Rapport 27 Vend An13.
126. SHDDT Xc 203 10e Chasseurs à Cheval. Dossier AN 13. Rapport 2 Fructidor An13.
127. SHDDT GR 2C 247 Bis Habillement.
128. SHDDT Xc 204 10e Chasseurs à Cheval. Dossier 1814. Rapport 1 Septembre 1814.
129. SHDDT Xc 204 10e Chasseurs à Cheval. Dossier 1814. Rapport 1 Septembre 1814.
130. SHDDT Xc 204 10e Chasseurs à Cheval. Dossier 1814. Lettre au ministre de geurre 12 Septembre 1814.
131. SHDDT Xc 204 10e Chasseurs à Cheval. Dossier 1815. Rapport 3 Avril 1820.
132. SHDDT Xc 206 11e Chasseurs à Cheval. Rapport 8 Prairial An XI.
133. SHDDT Xc 206 11e Chasseurs à Cheval. Rapport 16 Vendémiaire An XIII.
134. SHDDT Xc 206 11e Chasseurs à Cheval. Rapport 16 Vendémiaire An XIII.
135. SHDDT Xc 206 11e Chasseurs à Cheval. Rapport 29 Thermidor An XIII.
136. SHDDT GR C2 247 Bis Habillement.
137. SHDDT Xc 206 11e Chasseurs à Cheval. Dossier 1814.
138. SHDDT Xc 206 11e Chasseurs à Cheval. Dossier 1814.
139. SHDDT Xc 206 11e Chasseurs à Cheval. Dossier 1814.
140. SHDDT Xc 208 12e Chasseurs. Rapport 2 Vend An13.
141. SHDDT Xc 208 12e Chasseurs. Rapport 2 Vend An13.
142. SHDDT Xc 208 12e Chasseurs. Rapport 9 Thermidor An13.
143. SHDDT Xc 208 12e Chasseurs. Rapport 1 Janvier 1808.
144. SHDDT Xc 208 12e Chasseurs à Cheval. Dossier 1814.
145. SHDDT Xc 208 12e Chasseurs à Cheval. Dossier 1814.
146. SHDDT Xc 208 12e Chasseurs à Cheval. Dossier 1814. Rapport 26 Septembre 1814.
147. SHDDT Xc 208 12e Chasseurs à Cheval. Dossier 1815.
148. SHDDT Xc 208 12e Chasseurs à Cheval. Dossier 1815.
149. SHDDT Xc 211 13e Chasseurs. Dossier An 13. Rapport 10 Thermidor An13.
150. SHDDT GR C2 247 Bis Habillement.
151. SHDDT Xc 211 13e Chasseurs. Dossier 1808. Rapport 7 Fevrier 1808.
152. SHDDT Xc 211 13e Chasseurs. Dossier 1814. Rapport 1 Avril 1813.
153. SHDDT Xc 211 13[e] Chasseurs. Dossier 1814. Rapport 1 Avril 1813.
154. SHDDT Xc 211 13e Chasseurs. Dossier 1814. Rapport 1 Avril 1813.
155. SHDDT Xc 211 13e Chasseurs. Dossier 1814. Rapport 1 Avril 1813.
156. SHDDT Xc 211 13e Chasseurs. Dossier 1815. Rapport 1 Aout 1814.
157. SHDDT Xc 211 13e Chasseurs. Dossier 1815. Rapport 21 Novembre 1815.
158. SHDDT Xc 213 14e Chasseurs à Cheval. Dossier An14. Rapport 14 Vend An14.
159. SHDDT Xc 213 14e Chasseurs à Cheval. Dossier 1809. Rapport 25 Septembre 1809.
160. SHDDT Xc 213 14e Chasseurs à Cheval. Dossier 1814. Rapport 1 Octobre 1814.
161. SHDDT Xc 213 14e Chasseurs 1811–1815. Dossier 1815. Rapport 31 Décembre 1815.
162. SHDDT Xc 213 14e Chasseurs 1811 à 1815. Dossier 1815. Rapport 31 Décembre 1815.

163. Bibliotheque Musée de l'Armée. Fonds Rousselot. Cavalerie légère. Extraits de Livre d'Ordres du Colonel Faverot.
164. SHDDT Xc 215 15e Chasseurs. Dossier An 13. Rapport 19 Vend An13.
165. SHDDT Xc 215 15e Chasseurs. Dossier An 14. Rapport 25 Brumaire An14.
166. SHDDT Xc 215 15e Chasseurs. Dossier 1808. Rapport 26 Janvier 1808.
167. SHDDT Xc 215 15e Chasseurs 1812–1815. Dossier 1814. Rapport 1 Aout 1814.
168. SHDDT Xc 217 16e Chasseurs à Cheval An XI a 1811. Dossier An XIII. Rapport 2 Vendémiaire An XIII.
169. SHDDT Xc 217 16e Chasseurs à Cheval An XI a 1811. Dossier 1814. Rapport 21 Janvier 1821.
170. SHDDT Xc 217 16e Chasseurs An XI a 1811. Dossier 1814. Rapport 21 Janvier 1821.
171. SHDDT Xc 217 16e Chasseurs An XI a 1811. Dossier 1814. Rapport 21 Janvier 1821.
172. SHDDT Xc 217 16e Chasseurs An XI a 1811. Dossier 1814. Rapport 21 Janvier 1821.
173. SHDDT Xc 217 16^{e} Chasseurs An XI a 1811. Dossier 1808. Rapport 25 Janvier 1808.
174. SHDDT Xc 217 16^{e} Chasseurs AnXII a 1815. Dossier 1813. Rapport 19 Mars 1813.
175. SHDDT Xc 217 16e Chasseurs AnXII a 1815. Dossier 1813. Rapport 22 Mars 1813.
176. SHDDT Xc 217 16e Chasseurs AnXII a 1815. Dossier 1813. Rapport 29 Mars 1813.
177. SHDDT Xc 217 16e Chasseurs AnXII a 1815. Dossier 1813. Rapport 27 Mai 1813.
178. SHDDT Xc 188 2e Chasseurs à Cheval 1812–1815. Dossier 1814. Rapport 1 Aout 1814.
179. SHDDT Xc 188 2e Chasseurs à Cheval 1812–1815. Dossier 1814. Rapport 1 Aout 1814.
180. SHDDT Xc 218 17 et 18 Chasseurs. Dossier 17e Chasseurs.
181. SHDDT Xc 218 17e et 18e Chasseurs. Dossier 18e Chasseurs.
182. SHDDT GR C2 247 Bis Habillement.
183. SHDDT Xc 220 19e Chasseurs à Cheval AnXI a 1815. Dossier 1814. Rapport 29 Mai 1820
184. SHDDT Xc 204 10e Chasseurs à Cheval. Dossier 1814. Rapport 1 Septembre 1814.
185. SHDDT Xc 204 10e Chasseurs à Cheval. Dossier 1814. Rapport 1 Septembre 1814.
186. SHDDT Xc 220 19e Chasseurs AnXII a 1815. Dossier 1814. Rapport 1 Mai 1820.
187. SHDDT GR C2 247 Bis Habillement.
188. SHDDT Xc 220 20e Chasseurs à Cheval AnXI a 1815. Dossier 1812. Rapport 9 Juillet 1812.
189. SHDDT Xc 220 20e Chasseurs à Cheval AnXI a 1815. Dossier 1812. Rapport 19 Juillet 1812.
190. SHDDT Xc 220 20e Chasseurs à Cheval AnXI a 1815. Dossier 1812. Rapport 30 Juillet 1812.
191. SHDDT Xc 220 20e Chasseurs à Cheval AnXI a 1815. Dossier 1813 Rapport 9 Fevrier 1813.
192. SHDDT Xc 220 20e Chasseurs à Cheval AnXI a 1815. Dossier 1813 Rapport 13 Fevrier 1813.
193. SHDDT Xc 220 20e Chasseurs à Cheval AnXI a 1815. Dossier 1813 Rapport 4 Mars 1813.
194. SHDDT Xc 181 2e Lanciers 1811–1814. Dossier 1814.
195. Carnet de la Sabretache 1906. Vol. 1, pp.670–672.
196. SHDDT Xc 224 21e Chasseurs. Rapport 8 Fructidor An XIII.
197. SHDDT Xc 208 12e Chasseurs à Cheval. Dossier 1814.
198. SHDDT Xc 208 12e Chasseurs à Cheval. Dossier 1814.
199. SHDDT Xc 196 5e Chasseurs à Cheval 1811–1815. Dossier 1814. Rapport 1 Aout 1814.
200. SHDDT Xc 196 5e Chasseurs à Cheval 1811–1815. Dossier 1814. Rapport 1 Aout 1814.
201. SHDDT Xc 196 5e Chasseurs à Cheval 1811–1815. Dossier 1814. Rapport 1 Aout 1814.
202. SHDDT Xc 196 5e Chasseurs à Cheval 1811–1815. Dossier 1814. Rapport 1 Aout 1814.
203. SHDDT Xc 226 22e Chasseurs. Dossier An 13. Rapport 12 Thermidor An13.
204. SHDDT Xc 226 22e Chasseurs. Dossier 1807. Rapport 29 Décembre 1807.
205. SHDDT Xc 182 3e et 4e Lanciers 1811–1814. Dossier 3e Lanciers 1814.
206. SHDDT GR C2 247 Bis Habillement.
207. SHDDT Xc 228 23e Chasseurs. Dossier 1812. Rapport 30 Avril 1812.
208. SHDDT Xc 228 23e Chasseurs. Dossier 1814. Exercise 1814.
209. SHDDT Xc 228 23e Chasseurs. Dossier 1813. Letter Au Ministre de Geurre, 5 Avril 1813.
210. SHDDT Xs 528 'Les forme, coupes, longueurs, largeurs, distance et dimensions sous determines dans le décret du 19 Janvier 1812'.
211. Les Gupil (1812) No. 32 Devis de dragons.
212. SHDDT Xc 228 23e Chasseurs. Dossier 1814. Exercise 1814.
213. SHDDT Xc 228 23e Chasseurs. Dossier 1814. Exercise 1814.
214. SHDDT Xc 228 23e Chasseurs. Dossier 1814. Exercise 1814.
215. SHDDT Xc 228 23e Chasseurs. Dossier 1814. Exercise 1814.
216. SHDDT Xc 229 24^{e} Chasseurs. Dossier An 13. Rapport 19 Fructidor An13. See also Ibid Rapport 21 Vendemiaire An13.
217. SHDDT GR 2C 247 bis Habillement.
218. SHDDT Xc 230 24e Chasseurs. Dossier 1808. Rapport 23 Janvier 1808.
219. SHDDT Xc 230 24e Chasseurs. Dossier 1808. Rapport 1 Mars 1808.
220. SHDDT Xc 202 9e Chasseurs à Cheval. Dossier 1814. Rapport 9 Juin 1814.

221. SHDDT Xc 202 9e Chasseurs à Cheval. Dossier 1814.
222. SHDDT Xc 200 8e Chasseurs à Cheval. Dossier 1814. Rapport 21 Juillet 1814.
223. SHDDT Xc 200 8e Chasseurs à Cheval. Dossier 1814. Rapport 21 Juin 1814.
224. SHDDT Xc 200 8e Chasseurs à Cheval. Dossier 1815. Rapport 3e Décembre 1815.
225. SHDDT Xc 200 8e Chasseurs à Cheval. Dossier 1814. Rapport 21 Juin 1814.
226. SHDDT Xc 233 26e Chasseurs. Dossier An 13. Rapport 12 Thermidor An13.
227. SHDDT Xc 233 26e Chasseurs. Dossier 1807. Rapport 25 Novembre 1807.
228. SHDDT Xc 192 4e Chasseurs à Cheval AnXI a 1815. Dossier 1814.
229. SHDDT Xc 192 4e Chasseurs à Cheval AnXI a 1815. Dossier 1814. Rapport 6 Juillet 1814.
230. SHDDT Xc 192 4e Chasseurs à Cheval AnXI a 1815. Dossier 1814.
231. SHDDT Xc 208 12e Chasseurs à Cheval. Dossier 1814.
232. SHDDT Xc 208 12e Chasseurs à Cheval. Dossier 1814.
233. SHDDT Xc 208 12e Chasseurs à Cheval. Dossier 1814.
234. SHDDT Xc 234 27e Chasseurs à Cheval. 1807–1814. Dossier 1808. Rapport 19 Décembre 1807.
235. SHDDT Xc 198 7e Chasseurs. Dossier 1814. Situation Rapport 21 Aout 1814.
236. SHDDT Xc 192 4e Chasseurs à Cheval AnXI a 1815. Dossier 1814. Rapport 1 Aout 1814.
237. SHDDT Xc 192 4e Chasseurs à Cheval AnXI a 1815. Dossier 1814. Rapport 1 Aout 1814.
238. SHDDT Xc 192 4e Chasseurs à Cheval AnXI a 1815. Dossier 1814. Rapport 1 Aout 1814.
239. SHDDT Xc 234 27e Chasseurs à Cheval. 1807 a 1814. Rapport 1 Mai 1820.
240. SHDDT Xc 192 4e Chasseurs à Cheval AnXI a 1815. Dossier 1814. Rapport 6 Juillet 1814.
241. SHDDT Xc 211 13e Chasseurs. Dossier 1815. Rapport 1 Aout 1814.
242. SHDDT Xc 206 11e Chasseurs à Cheval. Dossier 1814.
243. SHDDT Xc 206 11e Chasseurs à Cheval. Dossier 1814.
244. SHDDT Xc 206 11e Chasseurs à Cheval. Dossier 1814.
245. SHDDT Xc 235 28e at 29e Chasseurs à Cheval. Dossier 28e Chasseurs à Cheval.
246. SHDDT Xc 206 11e Chasseurs à Cheval. Dossier 1814.
247. SHDDT Xc 206 11e Chasseurs à Cheval. Dossier 1814.
248. SHDDT Xc 235 28e at 29e Chasseurs à Cheval. Dossier 28e Chasseurs à Cheval.
249. SHDDT Xc 215 15e Chasseurs 1812 à 1815. Dossier 1814. Rapport 1 Aout 1814.
250. SHDDT Xc 180 5 1e Lanciers 1811–1814. Dossier 1814. Rapport 8 8bre 1814.
251. SHDDT Xc 180 5 1e Lanciers 1811–1814. Dossier 1814. Rapport 8 8bre 1814.
252. SHDDT Xc 235 28e at 29e Chasseurs à Cheval. Dossier 29e Chasseurs à Cheval.
253. SHDDT Xc 260 30e et 31e Chasseurs. Dossiers 30e Chasseurs. Rapport 5 Juillet 1811.
254. SHDDT Xc 260 30e et 31e Chasseurs. Dossiers 30e Chasseurs. Rapport fait au ministre 2 Mai 1811.
255. SHDDT Xc 184 7e, 8e, 9e Chevaux-Legere-Lanciers. Dossier 9e régiment.
256. SHDDT Xc 260 30e et 31e Chasseurs. Dossiers 31e Chasseurs. Rapport 18 Septembre 1811.
257. SHDDT Xc 260 30e et 31e Chasseurs. Dossiers 31e Chasseurs. Rapport 20 Septembre 1811.
258. SHDDT Xc 260 30e et 31e Chasseurs. Dossiers 31e Chasseurs. Rapport 12 décembre 1820.
259. SHDDT Xc 260 30e et 31e Chasseurs. Dossiers 31e Chasseurs. Lettre 7 7bre 1811.
260. SHDDT Xc 260 30e et 31e Chasseurs. Dossiers 31e Chasseurs. Rapport 1 7bre 1811.
261. SHDDT Xc 260 30e et 31e Chasseurs. Dossiers 31e Chasseurs. Rapport 12 Décembre 1820.
262. SHDDT Xc 213 14e Chasseurs 1811–1815. Dossier 1814. Rapport 1 Octobre 1814.
263. Yves Martin pers comm 19 August 2021.
264. SHDDT Xc 186 1e Chasseurs. Dossier 1814. Rapport 11 Octobre 1814.
265. SHDDT Xc 186 1e Chasseurs. Dossier 1814. Rapport 11 Octobre 1814.
266. SHDDT Xc 186 1e Chasseurs. Dossier 1814. Rapport 11 Octobre 1814.
267. SHDDT Xc 186 1e Chasseurs. Dossier 1815. Rapport 22 Xbre 1815.
268. SHDDT Xc 186 1e Chasseurs. Dossier 1815. Rapport 22 Xbre 1815.
269. SHDDT Xc 186 1e Chasseurs. Dossier 1815. Rapport 22 Xbre 1815.
270. SHDDT Xc 217 16e Chasseurs à Cheval AnXI a 1815. Dossier 1815 Chasseurs Belge. Rapport 1 Mai 1815.
271. SHDDT Xc 217 16e Chasseurs à Cheval AnXI a 1815. Dossier 1815 Chasseurs Belge. Rapport 12 Mai 1815.
272. SHDDT Xc 217 16e Chasseurs à Cheval AnXI a 1815. Dossier 1815 Chasseurs Belge. Rapport 15 Mai 1815.
273. Bibliotheque Musée de l'Armée. Fonds Rousselot. Fiche Dragons 1e Empire.
274. Bibliotheque Musée de l'Armée. Fonds Rousselot. Fiche Dragons 1e Empire.
275. SHDDT Xc 260 30e et 31e Chasseurs. Dossiers 31e Chasseurs. Rapport 12 décembre 1820.
276. Bibliotheque Musée de l'Armée Manuscrits Et Imprimés; Planche 135 du volume IV du projet de règlement sur l'habillement du major Bardin.
277. Les Gupil, p.12.
278. SHDDT Xs 525 PROJET D'ARRÊTÉ Relatif à l'Habillement des troupes pour l'an X.
279. Les Gupil Note 5 Surtout.
280. SHDDT Xs 525 Circulaire 1 Vend An14.

281. Les Gupil, No. 35 Devis des Hussards.
282. SHDDT Xs 525 Circulaire 21 Avril 1807.
283. SHDDT GR 1M 247 bis Habillement.
284. SHDDT Xc 240 2e Hussard Dossier 1808. Rapport 5 Janvier 1808.
285. Les Gupil, p.221.
286. Les Gupil Note 11 *Pantalons de drap*.
287. SHDDT Xs 525 Circulaire 7 Julliet 1809.
288. Bibliotheque Musée de l'Armée, Manuscripts and printed books, Volume 1 du projet de règlement sur l'habillement du major Bardin, pp.295–307.
289. Les Gupil, pp.247–248.
290. SHDDT Xc 238 1e Hussard. Rapport 1 8 Thermidor An XIII.
291. SHDDT Xc 238 1e Hussard. Rapport 18 Thermidor An XIII.
292. SHDDT GR C2 247 Bis Habillement.
293. SHDDT Xc 138 1e Hussard, rapport 16 Décembre 1807.
294. SHDDT Xc 138 1e Hussard, rapport 16 Décembre 1807.
295. SHDDT Xc 238 1e Hussard. Dossier 1814. Rapport 21 Juillet 1814.
296. SHDDT Xc 238 1e Hussard. Dossier 1814. Rapport 21 Juillet 1814231.
297. SHDDT Xc 240 2e Hussard. Rapport 21 Thermidor An XIII.
298. SHDDT Xc 240 2e Hussard, Dossier 1808. Rapport 8 Janvier 1808.
299. SHDDT Xc 241 2e Hussard. Dossier 1814. Rapport 16 July 1814.
300. SHDDT Xc 241 2e Hussard. Dossier 1814. Rapport 16 July 1814.
301. SHDDT Xc 241 2e Hussard. Dossier 1815. Rapport 25 9bre 1815.
302. SHDDT Xc 242 3e Hussard An XII a 1815. Dossier An XIII. Rapport 20 Thermidor An XIII.
303. SHDDT Xc 242 3e Hussard An XII a 1815. Dossier An XIII. Rapport 20 Thermidor An XIII.
304. SHDDT Xc 242 3e Hussard. Dossier 1808. Rapport 4 Janvier 1808.
305. SHDDT Xc 242 3e Hussard An XII a 1815. Dossier 1808. Rapport 4 janvier 1808.
306. SHDDT Xc 242 3e Hussard An XII a 1815. Dossier 1815. Rapport 3 Avril 1820.
307. SHDDT Xc 242 3e Hussard An XII a 1815. Dossier 1814. Rapport 1 Aout 1814.
308. SHDDT Xc 242 3e Hussard An XII a 1815. Dossier 1814. Rapport 1 Aout 1814.
309. SHDDT Xc 242 3e Hussard An XII a 1815. Dossier 1815. Rapport 25 Novembre 1815.
310. SHDDT Xc 242 3e Hussard An XII a 1815. Dossier 1815. Rapport 27 Novembre 1815.
311. SHDDT Xc 242 3e Hussard An XII 1815. Dossier 1815. Rapport 27 Novembre 1815.
312 SHDDT Xc 244 4e Hussard 1791–1815. Dossier 1814. Rapport 16 July 1814.
313. SHDDT Xc 244 4e Hussard 1791–1815. Dossier 1814. Rapport 16 July 1814.
314. SHDDT Xc 244 4e Hussard 1791–1815. Dossier 1814. Rapport 23 Novembre 1819.
315. SHDDT Xc 244 4e Hussard 1791–1815. Dossier 1815. Rapport 22 Novembre 1815.
316 SHDDT Xc 244 4e Hussard 1791–1815. Dossier 1815. Rapport 22 Novembre 1815.
317 SHDDT Xc 244 4e Hussard 1791–1815. Dossier 1815. Rapport 22 Novembre 1815.
318. SHDDT Xc 245 5e Hussard. Rapport 30 Thermidor AnXI.
319. SHDDT Xc 245 5e Hussard. Rapport 30 Thermidor AnXI.
320. SHDDT Xc 245 5e Hussard. Rapport 17 Pluvoise AnX.
321. SHDDT GR C2 247 bis Habillment.
322. SHDDT Xc 246 5e de Hussard 1811–1815. Dossier 1814. Rapport 11 Aout 1814.
323. SHDDT Xc 246 5e de Hussard 1811–1815. Dossier 1814. Rapport 11 Aout 1814.
324. SHDDT Xc 246 5e de Hussard 1811–1815. Dossier 1815. Rapport 14 9bre 1815.
325. SHDDT Xc 246 5e de Hussard 1811–1815. Dossier 1815. Rapport 14 9bre 1815.
326. SHDDT Xc 328 6e Hussard. Dossier 1808. Pully au Ministre de Geurre 20 Juillet 1808.
327. SHDDT Xc 328 6e Hussard. Dossier 1814. Rapport 25 Juillet 1814.
328. SHDDT Xc 328 6e Hussard. Dossier 1814. Rapport 1 décembre 1815.
329. SHDDT Xc 250 7e Hussard. Rapport 3 Prairial An XI.
330. SHDDT Xc 250 7e Hussard. Rapport 3 Prairial An XI.
331. SHDDT Xc 250 7e Hussard. 8 Thermidor An XIII.
332. SHDDT Xc 250 7e Hussard. Rapport 8 Thermidor An XIII.
333. SHDDT GR C2 247 Bis Habillement.
334. SHDDT Xc 250 7e Hussard. Rapport 20 Janvier 1808.
335. SHDDT Xc 250 7e Hussard. Rapport 20 Janvier 1808.
336. SHDDT Xc 251 7e Hussard. Rapport 2 7re 1814.
337. SHDDT Xc 251 7e Hussard. Rapport 2 7re 1814.
338. SHDDT Xc 253 8e Hussard. Dossier 1814. Rapport 14 Xbre 1814.
339. SHDDT Xc 242 3e Hussard An XII a 1815. Dossier 1814. Rapport 1 Aout 1814.
340. SHDDT Xc 242 3e Hussard An XII a 1815. Dossier 1814. Rapport 1 Aout 1814.

341. SHDDT Xc 246 5e de Hussard 1811–1815. Dossier 1814. Rapport 11 Aout 1814.
342. SHDDT Xc 255 9e Hussard. Dossier An11. Rapport 20 Prairial AnXI.
343. SHDDT Xc 255 9e Hussard. Dossier An13. Rapport 18 Fructidor AnXIII.
344. SHDDT Xc 255 9e Hussard 1811–1814. Dossier 1808. Rapport 19 Janvier 1808.
345. SHDDT Xc 255 9e Hussard 1811–1814. Dossier 1813. Rapport 29 Mai 1813.
346. SHDDT Xc 248 6e Hussard. Dossier 1814. Rapport 25 Juillet 1814.
347. SHDDT Xc 328 6e Hussard. Dossier 1814. Rapport 25 Juillet 1814.
348. SHDDT Xc 328 6e Hussard. Dossier 1814. Rapport 25 Juillet 1814.
349. SHDDT Xc 256 10e Hussard 1793–1811. Dossier An X. Rapport 22 Ventôse An X.
350. SHDDT Xc 256 10e Hussard 1793 –1811. Dossier An XI. Rapport 16 Thermidor An XI.
351. SHDDT Xc 256 10e Hussard 1793–1811. Dossier An XIII. Rapport 22 Thermidor An XIII.
352. SHDDT Xc 256 10e Hussard 1793–1811. Dossier 1808. Rapport 21 Janvier 1808.
353. SHDDT Xc 256 10e Hussard 1793–1811. Dossier 1808. Rapport 21 Janvier 1808.
354. SHDDT Xc 256 10e Hussard 1793–1811. Rapport 21 Avril 1821.
355 SHDDT Xc 241 2e Hussard. Dossier 1814. Rapport 16 July 1814.
356 SHDDT Xc 241 2e Hussard. Dossier 1814. Rapport 16 July 1814.
357. SHDDT Xc 242 3e Hussard An XII a 1815. Dossier 1814. Rapport 1 Aout 1814.
358. SHDDT Xc 246 5e de Hussard 1811–1815. Dossier 1814. Proces Verbal 11e regiment.
359. SHDDT Xc 260 12e Hussard 1812–1814.
360. SHDDT Xc 260 12e Hussard 1812–1814. Observations 10 Fevrier 1813.
361. SHDDT Xc 260 12e Hussard 1812–1814. Minute de la Lettre Ecrit 3 Mars 1813.
362. SHDDT Xc 183 5e et 6e Lanciers 1811–1814.
363. SHDDT Xc 183 5e et 6e Lanciers 1811–1814.
364. SHDDT Xc 183 5e et 6e Lanciers 1811–1814.
365. SHDDT Xc 183 5e et 6e Lanciers 1811–1814.
366. SHDDT Xc 261 13e at 14e Hussard. Dossier 14e Hussard. 13 xbre 1813.
367. SHDDT Xc 261 13e at 14e Hussard. Dossier 13e Hussard. Rapport 14 7bre 1813.
368. SHDDT Xc 261 13e at 14e Hussard. Dossier 13e Hussard. Rapport 3 Juillet 1813.
369. SHDDT Xc 261 13e at 14e Hussard. Dossier 13e Hussard. Proces Verbal 3 Aout 1813.
370. SHDDT Xc 261 13e at 14e Hussard. Dossier 13e Hussard. Proces Verbal 3 Aout 1813.
371. SHDDT Xc 261 13e at 14e Hussard. Dossier 13e Hussard. Rapport 11 Xbre 1813.
372. SHDDT Xc 261 13e at 14e Hussard. Dossier 13e Hussard. Grundler to MacDonald 22 Xbre 1813.
373. SHDDT Xc 261 13e at 14e Hussard. Dossier 13e Hussard. Grundler to MacDonald 23 Xbre 1813.
374. SHDDT Xc 261 13e at 14e Hussard. Dossier 13e Hussard. Rapport 31 Xbre 1813.
375. SHDDT Xc 261 13e at 14e Hussard. Dossier 13e Hussard. Rapport 9 Fevrier 1814.
376. SHDDT Xc 261 13e at 14e Hussard. Dossier 13e Hussard. Rapport 9 Fevrier 1814.
377. SHDDT Xc 261 13e at 14e Hussard. Dossier 13e Hussard. Lettre 12 Fevrier 1814.
378. SHDDT Xc 261 13e at 14e Hussard. Dossier 13e Hussard. Lettre 16 Fevrier 1814.
379. SHDDT Xc 183 5e et 6e Lanciers 1811–1814.
380. SHDDT Xc 183 5e et 6e Lanciers 1811–1814.
381. www.napoleon-series.org/military/Despeche/Issue1/c_13thHussards.html accessed 21/04/2016 at 13.54.
382. SHDDT Xc 261 13e at 14e Hussard. Dossier 14e Hussard. Rapport 3 Mars 1813.
383. SHDDT Xc 261 13e at 14e Hussard. Dossier 14e Hussard. 13 xbre 1813.
384. SHDDT Xc 261 13e at 14e Hussard. Dossier 14e Hussard. 13 xbre 1813.
385. SHDDT Xc 244 4e Hussard 1791–1815. Dossier 184. Rapport 16 July 1814.
386. SHDDT Xc 244 4e Hussard 1791–1815. Dossier 1814. Rapport 16 Juillet 1814.
387. SHDDT Xc 238 1e Hussard. Dossier 1814. Rapport 21 Juillet 1814.
388. SHDDT Xc 238 1e Hussard. Dossier 1815. Rapport 26 9bre 1815.
389. SHDDT Xc 238 1e Hussard. Dossier 1815. Rapport 26 9bre 1815.
390. Bibliotheque Musée de l'Armée. Fonds Rousselot. Fiche Dragons 1e Empire.
391. Bibliotheque Musée de l'Armée. Fonds Rousselot. Fiche Dragons 1e Empire.
392. SHDDT Xc 260 30e et 31e Chasseurs. Dossiers 31e Chasseurs. Rapport 12 décembre 1820.